THE MYSTERIES OF THE GREAT PYRAMIDS

Thousands of years ago they were built on the Egyptian desert—awesome, inspiring, symbolic, yet seemingly, utterly useless. Clearly they were meant as tombs for mighty Pharaohs, but was that all? To what other ends were the millions of grueling man-hours spent? What do the pyramids really stand for? Will their secrets ever be revealed?

This book takes the reader from the external dimensions of the Great Pyramid of Giza, where the solstices, the equinoxes, and the solar noon can all be calculated; to its internal structure, Cheops' sepulchral crypt; to unravel the mystical, mathematical, and astronomical enigmas that have intrigued man for centuries.

THE MYSTERIES OF THE GREAT PYRAMIDS is one of a series of Avon Books dedicated to exploring the lost secrets of ancient peoples and earlier times . . . secrets which challenge mankind today—and which may hold the key to our own future.

THE MYSTERIES OF THE GREAT PYRAMIDS

"The Luminous Horizons of Khoufou"

A. Pochan

AVON
PUBLISHERS OF BARD, CAMELOT AND DISCUS BOOKS

THE MYSTERIES OF THE GREAT PYRAMIDS was
originally published as *L'Enigme de la grande pyramide.*

AVON BOOKS
A division of
The Hearst Corporation
959 Eighth Avenue
New York, New York 10019

Copyright © 1971 by Editions Robert Laffont
Published by arrangement with Editions Robert Laffont.
Library of Congress Catalog Card Number: 77-92348
English translation copyright © 1978 by Avon Books
ISBN: 0-380-00881-5

First Avon Printing, January, 1978

AVON TRADEMARK REG. U.S. PAT. OFF. AND IN
OTHER COUNTRIES, MARCA REGISTRADA,
HECHO EN U.S.A.

Printed in the U.S.A.

Such a vanity as that which produced the great Pyramid, that has withstood the ravages of three or four thousand years, must certainly, in the end, be accounted as something.

CHATEAUBRIAND
Travels to Jerusalem and the
Holy Land through Egypt

CONTENTS

FOREWORD

A new book about the pyramids might seem superfluous in view of the impressive number of books on the subject already available. This book, however, provides an indispensable focus for questions over which mysticism, skepticism, and charlatanism have managed to provoke a veritable contagious psychosis.

The pyramids, those wonders of the ancient world, have always been the object of man's curiosity. The Arab authors are prolix on the subject, but their descriptions have traditionally been consigned to the realm of fabrication. The Greek and Roman authors, though regarded as more serious, have also come under much criticism. Numerous Western travelers have provided us with imprecise descriptions, and it was necessary to await the French Expedition to Egypt (1799–1801) in order to obtain the valuable data that modern Egyptologists further specified through the painstaking excavation of the mounds of ruins, which continues to this day.

Although the Egyptian pyramids were plundered long before the Arab invasion, it was after the reign of Al Mamun that they underwent the severest depredations. The removal of the facings of the two great pyramids of Giza destroyed an invaluable historical and scientific treasure, for according to accounts by Arab historians, the casing blocks were covered with hieroglyphic inscriptions.

This book is primarily confined to a study of the Great Pyramid of Giza, although the latter is far from being unique in the world. Aside from the Chaldean step ziggurats, one might cite the fields of pyramids at Meroe and at Napata in Nubia. Central and Latin America (Mexico, Guatemala, Costa Rica, Colombia, etc.) also boast a good many pyramids, including the largest in the world (in terms of volume), that of Cholula (base, 439 meters; height, 54 meters). This curious presence of pyramids at the same latitude as those in Africa might be considered a serious argument in favor of Wegener's theory of continental drift and even Plato's statements concerning Atlantis.

In the abundant "pyramidal literature" there are two opposing tendencies: some Egyptologists maintain that the scientific knowledge of the ancient Egyptians was very advanced; others consider it virtually negligible. To the adherents of a disconcerting modern mysticism, the builders of the Great Pyramid were unwittingly endowed with divine wisdom so that they *unconsciously* set in stone humanity's past, present, and future history; the Great Pyramid in this view is a gigantic Bible that the profane world has thus far been unable to decipher.

I will begin with a detailed description of the Great Pyramid as it now stands, including its precise dimensions, based on modern measurements collated with my own. The photographs, some of which can never be duplicated, should contribute to a better understanding of the text.

The general description of the monument will be followed by major extracts from the ancient, Arab, and modern sources.

Then the question of the Great Pyramid's destination will be broached. Having provided the most likely etymology of the word *pyramid* and the Egyptian name for the Great Pyramid, I will discuss the various theories, mystical as well as mathematical and astronomical. Two recent books, one by Jean-Philippe Lauer and one by Julian Bruchet, will be closely examined.

Finally, since I feel I know the Great Pyramid well (having studied it for seven years), I will set forth my own position, after having briefly reviewed the religious concepts of the Old Kingdom.

The book will end with an attempt at a historical account of the Great Pyramid from the time of its construction up to the present. This account will set the construction of the monument back to 4800 B.C., according to the Egyptian chronology that I have reestablished.[1] The Egyptologists who place Cheops' reign around 2700 B.C. are thus off by 2,100 years!

I hope this book will afford the reader some fresh insights on the subject.

NOTE

1. André Pochan, *Chronologie Egyptienne* (Montessori: Editions Maât, 1968).

INTRODUCTION

WHO IS CHEOPS?

According to Manetho, Suphis is the second king of the Fourth Dynasty, whose members belonged to a line different from that of the Third. He was the son of Soris (Sneferu) and married his own sister, Mertitefs. He reigned for sixty-three years, from 4829 to 4766 B.C.

Different names have been attributed to him: Cheops (Herodotus), Sufis (Africanus and Eusebius), Saophis (Eratosthenes). These distorted names are all recognizable, however, for his hieroglyphic name is Khnum-Khufu, in which we recognize the name Chemmis, given to him by Diodorus Siculus.

The most commonly occurring cartouche is:

Khufui: "He protects me."

The full name, found in the Great Pyramid's relieving chambers and in a bas-relief discovered on a stone at Wadi Magharah, is:

Hrw-Khnum-Khufu: "the most high"—"Khnum protects me."

This name of his pyramid is:

Akhet Khufu: "Khufu's Luminous Horizon."

An inscription discovered by George A. Reisner in the mastaba of Pen-Meruw at Giza is of primary importance because the determinative used for the pyramid is that of solar temples. As I shall prove in this book, the Great Pyramid was both the tomb of Cheops and the temple of the sun god Khnum.

Two questions arise: Why was Cheops' cartouche simplified and why does it bear only the mark *Khufui* ("He protects me").

The point could be argued, but in my opinion the best solution is the following: Khnum, a ram-headed sun god native to Upper Egypt (Elephantine), was often associated during the New Kingdom with Ra and Amon. It is possible that the Fourth Dynasty originated around Beni-Hassan, for there is in this area a village called Monet-Khufu ("Khufu's nurse"). Moreover, the majority of the princes of the "nome of the Gazelle" bore the generic name *Khnumhotep* ("gift of the god Khnum").

In the nomes of Memphis and Heliopolis this god (Khnum) was considered a *usurper*; thus the royal name in itself constituted a provocation. It is therefore understandable that the sacerdotal colleges should have exhibited strong opposition and manifested their vengeance at the time of Kephren's death, as Herodotus and Diodorus Siculus inform us. However, a temporary accord may have been reached. All that was necessary, in fact, was to delete from the royal cartouche the name of the intruder, Khnum; once the cartouche had been reduced to *Khufui* ("He protects me"), the indefinite pronoun *he* could thenceforth be applied to all the gods in the Egyptian pantheon.

There still remains the problem of explaining the names Surid, Saurid, and Soris, which were handed down to us by the Arab authors. Now, Khnum is a ram-headed sun god, and the hieroglyph meaning "ram" is:

Sri.

which seems to be a satisfactory solution.

ETYMOLOGY OF THE WORD *PYRAMID*

Many explications of the word *pyramid* have been proposed; none, in my opinion, is acceptable.

Some have seen in it the Greek root *pyr* (fire), because of the resemblance between the geometric shape and that of a flame. Some have noted the root Πυρος (wheat) and deduced that the pyramids were none other than "Joseph's granaries" (*haramât Jussef*). Adler believes the word derives from *pi-rama:* "the height; the raised monument." Volney derives the etymology from the Hebrew *bur a-mit:* "the vault of the dead; the tomb."

Sir Gaston Maspero finds none of the proposed etymologies satisfactory. He believes the least farfetched is that of Morris Benedict Cantor and August Eisenlohr, according to which "pyramid" is the Greek form of the compound *peri m uisi,* which in the Egyptian mathematical language is used to designate the sharp projection or ridge of the pyramid.

The hieroglyphic representation of the word is:

mr: "stairway."

Since the phonetic value of the hairpin is *mr,* there is thus a redundancy in the hieroglyphic representation, which often occurs in Egyptian; this word, however, does not provide the etymology of the word *pyramid.*

In my opinion, the solution is as follows. The word *pyramid* derives from the Egyptian

pr. m it: "abode of laments"; "house of the dead."

Thus the word *pyramid* signifies, quite simply, "tomb."

Another representation, having the same sense, is equally suitable:

pr m mwt: "abode of the sarcophagus."

Each royal pyramid had its own name. The three great pyramids of Giza were called "Khufu's Luminous Horizon," "Khefra the Great," and "Menkaura the Divine."

CHAPTER 1

THE PRESENT STATE
OF THE GREAT PYRAMID

Stripped of its facing, the blocks of which were used to build the citadel of Cairo, the Great Pyramid now appears as a prodigious mound of blocks laid out in 203 superincumbent courses. Originally it must have been comprised of 210 ($2 \times 3 \times 5 \times 7$) courses. According to the accounts of the Arab authors, this facing was covered with hieroglyphs incomprehensible to them; its disappearance thus constitutes an irremediable loss for Egyptology. Abd-al-Latif says the dismantling was ordered by Karakush, intendant of Saladin (1169–96 B.C.).

Built on the Giza Plateau, 41 meters above the farmlands, with a base covering over 5 hectares and a present height of 139 meters, the Pyramid dominates the Nile Valley at the apex of its delta. The Pyramid's volume is estimated as about 2.6 million cubic meters and its mass as 7 million metric tons.

The date of its erection is assigned to the reign of Cheops (Khnum-Khufu, 4829–4766 B.C.), the second king of the Fourth Dynasty, according to Manetho, and the twenty-eighth king of Egypt, starting with Menes.

In the following pages I will provide all the data from the modern measurements made of the monument by Petrie, the Survey of Egypt, and myself. However, it is necessary to

1

note that, given the Pyramid's present state and despite the great care with which these measurements were taken, the dimensions of the sides of the base are only accurate, at most, to the nearest decimeter. As for the original height, calculated according to the slope (known only to the nearest minute), the approximation only falls within 0.5 meter.

It is also necessary to note that the Pyramid was but one element in the important complex making up the royal hypogeum, which included: the valley reception temple, the covered causeway, the mortuary temple, and, to the west of the last, the Pyramid. (It is remarkable that pyramids are always located west of their temples, like the bell towers of our churches and the minarets of mosques.)

From afar, despite the absence of the facing, the Pyramid's faces appear to be flat; all four, however, are curiously hollowed toward the center. (In the section "The Great Pyramid and the Determination of Equinoxes and Solstices," I will examine the reasons for this unusual hollowing.) Therefore, in order to keep rainwater from streaming into the Descending Passage, the Pyramid's entrance, located on the north face, was displaced 7.35 meters (14 cubits) east of the face's apothem.

The entrance to the Descending Passage is found at the level of the fifteenth course; it must have been at the level of the sixteenth or seventeenth course before the dismantling. It should be noted that in order correctly to fit and place the blocks constituting the Descending Passage's floor at the level of the swivel door, it was necessary to add, between the fourteenth and fifteenth courses (which are 0.748 and 0.715 meters high), a supplementary row only 0.11 meter thick.

Of the Pyramid's facing there remain in place only a few blocks toward the middle of the north face. These blocks, fairly well preserved, have allowed the Pyramid's slope to be determined, approximately, as 51° 51'. The dimensions of the outline of one of them can be found at some distance. At the foot of the west side the facing blocks have been extremely damaged and worn away by sandstorms.

The Descending Passage is surmounted by a ridged double discharging arch formed by four blocks resting on an enormous lintel. On the upper west side of the discharging arch is a ridiculous hieroglyphic inscription (fortunately nearly invisible today) by the German Egyptologist Karl Richard

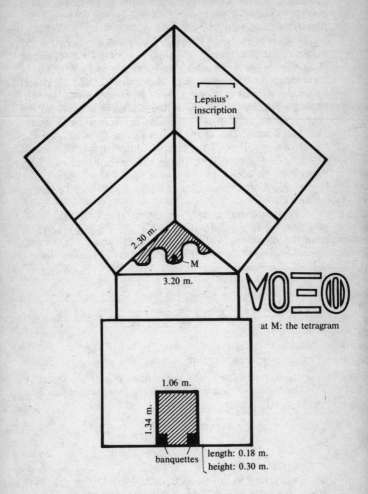

THE GREAT PYRAMID'S ENTRANCE

Dimensioned sketch of the entrance to the Great Pyramid's Descending Passage, and the enigmatic tetragram carved inside the "sign of the horizon."

Lepsius in which Kaiser Friedrich-Wilhelm IV of Prussia is called "King of Upper and Lower Egypt," "Son of Ra, blessed with eternal life"!

The present entrance to the Great Pyramid, situated at the height of the fifth course, is simply a very old tunnel dating from the Seventh through the Ninth Dynasty (4123–3568 B.C.), plugged up again under Ramesses II, and reopened under Al Mamun (815 A.D.). Seen from a distance, the triangle formed by the blocks of the discharging arch and the lintel seem to have an eye at the center. According to Walter Marshal Adams, this triangle was meant to symbolize the "door of the horizon," the hieroglyphic sign for the horizon ⌒ having been carved inside the triangle, which, from a distance, assumes the form of a pupil. Thus, Adams believes, the hieroglyphic sign must be the Pyramid's divine name.

A convincing argument? Not to the hermetics, who maintain that the Great Pyramid's divine name was kept secret from the profane world. This, however, was not the case, since the name of the Great Pyramid crops up in many tombs in the Giza Plateau:

A mastaba studied by Reisner, that of Pen-Meruw, mentions the name of the Great Pyramid with the determinative reserved for solar temples—a platform pyramid topped by a small obelisk.

We will return to this important fact later.[1] Here one detail that is unknown to the hermetics can be pointed out. At the center of the pupil, deeply carved in letters 6 centimeters high, is a curious tetragram (reproduced in the sketch of the Pyramid's entrance). Admitting my own incompetence, I will leave it to them to interpret the inscription. Since it almost

GREAT PYRAMID
MERIDIAN CROSS SECTION

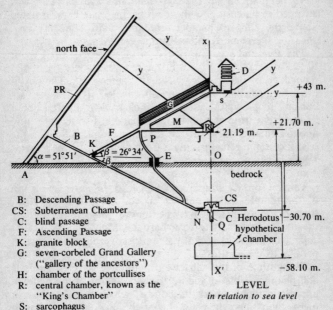

B: Descending Passage
CS: Subterranean Chamber
C: blind passage
F: Ascending Passage
K: granite block
G: seven-corbeled Grand Gallery
   ("gallery of the ancestors")
H: chamber of the portcullises
R: central chamber, known as the
   "King's Chamber"
S: sarcophagus
D: relieving chambers
M: passage to middle chamber
R: middle chamber, known as the
   "Queen's Chamber"
J: corbeled niche
P: shaft known as the "well"
E: excavation known as the "grotto"
N: nook, west wall of passage
PR: the Pyramid's missing casing
X X': the Pyramid's axis
Y: so-called ventilation ducts

bedrock

LEVEL
in relation to sea level

Plateau of the pyramids 58.60 m.

The Nile today

Bed	+10.00 m.
Low water	+12.25 m.
High water	+20.63 m.

The Nile in Cheops' time

Bed	+1.50 m.
Low water	+3.75 m.
High water	+10.25 m.

certainly is not contemporary with the building of the monument, one must congratulate the audacious person who, as a joke, dared risk his life in order to carve this mysterious tetragram in the Great Pyramid's pupil.

Aside from this curious tetragram, no ancient inscriptions have been found on the exterior since the Pyramid was stripped of its casing. Only the relieving chambers, situated above the King's Chamber, contain graffiti from the time, showing the name Khnum-Khufu.

The Pyramid's casing rested on a socle exactly 1 cubit (0.525 meter) thick, except at the corners, where the socle, embedded by 0.27 meter, was 0.795 meter thick. The northern esplanade had been carefully leveled. It contains, according to Howard-Vyse, a curious trench situated about 91.4 meters from the north face, parallel to the latter and about 2 meters deep. Of the funerary temple adjoining the east face there remains only a trace of the basalt pavement; Lauer has nevertheless attempted to reconstruct the original plan.[2]

Parallel to the Pyramid's east face, to the north and south of the temple, two elongated alveoli carved in the rock, though long considered to be mortar pits, were actually meant to accommodate solar barques. Moreover, two other solar barques have recently been discovered, still in place, parallel to the south face.

The outline of the causeway mentioned by Herodotus is still plainly visible on the northeastern slope of the plateau; enormous blocks mark its course, which vanish where it meets the Arabic village of Nazlet el-Samman. According to Herodotus, the causeway was 5 stades (923.45 meters) long, 10 orgyie (18.47 meters) wide, and 8 orgyie (14.77 meters) high at its highest point.

I've discovered numerous remnants of the exterior part of the Pyramid's casing; they are of a curious deep brick-red hue attributable to paint with a ferrous oxide base. I shall come back to this subject later.

At present, the Pyramid ends in a platform whose sides measure about 11 meters. In Pliny's time this platform measured 4.88 meters along the side, a figure confirmed by Claude François Lambert (in 1630) as 20 spans (4.80 meters).

It is certain that the Great Pyramid never ended in a point and was never capped with a pyramidion analogous to those

LEVELS OF THE GREAT PYRAMID

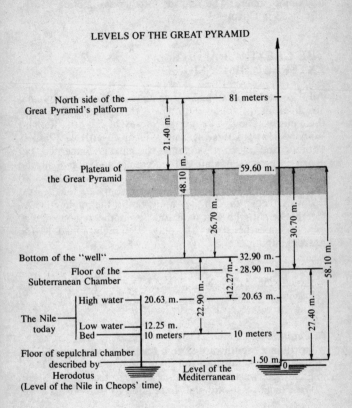

North side of the Great Pyramid's platform — 81 meters

21.40 m.

48.10 m.

Plateau of the Great Pyramid — 59.60 m.

26.70 m.

30.70 m.

58.10 m.

Bottom of the "well" — 32.90 m.

Floor of the Subterranean Chamber — 28.90 m.

12.27 m.

High water — 20.63 m. — 20.63 m.

22.90 m.

The Nile today

Low water — 12.25 m.

Bed — 10 meters — 10 meters

27.40 m.

Floor of sepulchral chamber described by Herodotus (Level of the Nile in Cheops' time) — 1.50 m. — 0

Level of the Mediterranean

of the pyramids of the Sesostrises and the Amenemhets of the Twelfth Dynasty. It was a solar temple and, as such, must have been topped with a small obelisk or perhaps a gnomon sphere. The reasons for this assumption will be discussed in Chapter V.

THE GREAT PYRAMID'S EXTERNAL DIMENSIONS

All the external sizes and dimensions of the Great Pyramid are given in the following table so the reader can refer to them easily. The figures are the Survey of Egypt's, Richard William Howard-Vyse's, and William Matthew Flinders Petrie's, and my own. As far as the base is concerned, because of the present state of the Pyramid and, above all, the incurvation of its faces (which has never been taken into account), the measurements are valid only to the nearest decimeter, even though they are given to the millimeter. As for the height, the approximation is in the region of 0.50 meter, since the slope has only been determined to the nearest minute.

Geographical position (Survey):
  Lat. 29° 58′ 51″ N; long. 31° 9′ E
  Previous determination:
  Lat. 29° 59′ 6″ N; long. 31° 7′ 47″ E

Orientation
  North face: southward shift in relation to true west, 2′ 28″
  South face: southward shift in relation to true west, 1′ 57″
  East face: westward shift in relation to true north, 5′ 30″
  West face: westward shift in relation to true north, 2′ 30″

Average value of the degree of the meridian
  Between Philae and Alexandria: 110,818 m.
  Value of the half-minute, Philae-Alexandria: 923.48 m.
  Value of the half-minute, Meroe-Philae: 922.71 m.
  Value of the half-minute at the latitude of Cairo: 923.80 m.

  Average altitude of the Pyramid's corners: 59.63 m. above
    the Mediterranean

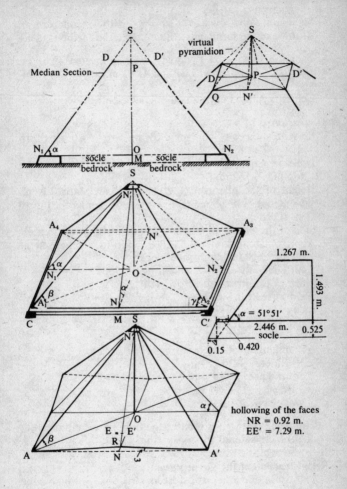

Altitude of the *bed* of the Nile: 10 m. above the Mediterranean

Average low water of the Nile: 12.25 m. above the Mediterranean

Maximum flood level: 20.63 m. above the Mediterranean

Altitude of the farmlands: 18 m. above the Mediterranean

Therefore the Great Pyramid's base is located 49.63 m. above the Nile's *present* bed and 41.63 m. above the farmlands.

Centenary alluvion-production coefficient: 0.130 m.

Dimensions

Present number of courses: 203; number of courses torn down: 7 or 8

Average height of courses: 0.685 m.; average height of the top ten: 0.562 m

Height of the platform: 139.117 m. (Jean Marie Joseph Coutelle), 138.30 m. (Edmé-François Jomard), 139.40 m. (Petrie)

Side of the platform: 9.96 m. (Coutelle), 11.7 m. (Petrie)

Approximate volume: 2,632,000 cubic m., composed of about 2,600,000 limestone blocks

Approximate weight: 7 million metric tons

Slope of the Pyramid: $51° 41' (\pm 1')$

sin 51° 51': 0.7863963

cos 51° 51': 0.6177224

tan 51° 51': 1.2730578

ctn 51° 51': 0.7855103

Actual lengths of the bases *upon the socle*:

North base: 230.253 m.

South base: 230.454 m.

East base: 230.391 m.

West base: 230.357 m.

The value of the north base, the only base fully cleared, should be considered the most valid.

Reconstruction of the Great Pyramid

This purely mathematical reconstruction presumes the Great Pyramid is perfectly regular. It is based on the measurement of the north base upon the socle (230.253 meters), the only measurement that is fairly certain.

The height is thus a function of the angle α of the slope used, for which four values can be found:

1. Angle of the casing block:
   51° 51 (±1′) . . . h = 146.563 m.
2. The slope *pi* = 3.1416:
   51° 50′ 14″ . . . h = 146.584 m.
3. The slope *pi* = 22/7:
   51° 50′ 34″ . . . h = 146.525 m.
4. The slope *phi* = 0.618034:
   51° 49′ 38″ . . . h = 146.443 m.

I shall use the first value, which corresponds to my measurement of the slope of the casing block.

The virtual pyramidion
We can determine the height of the virtual pyramidion from Pliny's datum of 16½ Roman feet (4.88 meters) for the platform's side. In this case, the imaginary height of the pyramidion would have been 3.106 meters.

Side DD′ .... 4.88 m.
Height SP .... 3.106 m.
Ridge SQ .... 4.63 m.
Apothem SN .... 3.94 m.

Consequently, the positions of the graphic summit and the platform are established thus:

Height	Graphic Summit	Platform
Above the socle:	SO = 146.563 m.	PO = 143.457 m.
Above the bedrock:	SM = 147.088 m.	PM = 143.982 m.

Measurement of the north base upon the bedrock
   231.393 m. (my measurement: 231.40 m.)
Measurement of the edge of the socle:
   231.093 m. [231.393 − (2 × 0.15)]
Width of the socle on the bedrock:
   0.470 m.
Upper width of the socle:
   0.420 m.
Batter of the socle down to the bedrock:
   0.150 m.

Thickness of the socle:
    0.525 m. (exactly 1 cubit)

True perimeter of the base: $230.253 \times 4 = 921.012$ m.
Perimeter of the socle upon the bedrock:
                        $231.393 \times 4 = 925.572$ m.
Perimeter of the edge of the socle:
                        $231.093 \times 4 = 924.372$ m.

Thickness of the facing blocks at the base: vary from 1.10 to 1.80 m. Probable thickness of the facing blocks at the summit: 1.22 m.

The most remarkable fact is the *hollowing of the faces,* which obliged the architect to displace the Descending Passage's axis 7.29 meters (14 cubits) east of the north apothem. This displacement of the axis was necessary in order to avoid inundating the Subterranean Chamber, as each face's hollow constituted a vast gutter capable of draining more than 2,000 cubic meters of water during a rainstorm. I will explain this curious hollowing later in the book.

Apothem of the complete Pyramid: NS = 186.37 m.
Apothem up to the platform: NN' = 182.43 m.
Ridge of the complete Pyramid: SA = 219.062 m.
Ridge up to the platform: 214.43 m.
                        (Pliny 725 feet = 214.26 m.)
Diagonal of the actual base: $A_1A_3 = 325.627$ m.
Angle of the slope . . . .   51° 51'
Angle of the ridge with the base . . . .   41° 59' 50"
Angles of the faces with the base . . . .   58° 17'
Angle of the summit of each face A_1SA_2 . . . .   63° 26'
Dihedral angle of the faces . . . .   112° 26'

THE GREAT PYRAMID'S INTERNAL STRUCTURE

The Descending Passage and the Subterranean Chamber

According to Petrie, the Pyramid's entrance is located 16.97 meters above the pavement, 13.31 meters horizontally inside the north base, and 7.29 meters east of the meridian plane.

THE PRESENT STATE OF THE GREAT PYRAMID

THE DESCENDING PASSAGE AND
THE SUBTERRANEAN CHAMBER

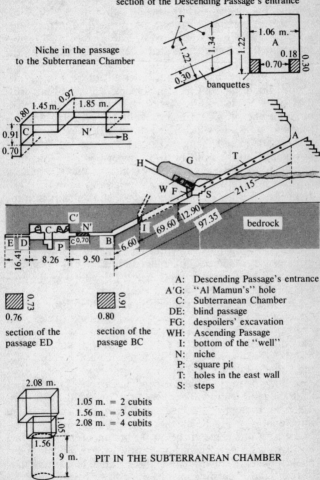

section of the Descending Passage's entrance

Niche in the passage
to the Subterranean Chamber

banquettes

bedrock

section of the
passage ED

section of the
passage BC

A: Descending Passage's entrance
A'G: "Al Mamun's" hole
C: Subterranean Chamber
DE: blind passage
FG: despoilers' excavation
WH: Ascending Passage
I: bottom of the "well"
N: niche
P: square pit
T: holes in the east wall
S: steps

1.05 m. = 2 cubits
1.56 m. = 3 cubits
2.08 m. = 4 cubits

PIT IN THE SUBTERRANEAN CHAMBER

depth reached by Perring: 11.60 m.

13

The Descending Passage, plunging into the Pyramid's interior from the present fifteenth course (the sixteenth or seventeenth course when the casing was intact), burrows at an angle of 26° 34' (corresponding to the cotangent 2), and descends obliquely for 97.25 meters—not taking into account the missing casing—before leading into a narrow (0.91-by-0.80-meter) horizontal passage measuring 9.50 meters long, which includes on its right (west) side a niche 1.85 meters long and 0.97 meter deep that is the same height as the passage.

The horizontal passage ends, after a 0.70-meter step, in a chaotic Subterranean Chamber (14 meters along its east-west axis and 8.23 meters along its north-south axis with a maximum height of 3.48 meters), with an irregular floor of rounded stones in which there appears a hole originally 4 cubits (2.08 meters) square. The sides of this square pit are not parallel to the walls of the chamber but are perceptibly parallel to its diagonals. The pit's total depth must originally have been 5 cubits (2.60 meters). Howard-Vyse, in 1837, had John Shae Perring extend it circularly 11.58 meters into the rock, hoping thus to discover the subterranean chamber described by Herodotus. Worth noting are the six curious enigmatic marks carved in the rock of the ceiling. (See photos.) This chaotic Subterranean Chamber, known as the "unfinished chamber," extends southward into a narrow horizontal blind passage 16.41 meters (35 cubits) long with a section measuring 0.76 by 0.73 meters.

Leaving this strange chamber and climbing back up the Descending Passage, we find, on the left-hand (west) side, 8 meters after leaving the low, narrow corridor with its niche, the bottom of the Pyramid's "well" (which is actually only a shaft), the upper end of which is located at the entrance to the Grand Gallery's landing.

Continuing to climb the Descending Passage, 21.15 meters from the present entrance we perceive, overhanging the passage, the bottom of the Ascending Passage, obstructed by three enormous granite blocks, each about 2.30 meters long. In the west wall, 3 meters below the bottom of the Ascending Passage, is located the ancient narrow excavation later used by despoilers to get around the three granite blocks and thus to reach the Ascending Passage.

Note that the walls of the Descending Passage show no

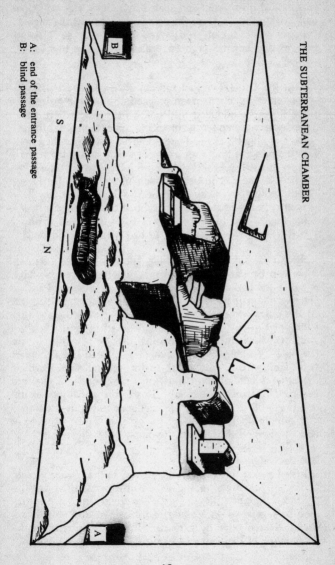

THE SUBTERRANEAN CHAMBER

A: end of the entrance passage
B: blind passage

S ⟶ N

signs of serious damage. Thus it is certain that, if the passage was indeed obstructed and sealed by blocks, this was done only within the depth of the casing that is now missing.

Petrie was of the opinion—one I share—that the Descending Passage had never been sealed with plug blocks. He writes:

> In the Great Pyramid the entrance passage is often spoken of as having been plugged up; and the holes in the floor are adduced in proof, as showing where the destroyers got under the blocks to force them out. Moreover, if plug-blocks had been dragged out, or broken up in the passage, the walls and roof would inevitably have been bruised or broken where each block was attacked; whereas, there is no trace of such injury visible. Besides these points, in the upper corners of the passage may be seen remains of the plaster, rubbed by the fingers into the angle; and this would have been displaced if any blocks that were cemented in had been dragged out.[3]

Strabo mentions a swivel door, and this seems to be corroborated by the existence of a banquette 0.30 meter high and 0.18 meter deep on each side of the Descending Passage and extending up to the plumb line of the Ascending Passage. At the latter level it is curious to discover three steps (not mentioned in any of the accounts) carved in the rock. Also worth noticing, in the Descending Passage's east wall, are ten holes, 4 centimeters in diameter, spaced equally apart (1.56 meters, or 3 cubits) up to the second step. Perhaps these holes held support rods for a ramp or for a handrail designed to facilitate descent. This entire apparatus would seem to confirm Strabo's statement concerning the existence of a mobile door. Moreover, traces of a similar door have been discovered in the great pyramid of Dashur.

The Ascending Passage

In order to reach this passage visitors to the Great Pyramid once had to climb up the despoilers' excavation and go around the granite blocks, since the tunnel entrance attributed by legend to Al Mamun had been blocked up and entirely covered over by a pile of debris resulting from the dismantling of the Pyramid's sides. This entrance could not be used again until Emile Baraize's excavation in 1917. The tunnel meets that of the first despoilers at the point where the Ascending Passage begins.

BLOCKAGE OF THE ASCENDING PASSAGE

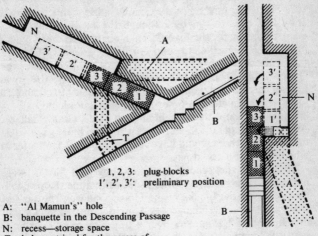

1, 2, 3: plug-blocks
1', 2', 3': preliminary position

A: "Al Mamun's" hole
B: banquette in the Descending Passage
N: recess—storage space
T: hole contrived for the egress of
    workers, later reopened by despoilers

This passage has a slope equal to, but the inverse of, the Descending Passage's slope; that is, 26° 34', corresponding to cotangent 2. Its total length is 37.49 meters. Petrie gives the slope as 26° 12' 50". His error is attributable to the state of the passage's floor and the difficulty of measuring an angle with the horizontal in a narrow shaft, for there is no doubt that the slope must correspond to cotangent 2, an angle whose gauge is the simplest to realize.

The three enormous granite blocks obstructing the Ascending Passage have a total length of 4.53 meters, with a section 1.194 by 1.052 meters. They each weigh over 5 metric tons. So far, the problem of their placement has not met with any logical solution.

Two questions arise regarding these blocks: Where were they stored before the passage was blocked? How were they moved to their present location?

The following solutions have been proposed in response to the first question:

1. The passage leading to the Queen's Chamber. Since the section of this corridor is smaller than that of the blocks, this solution is implicitly impossible.

2. The lower landing of the Grand Gallery. This landing is only 4.77 by 1.052 meters; though the blocks could have been stored there, they would have obstructed the Ascending Passage as well as the corridor of the Queen's Chamber.

3. The middle of the Grand Gallery, which overhangs the Queen's Chamber by 2.18 meters. If so, during the royal funeral ceremony it would have been necessary to climb 3.50 (2.18 + 1.32) meters in order to get over the blocks.

4. On the ramps to the right and left of the Grand Gallery. As these are only 0.536 meter deep and the blocks are 1.052 meters wide, there would have remained only 0.516 meter in which the coffin could pass.

To answer the second question—how the blocks were moved to their present location—let us assume the possibility of storing the blocks in the Grand Gallery. The task of lowering blocks weighing over 5 metric tons each, located at a height of 2.18 meters over a tiny landing, would have constituted an arduous operation. How was it possible to slide them down a 39.25-meter-long passage having the same section as that of the blocks themselves, thus barring the possibility of using ropes or dowels? Since the slope of the passage is only 26° 24′, it would have required that an enormous push be given in a corridor where *only* one man could fit! This descent alone would have constituted the most prodigious exploit of all time! I think it impossible.

In his book, J. Bruchet[4] offers the hypothesis that the blocks were put in place at the time of construction, which was possible, he says, because the Pyramid never served as a tomb but only as a cenotaph. He is mistaken: the Ascending Passage was not obstructed until *after* the isiac ceremony of the transferral of the *ka* had taken place in the upper chamber.

Then where were these three blocks stored? The solution is simple; it's quite astonishing that no one has ever thought of it, except the first despoilers of the Pyramid. The three blocks were stored in a niche constructed in the west wall near the bottom of the Ascending Passage, parallel to the latter and connected, by means of a narrow shaft, with the Descending Passage. By simply being tipped over, and then allowed to slide for 2.50 meters, the blocks would arrive at their final position. Once the job was completed, the workers could regain the Descending Passage through the narrow shaft, which would itself eventually be sealed with cemented limestone blocks.

It was by means of the rather easy reopening of this shaft that the first despoilers were able to reach the Ascending Passage. We can assume that they knew the niche existed, and for this reason these despoilers were probably none other than the priests of the Pyramid. This niche–storage space is no longer distinguishable because it was much enlarged by "Al Mamun's" extensive excavation.

The Great Shaft or "Well"

This shaft, improperly called a "well," which originally started at the level of the bedrock, was designed for the descent of the workers. The Descending Passage was reserved for the exit of workers carrying out stone-cutting debris.

It is located about 5 meters to the west of the Descending Passage, on a parallel plane. Having served its purpose once the Subterranean Chamber had been carved out, it was obstructed while the Pyramid's core was being set in place with a plug made of desert pebbles mixed with cement, as examination of the excavation known as the "grotto" will reveal. When the Pyramid was completed the "well" was thus *totally* cut off from the Grand Gallery. It was only recently extended *through the masonry* up to the gallery's entrance, on which it now opens.

Petrie writes:

The shaft, or "well," leading from the N. end of the gallery down to the subterranean parts, was either not contemplated at first, or else was forgotten in the course of building; the proof of this is that it has been cut through the masonry after the courses were completed. On examining the shaft, it is found to be irregularly tortuous through the masonry, and without any arrangement of the blocks to suit it; while in more than one place a corner of a block may be seen left in the irregular

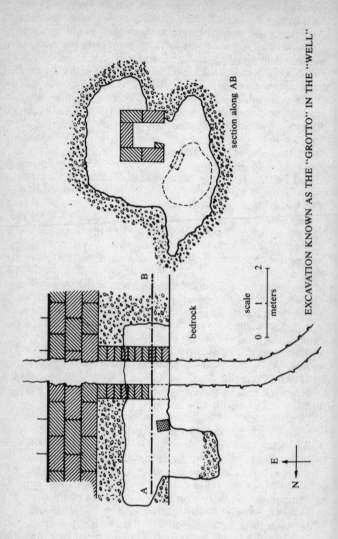

section along AB

bedrock

scale

0   1   2

meters

E

N

EXCAVATION KNOWN AS THE "GROTTO" IN THE "WELL"

curved side of the shaft, all the rest of the block having disappeared in cutting the shaft. This is a conclusive point, since it would never have been so built at first. A similar feature is at the mouth of the passage, in the gallery. Here the sides of the mouth are very well cut, quite as good work as the dressing of the gallery walls; but on the S. side there is a vertical joint in the gallery side, only 5.3 inches from the mouth. Now, great care is always taken in the Pyramid to put large stones at a corner, and it is quite inconceivable that a Pyramid builder would put a mere slip 5.3 inches thick beside the opening to a passage.[5]

The Pyramid's "well" is mentioned by Pliny, who gives its correct depth, though he obviously did not descend into the "well" because he reported that it was said to connect with the Nile. The depth was probably revealed to him by one of the priests still attached to the Pyramid.

At the time of the Expedition to Egypt Coutelle found the bottom of the "well" to be filled with pebbles from an excavation made in the cement, an excavation known as the "grotto." He attempted to excavate the "well" but military operations prevented him from completing the project. Therefore, since the Descending Passage was itself obstructed by debris from the despoilers' tunnel made at the level of the granite blocks in the Ascending Passage, Coutelle was unable to discover the Subterranean Chamber. The excavation of the "well" was completed by Giovanni Battista Caviglia in 1817.

Frederick Louis Ludwig Norden, who visited the Great Pyramid in 1737, provides a section of it that correctly places the well *and the Subterranean Chamber*. Since the Descending Passage ends beneath the granite blocks of the Ascending Passage, it must have been obstructed at the time, yet Norden writes, concerning his descent into the well:

After having suffered much discomfort there, one is annoyed to find that one cannot see its ultimate disposition because of the sand that plugs it up.

Did Norden get his information from an Arab who had succeeded in sliding into the interior? This is very doubtful, because Benoît de Maillet writes that in his time (*c.* 1700) the "well" was plugged up by sand and pebbles to a depth of 133 feet (43.20 meters), a fact John Greaves had already noted (in 1639).

The sand and pebbles obstructing the lower end of the "well" came from the excavation known as the "grotto" made by treasure seekers. I provide here an outline and section of this excavation. I myself experienced the adventure Coutelle describes (see pp. 85–88) when I descended into the shaft.

The *Serdab*, Known as the "Queen's Chamber"

The Ascending Passage opens into the Great Hall, or Grand Gallery, on a landing 4.77 meters deep, which a wall 2.18 meters high delimits to the south. The two lateral walls of this lower landing of the Grand Gallery each contain five facing holes, which once held beams designed to support a floor that extended the Ascending Passage and allowed one to climb the 2.18-meter-high step from the Horizontal Passage of the Queen's Chamber.

This north-south Horizontal Passage is 1.185 meters high, 1.042 meters wide, and 33.56 meters long. It leads into the Queen's Chamber, which is actually the Pyramid's secret *serdab*. At a distance of 28.56 meters along the passage's floor can be seen a curious drop of 0.52 meter (1 cubit): the passage's height thus becomes 1.695 meters and its floor is then level with that of the chamber.

This chamber, which certainly never served as a tomb, was the secret abode of the king's "double"—that is, his diorite or basalt statue[6] brought to life through the isiac rituals of the opening of the mouth and eyes.

With its ridged roof, which seems to have been colored blue, the chamber has the following dimensions: east-west length, 5.75 meters (11 cubits); north-south length, 5.23 meters (10 cubits); height of the walls, 4.17 meters (8 cubits) and 6.30 meters (12 cubits) up to the ceiling's apex. The chamber is constructed of Turah limestone.

Carved in the east wall and curiously displaced 0.60 meters southward in relation to the ceiling's apex—that is, the chamber's east-west axis—is a four-corbeled niche, the edges of which, like the ceiling, seem to have been colored blue. Its depth is 1 cubit (0.52 meter). A tunnel about 5

GRAND GALLERY

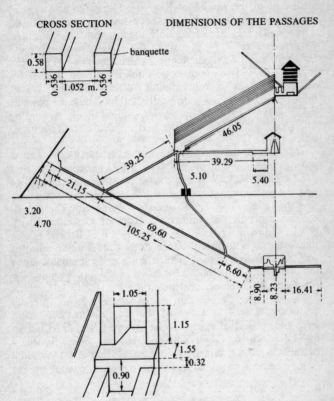

CROSS SECTION

DIMENSIONS OF THE PASSAGES

banquette

0.58

0.536 1.052 m. 0.536

46.05

39.25

39.29

5.10

5.40

21.15

3.20
4.70

69.60

105.25

6.60

8.90 8.23 16.41

1.05

1.15

1.55

0.32

0.90

ENTRANCE TO THE CHAMBER OF THE PORTCULLISES
"THE GREAT STEP"

meters deep has been made there; traces of hammering are visible on the chamber's walls, and on the floor five imprints of column bases can be made out, three to the south and two to the north. In front of the niche traces of a stairway or a table for offerings are very clear. The layout seems identical with that of the *serdab* of Kagemni Mereruka at Saqqara.

Two openings are visible at eye level in the north and south walls; they are perceptibly square, with sides of about 22 centimeters. They constitute the ends of two ducts extending all the way out to the Pyramid's casing. The existence of these two conduits was unknown until August 14, 1872, when they were accidentally discovered by J. Waynman Dixon. They had been obstructed by limestone plaques 0.127 meter thick made by carving a mural block. According to Petrie, the angles with the horizontal are the following: north shaft, 37° 28′; south shaft, 38° 28′.

The level of the chamber's floor and of part of the access passage poses a difficult problem: it lacks a course 1 cubit (0.52 meter) thick. Was this course omitted intentionally, or was it simply dug up and carried off by treasure seekers, as was the case in the second and third pyramids? The travelers' accounts are unanimous: the chamber was littered with blocks. Jomard writes: "The room is full of debris; sometimes the air is so foul that one cannot remain five minutes without suffocating. . . ." This is quite understandable since the chamber was without ventilation at the time because the plaques, still in place, obstructed the ducts.

The so-called ventilation ducts—those of the Queen's Chamber as well as those of the King's Chamber—have been the subject of many diverse theories, which I shall go into later. Morton Edgar, with good reason, sees in the ducts of the Queen's Chamber formal proof that the Pyramid's design was not modified in the course of its execution. He writes:

The air channels in the Queen's Chamber are very interesting; their existence was not known before 1872. In *Our Inheritance in the Great Pyramid*, Professor Piazzi Smith relates how Waynman Dixon, noticing a crack in the south wall of the chamber, pushed an iron wire into it to a great depth. Then he had his man, Bill

THE PRESENT STATE OF THE GREAT PYRAMID

THE PYRAMID'S *SERDAB*, KNOWN AS THE "QUEEN'S CHAMBER"

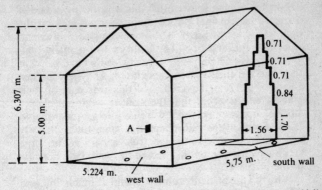

A: opening of the north "psychic" duct; the opening of the south "psychic" duct (not shown) is located exactly opposite it

The "double" faced toward the west—"Amenti," the western horizon

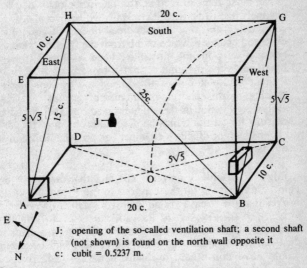

J: opening of the so-called ventilation shaft; a second shaft (not shown) is found on the north wall opposite it

c: cubit = 0.5237 m.

THE CHAMBER OF THE TRANSFERRAL OF THE *KA*, KNOWN AS THE "KING'S CHAMBER"

Grundy, drive a chisel into the opening, and a cavity soon appeared.

Further digging showed that this was the lower end of a square air channel. Proceeding the same way on the opposite side, Mr. Dixon discovered a second canal, similar to the first one. The builders had actually constructed two air channels to the Queen's chamber, but they had left their extremities closed. They left the last 5 inches (0.127m) covered, and this was part of their plan. There is proof that the orifices were not simply stopped up, because there were no joints. According to Piazzi Smith, "the thin plaque (127 mm.) was cleverly and symmetrically fashioned from a part of the large stone which made up this part of the wall on either side of the channel."

Why did the ancient architect spend so much time and effort constructing two long air channels when they could not have served as conductors until someone found and broke the tympanum?

We must remember that the interior blocks of the channels had to be placed gradually as the pyramid was constructed and that the hundreds of feet of carefully executed channels which climb from the Queen's chamber at a steep incline must have been fashioned stone-by-stone as the pyramid rose step-by-step.

Since examination of the many and various facts relating to this enormous monument proves that its architect was not in the slightest mad and that he had reasons for all the things he did, the problem of the air channels of the Queen's chamber has preoccupied many minds.

Edgar is absolutely correct. The fact that the two "psychic" ducts extend all the way out to the Pyramid's casing proves that the Great Pyramid's design *was not corrected or modified in the course of its execution,* for to complete communication channels with the "beyond" from a chamber destined to be abandoned once the Gallery had been built would have constituted a totally pointless task. We can assume the architects were not stupid, so it is obvious that Ludwig Borchardt's statements regarding this subject are totally erroneous.

Petrie was the first to realize that the Queen's Chamber was actually the Pyramid's *serdab*. The ducts, intentionally obstructed at both ends, were reserved for the king's "psyche"—that is, his soul or *ba*. I shall refer to them as *psychic ducts* rather that *ventilation ducts,* although they have become the latter since the perforation of their plaques.

Why two shafts? Wouldn't one have sufficed? Were two made in anticipation of a possible obstruction in one of them, or out of concern for symmetry? Or could it have been that one of the ducts was reserved for the psyche's arrival and the other for its departure? It should be noted that the wells of mastabas served the same purpose. At Meroe the points of certain pyramids house, at an inaccessible height, an open lucarne—a true "chamber of the soul," to use Marcelle Baud's expression—that served as a resting place for the soul of the deceased before it soared to heaven or descended to the tomb. It was in one of these small chambers that the treasure of Queen Candace was discovered.

The two ducts in the Queen's Chamber (*serdab*) are perpendicular to the Pyramid's north and south faces and terminate near the middle of their respective apothems. The ducts' openings are at the level of the 116th course, about 69 meters above the Pyramid's base. Since the ducts are perpendicular to the faces, they undeniably represent the shortest possible distance for the soul traveling to visit its double in the *serdab*.

Since these two ducts were hermetically sealed at both ends and thus could not have served as ventilation ducts, Bruchet has put forth the singular hypothesis that they might have been acoustic vents ending in a sound box connected to secret chambers not yet discovered—a rather fanciful hypothesis coming from such a practical, serious author.

The question of the ducts in the King's Chamber is much more delicate and difficult to solve. According to Petrie, the north duct measures about 71 meters, the south 53 meters; their respective slopes are 31° 33' and 45° 14'.

Are these shafts really ventilation ducts or were their plaques, like those in the Queen's Chamber, perforated *after* the Pyramid was completed? We must keep in mind that the walls of the *serdab* are made of limestone, while those in the King's Chamber are granite. Now, it was 6,700 years before the plaques of the *serdab* were discovered. Is it possible that those in the King's Chamber were discovered and punctured much earlier?

Perhaps these ducts were never closed? But then, they would have inevitably been clogged by the Aeolian desert sand. In 1935 Baraize had both the Descending Passage and the Subterranean Chamber entirely cleared of debris. At the present time (1970) Aeolian sand and debris from eroded rocks have partly filled the Subterranean Chamber and have completely blocked the opening and the access passage. It is thus unlikely that the ducts in the King's Chamber were originally open at both ends.

Two hypotheses should, however, be entertained:

1. If the two conduits were originally ventilation ducts, the unavoidable conclusion is that the Great Pyramid's upper chamber was not the site of the royal sepulcher. Continuous ventilation would have inevitably resulted in not only the putrefaction of the mummy, but also the rapid destruction of all the funerary furniture indispensable to the deceased for his life in the beyond.

2. If the two conduits, like those of the *serdab*, were "psychic" ducts closed off at both ends, it might be concluded that their lower plaques were punctured when the Pyramid was first broken into. This date is uncertain. Petrie thinks the violation was the work of the same hands that destroyed the statues and temples of Kephren and Mykerinos, as well as the pyramids of Abu Roash, Abusir, and Saqqara—that is, that it probably occurred during the civil wars of the Seventh through the Tenth Dynasty (*c.* 4100–3500 B.C.). At that time the necessary existence of "psychic" ducts was known.

But if determining the *sources* of the ducts was relatively easy, through sounding, this did not hold true for their outer ends, which the Pyramid's casing rendered virtually inaccessible. In order to carry out the delicate and dangerous search for and perforation of the upper plaques, specially equipped workers would have been indispensable, and they would have to have worked in broad daylight and in plain view. If their sole purpose was to locate and carry off the treasure amassed in the Pyramid, the despoilers would have worked secretly; perforating the exterior drums could not have interested them in the least.

It is possible that an additional goal of the first despoilers was vengeance. Diodorus Siculus reports that:

> . . . And though the two kings [Chemmis and Cephren] built the pyramids to serve as their tombs, in the event neither of them was buried in them; for the multitudes, because of the hardships they had endured in the building of them and the many cruel and violent acts of these kings, were filled with anger against those who had caused their sufferings and openly threatened to tear their bodies asunder and cast them in despite of the tombs. Consequently each ruler when dying enjoined upon his kinsmen to bury his body secretly in an unmarked place.

It is quite certain that the sacerdotal colleges of Ptah in Memphis and of Ra in Heliopolis contributed to the devastation and pillage of the Great Pyramid. They found it necessary to put an end to the interference of the usurper god Khnum in the territory of Lower Egypt, and to this purpose they sought to discredit Cheops by accusing him of having indulged in all sorts of cruel acts and of having closed the temples while forbidding the Egyptians to conduct sacrifices. Pushing their calumny to the point of opprobrium, they invented the preposterous legend that Cheops had prostituted his own daughter.

To return to the ducts in the King's Chamber: Whereas the entrance to the south duct has been enlarged to proportions that would admit a human body, the north duct's entrance seems to have undergone no appreciable violence.

The Grand Gallery of
King Cheops' Ancestors

The length of the Grand Gallery, from the north wall to where the south landing juts out, is 46.04 meters; its total width (including the two lateral banquettes) is 2.092 meters (4 cubits).

The lateral walls, comprising seven corbels, form an arch, the ceiling of which is the same width as the sunken ramp between the two banquettes; their vertical height is 8.70 meters (including the height of the banquettes).

The forty slabs forming the ceiling, plainly colored a dark red, overlap like roof tiles.

The edges of the corbels, measuring about 7 centimeters, are of a red-brown hue, a color that gives the impression of granite, although the blocks are Turah limestone. All along and above the third corbel can be seen significant evidence of continual hammering activity.

Each of the two lateral banquettes is 0.51 meter (originally 1 cubit) wide and 0.58 meter high; the section perpendicular to their slope measures 0.52 meter (1 cubit) high. The east banquette, starting flush with the north wall, contains twenty-eight curious slots. The west banquette does not adjoin the north wall because the site of the twenty-eighth slot is taken up by the end of the Pyramid's "well." Thus the right banquette has only twenty-seven slots. These slots are, on the average, 0.52 meter (1 cubit) long, 0.16 meter wide, and 0.21 meter deep; they are spaced 1.74 meters apart on the average.

Directly behind each of the slots the surfaces of the walls show extensive chipping, attesting to significant hammering activity. What, then, was the purpose of these twenty-eight slots?

Various hypotheses, each as unlikely as the next, have been put forth concerning these slots. One theorist would have it that the slots served to hold a scaffold designed to support a platform for storing the plug blocks. But the number of slots (twenty-eight) should have attracted the attention of Egyptologists. Wasn't Cheops the twenty-eighth King of Egypt after Menes? I propose that the twenty-eight slots are twenty-eight bases for twenty-eight facing royal statues, and that the Grand Hall is actually the *gallery of King Cheops' ancestors!*

The absence of the twenty-eighth slot in the west banquette, whose place is now taken up by the opening of the "well," serves to confirm the views expressed by Petrie: to wit, that the connection of the Grand Gallery with the primitive shaft used by descending stonecutters, a hole drilled *through the masonry,* was a task undertaken *after* the Pyramid had been built.

That the Grand Gallery is simply the gallery of the ancestors is corroborated by two ancient Arab authors. Muhammed ibn Ishaq Ibn al-Nadim, quoted by Ahmad ibn Ali al-

THE GALLERY OF THE ANCESTORS

An attempt to reconstruct the gallery of King Cheops' ancestors

Fig. 2: Method of setting the poles used for temporarily restraining the portcullises

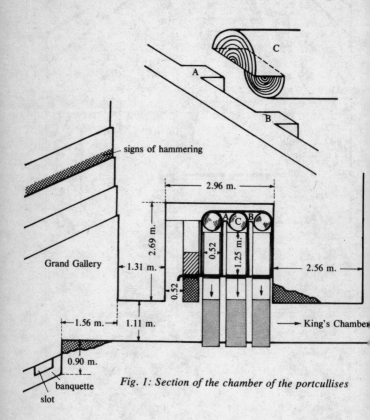

signs of hammering

2.96 m.

2.69 m.

Grand Gallery — 1.31 m.

0.52

1.25 m.

2.56 m.

0.52

— 1.56 m.— 1.11 m.

King's Chamber

0.90 m.

banquette

slot

Fig. 1: Section of the chamber of the portcullises

Maqrizi, writes: ". . . A passage pierces this pavement . . . ; the arch is made of stone and one sees there portraits and statues standing or resting and a quantity of other things, the meaning of which we do not understand." And Ibrahim Wassif Shah writes: ". . . In the eastern pyramid, chambers had been built in which the stars and heavens were depicted, and in which was amassed what Surid's forebears had accomplished in the way of statues." (Undoubtedly, the manuscript's text has been misreported; it should read: ". . . in which were amassed the statues that were done of Surid's forebears.")

I am convinced my theory is correct—that Surid (Cheops) and his twenty-seven forebears were each represented by two facing statues placed in successary order. I believe (and I will come back to this later) that the site of the twenty-eighth statue in the west banquette was taken up by the extension of the primitive shaft through the masonry carried out under Ramesses II, 3,500 years after the Pyramid was built. The hammered area all along and above the third corbel might have contained an inscription now lost—alas!—or, perhaps, royal cartouches.

At the top of the gallery, on a projection 0.90 meter above the gallery's floor between the two banquettes, is found a landing 1.557 meters (3 cubits) deep, bounded by the south wall. An opening 1.049 meters (2 cubits) wide, 1.110 meters high, and 1.311 meters deep leads to the hall of the portcullises, known as the "Antechamber." This hall, whose walls are made of granite, measures 2.96 meters long (north-south), 1.70 meters wide (east-west), and 3.80 meters high in relation to the corridor's floor. According to Petrie, the Antechamber's floor is located 43 meters above the Pyramid's base, level with the King's Chamber. A passage 1.112 meters high, 1.050 meters wide, and 2.562 meters long connects it with the latter.

The Chamber of the Portcullises, or Antechamber

The chamber of the granite portcullises, known as the "Antechamber," is characterized by:

1. Four vertical slots carved in the south wall (their purpose, in all probability, was to hold ropes used during the final lowering of the portcullises).

2. Three grooves carved in the east and west walls (these grooves served as runners for the three now-absent portcullises).

3. Three *semicylindrical* projections atop the three grooves in the west wall. On the opposite side, on the east wall, *at the same height* as the curve of the semicylinders, three *flat* projections cap the runners.

There is no doubt that this apparatus was designed to hold three poles about 0.50 meter in diameter, the west ends of which were to be inserted in the semicylindrical cavities, while their east ends, notched halfway, were to rest on the *flat* upper surfaces, with their sides wedged between the projections (see figure p. 32). Therefore these poles could not turn, so Borchardt's pulley hypothesis, adopted by Lauer, is untenable. It was, moreover, the wood's friction against the ropes that played the major role in temporarily restraining the portcullises.

4. A fourth characteristic of the Antechamber is the presence of a suspended lintel 0.40 meter thick. This is still in place, and is made up of two superimposed parts with respective heights of 0.70 and 0.61 meter, resting on projections of the east and west walls. The upper part of this lintel contains a horseshoe-shaped projection. There is no way this lintel could be a portcullis suspended for some unknown reason, because no slot extends into its groove.

Since the upper part of this lintel can be raised by means of its projection, the lintel constituted *an enormous flange* that gripped and held the ends of the four ropes designed to sustain the portcullises while the relieving props lodged in the east and west grooves were being removed. The lowering of the portcullises was then easily effected by cutting, flush with the north portcullis, the four ends of the portions of the ropes passing *under* the portcullises. Since the length of the portions of rope now hanging was less than the height to which the portcullises were originally raised, these freed rope ends could not be caught by the bottom of the portcullises. Therefore the ropes could easily be raised from above the lowered portcullises and then detached from the lintel-flange.

Contrary to the claims made by certain authors, the most recent of whom is Bruchet, the three portcullises were *actually set in place and lowered*. The south wall, in fact, shows clear, significant traces of damage, which would be totally inexplicable had the passage to the King's Chamber been open. It is obvious that the damage done to the Antechamber's south wall was effected from the space located above the lowered portcullises. The first despoilers, having experienced great difficulty in trying to raise the granite block closing off the entrance to the Antechamber, were unable to force the portcullises and had to settle for making a man-sized hole in the upper part of the corridor's wall, opening onto the chamber of the sarcophagus.

I will return to this subject at the end of this work when I attempt to provide a historical account of the Great Pyramid.

The King's Chamber

Constructed entirely of Aswan granite, its dimensions are the following: length, 10.481 meters (20 cubits); width, 5.235 meters (10 cubits); height, 5.858 meters (5 $\sqrt{5}$ cubits).

The walls comprise five courses; the roof is formed by nine enormous granite slabs weighing about 400 metric tons.

Two so-called ventilation ducts are located in the north and south walls, and climb through the masonry at angles of 31° 33' (north duct) and 45° 13' 40" (south duct). The beginning of the south duct is in the form of a barrel 1.50 meters deep horizontally and 0.45 meter in diameter. In its ascending part, its section is a square measuring 0.221 meter along the side, identical to that of the north duct.

According to Howard-Vyse, the lengths of the ducts are the following: north duct, 71.02 meters; south duct, 53.04 meters. The part of the wall next to the start of the south duct has been hammered so as to give the impression of a lion grasping the entrance to the duct with its paws. We can assume that the "ventilation" ducts were originally obstructed. It is obvious that if this chamber served as a sepulchral chamber, it would have been *absolutely* necessary to seal these ducts in order to prevent the putrefaction of the mummy and the destruction of its funerary furniture. Although it is within the realm of possibility, it is very unlikely that this chamber ever held the royal remains. Then why these ducts? As I said earlier, I believe they were installed to allow the royal soul to leave the body and ascend toward heaven in order to join Ra's barque, after the transferral of the divine *ka* (brought about by passes and magical incantations) from the body of the deceased king to that of his successor.

The King's Chamber is surmounted by five chambers of construction; the only interest these offer are the quarriers' graffiti found therein, sole evidence of the era during which the Pyramid was built, providing the royal name "Khnum-Khufu" or "Soris-Khufu" (the Arab authors' Surid).

According to Petrie, the King's Chamber was placed at a level such that the surface of the Pyramid's horizontal section at that height would be equal to half that of its base—or, consequently, either the diagonal of the square section would be equal to the length of the base or the side of the square section would be equal to half the diagonal of the Pyramid's base.

From the dimensions of the King's Chamber, Petrie determined the value of the cubit used under the Fourth Dynasty: 0.5237 meter, which is certainly very close to the true value.

The dimensions of the King's Chamber are such that the triangle AHB is isiac, as its sides measure 15, 20, and 25 cubits, respectively (see figure 25), and the chamber's height is exactly half the diagonal of its base ($5\sqrt{5}$ cubits).

According to Bruchet, the chamber is located at two sevenths the total height of the Pyramid, while the middle chamber is situated at one-seventh the Pyramid's height.

Petrie's and Bruchet's accounts are very similar: according to Petrie's rule, the King's Chamber would be located at $\frac{2 - \sqrt{2}}{2}$ the height. Now, $\frac{2 - \sqrt{2}}{2} = 0.293$, and $\frac{2}{7} = 0.286$.

The Sarcophagus

In the western part of the chamber is found the famous granite sarcophagus. Since this sarcophagus has been the object of much speculation, a precisely dimensioned sketch is essential. After measuring with the greatest care, I determined that its exterior dimensions are: length, 2.292 meters; width, 0.984 meters; height (without lid), 1.053 meters.

This sarcophagus, made of Aswan granite, was equipped with a sliding dovetailed lid; it is similar to many other sarcophagi, particularly that of Unas and most especially those of the great mastaba of Medum and the pyramid of Kephren. Upon closing, three rods inserted in holes in the lid

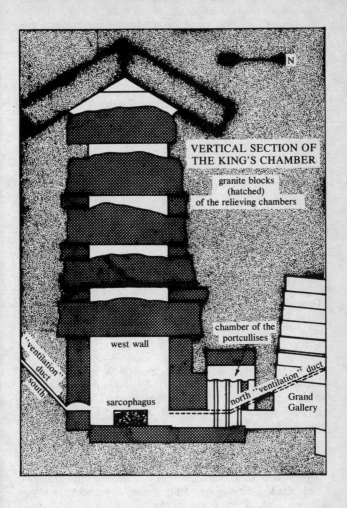

N

VERTICAL SECTION OF
THE KING'S CHAMBER

granite blocks
(hatched)
of the relieving chambers

chamber of the
portcullises

"ventilation"
duct
south

west wall

sarcophagus

north "ventilation" duct

Grand
Gallery

dropped into three corresponding holes in the cask, which were not as deep as the length of the rods.

A strange, unusual standard of volume and weight, this coffer with its sliding lid and automatic, unpickable lock!

One could validly object that the dimensions of the sarcophagus are too small for it to have contained a royal mummy equipped with several coffins, one within the other, as was the case with Tutankhamen. Its inner dimensions are, in fact, 1.985 by 0.675 meters, and its depth is 0.837 meter. If the cask did serve as Cheops' sarcophagus, one must conclude that he had less taste for ostentation than did his Eighteenth Dynasty successors.

But I am convinced that the cask merely held Kephren's body for two or three days, the length of time necessary for the transferral of the divine *ka*. Once the magical rites had been completed, the *empty* coffin, now considered sacred, was closed, the portcullises were lowered, and the Ascending Passage was blocked.

The sarcophagus discovered embedded in the pavement of Belzoni's Chamber in the pyramid of Kephren has more or less the same dimensions as the one found in the King's Chamber. These limited dimensions are sufficient to house a medium-sized mummy placed in *a single coffin* a maximum of 3 centimeters thick. Consequently, it is not unlikely that these two sarcophagi served not as sepultures but as cenotaphs of Osiris during the magical transferral of the divine *ka*. It is certainly for this reason that various initiated authors designate the great pyramids as the tombs of Osiris.

The sarcophagus was forced open, and the upper left-hand part of the eastern side is broken. The lid is missing, and no author mentions it prior to the French Expedition to Egypt. Only one member of the Expedition, General Baron Desvernois, notes, in his *Mémoires:*

> It is the chamber of King Cheops, with the sarcophagus of this prince located to the right of the entrance against the wall, but uncovered, containing only granular blackish-brown dust, rather similar to poor-quality loose tobacco, but odorless; *the lid, broken vertically in two, is propped up against the wall* right next to the sarcophagus.

THE SARCOPHAGUS IN THE KING'S CHAMBER

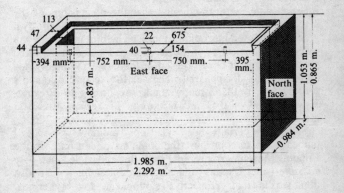

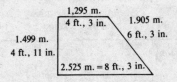

Section of one of the facing blocks still in place along the Great Pyramid's north face (according to Petrie)

Desvernois must have been mistaken: the granite block in question is certainly not the lid of the sarcophagus; it came from a probe made in the chamber's floor north of the cask.

Concerning the dimensions of the sarcophagus in the King's Chamber, I should point out that its exterior height (with the lid missing) is exactly 2 cubits, while the ratio of its length to its width is exactly 7:3. I might add that the thickness of the paving blocks under the sarcophagus is 1.05 meters (2 cubits).

I shall return later to the subject of the King's Chamber and its sarcophagus, the source of some absurd speculations by certain "pyramidal visionaries."

Since many authors contend that the dimensions of the sarcophagus are insufficient for it to have housed the royal mummy enclosed in a coffin, it may be helpful to provide the respective dimensions of the sarcophagi located in the three great pyramids of Giza. The lid of the Great Pyramid's sarcophagus has disappeared. That of the second pyramid's sarcophagus is 0.252 meter thick. According to Howard-Vyse, the lid of the sarcophagus at Mykerinos was 0.23 meter thick.

Since it is certain that Mykerinos' mummy was indeed placed in its sarcophagus (the coffin's wooden lid is in the London Museum at present) it is thus possible—but only *possible*—that Cheops' and Kephren's mummies were also inhumed in their respective sarcophagi, for Mykerinos' sarcophagus was the smallest of the three. From the dimen-

	CHEOPS granite	KEPHREN granite	MYKERINOS blue basalt
External dimensions (in meters)			
Length	2.292	2.630	2.470
Width	0.984	1.065	0.940
Height	1.053	0.965	0.889
Internal dimensions (in meters)			
Length	1.985	2.150	1.850
Width	0.675	0.676	0.600
Depth	0.837	0.750	0.620

sions of their sarcophagi, we can deduce that Kephren was bigger than Cheops and Mykerinos smaller.

If this was indeed the case, we must conclude that the pharaohs of the Fourth Dynasty were more modest than their ostentatious successors. Amenemhet III, whose brick pyramid at Hawara dominates the side of the Labyrinth, had, as a sarcophagus, a quartzite monolith weighing 110 metric tons, with an interior length of 7 meters and walls 1 meter thick! Psusennes had a silver mummy-shaped coffin inside two sarcophagi laid one within the other. Tutankhamen, an insignificant king alongside Cheops and Kephren, had three coffins; his sarcophagus measures 2.75 meters long.

It is clear from the limited dimensions of the three sarcophagi found in the great pyramids of Giza that if they did hold the royal mummies, each mummy had a single, rather thin coffin, since the breadth of an average-size man at the time was 0.56 meter.

NOTES

1. Henri Gauthier, *Le Livre des rois d'Egypte* [Book of the Kings of Egypt] (Cairo: Imprimerie de l'Institut Français d'Archéologie, 1907–17), vol. 1, p. 6.
2. Jean-Philippe Lauer, *Les Problèms des pyramides d'Egypte* (Paris: Payot, 1948), p. 95.
3. William Matthew Flinders Petrie, *The Pyramids and Temples of Gizeh* (London: Field & Tuer, 1883).
4. *Nouvelles recherches sur la Grande Pyramide* (Aix-en-Provence: La Pensée Universitaire, 1965).
5. Petrie, *Pyramids and Temples of Gizeh.*
6. Petrie points out that a quantity of debris from a black rock was found near the niche in the Queen's Chamber.

CHAPTER 2

THE PYRAMIDS THROUGH HISTORY

THE GREEK AND ROMAN AUTHORS

Many of the ancient authors, from Herodotus on, wrote about the Egyptian pyramids. However, so far no significant hieroglyphic text from the era has come down to us; only certain names of royal pyramids have been recovered, particularly—and fortunately—that of the pyramid of Cheops.

Herodotus (c. 430 B.C.)

History, II, 124–35: Now unto the time of King Rhampsinitus they said that Egypt was in all things well governed and flourished greatly; but Cheops, who became king after him, speedily brought Egypt into all manner of misery. For he shut up all the temples, and prevented them from sacrificing. And secondly he commanded all the Egyptians to labor for him. Some were enjoined to drag stones to the Nile from the quarries in the Arabian mountain; and he appointed others to receive the stones when they were brought over the river in ships, and drag them to the mountain called Libyan. And there were ever a hundred thousand men laboring at one time, three months apiece. And the time which passed upon the people in their oppression was firstly the ten years wherein they built the road by which the stones were dragged, a work, as it seemeth me, not very much less than the pyramid itself, for the length of it is five stades and the breadth ten fathoms, and the height, where it is highest, eight fathoms [5 stades = 923.50 m.; 10 fathoms = 18.47 m.; 8 fathoms = 14.78 m.] and it is of polished stone and figures are graven thereon. *So the ten years were for this, and also for the underground chambers on the hill where the pyramids stand, which he made as a tomb for himself in an island, bringing a channel from the Nile.* But the pyramid itself took twenty years to make. Each front thereof is eight plethra [8 plethra = 246.26 m.] long, (for it is square), and the height is the same. It is of polished stone fitted perfectly, and none of the stones is less than thirty feet [30 feet = 9.24 m.] long. And this pyramid was made thus. They made it first in the shape of stairs, and lifted up the stones which remained with engines made of short timbers. From the ground they raised them to the first range of stairs; and when the stone came up to this, it was set in another engine that stood on the first range, and drawn up from this to the second range, and thence by another engine to the third; for there were as many engines as there were ranges of stairs. (Or peradventure there was only one engine, and that easy to carry, which they moved from range to range, after taking out the stone; for I will give both accounts as both are told.) Howsoever, the topmost parts of the pyramid were finished first, and then the next, and lastly the parts at the bottom near the ground. And it is recorded in Egyptian writing on the pyramid how much was spent on radish and onion and garlick for the labourers. And if I well remember what the interpreter told me reading the writing, a thousand and six hundred talents of silver were expended. [1,600 talents = 41,884 kg.] And if this is indeed so, how much more must have been expended on the tools they worked with, and on bread and clothing for the labourers, seeing they were the aforesaid time in building the works, and no little time besides, as I deem, in cutting the stones and bringing them, *and building the chambers under the earth.* And Cheops came to such wickedness that, when he lacked money, he set his daughter in a brothel and enjoined her to charge thus and thus much; but they told me not how much. And she demanded the sum enjoined by her father, and also resolved to leave a memorial of her own. And she besought each man that went in unto her to give her a present of one stone. And from these stones, they said, was made the pyramid that standeth in the midst of the three in front of the great pyramid; and each face thereof is one plethrum and an half long. [1½ plethra = 46.17 m.]

And the Egyptians said that this Cheops reigned fifty years, and when he deceased, his brother Chephren received the kingdom. And he walked in the same way as the other in all things, and builded a pyramid likewise. This pyramid attaineth not the dimensions of the former (for I myself measured them); *for there are neither chambers under the earth beneath it, nor doth a channel come into it from the Nile, like that which floweth into the other through a conduit of masonry and encircleth an island within, where Cheops himself is said to lie;* but the first course is made of Ethiopian stone of many colours. And it adjoineth unto the other; and they both stand on the same hill, which is about an hundred feet high. And Chephren, they said, reigned six and fifty years.

And after this king they said that Mycerinus the son of Cheops reigned over Egypt. . . .

This king also left a pyramid, much less than his father's: each face thereof—for it is square—wanteth twenty feet of three plethra, and half thereof is of Ethiopian stone. Now divers of the Greeks say that this pyramid pertaineth unto Rhodopis the whore. But they speak not rightly; and it seemeth me that they know not even who Rhodopis was, when they speak thus; for else they had not ascribed unto her the making of such a pyramid, whereon countless thousands of talents have been expended. . . .

Concerning the Labyrinth:

But after Mycerinus the priests said that Asychis became king of Egypt. . . . And this king, desiring to excel all the kings of Egypt that were before him, left for memorial a pyramid made of bricks; and carved on a stone in it is writing which saith thus: Contemn me not beside the pyramids of stone; for I surpass them as much as Zeus surpasseth the other gods. With a pole they dipped down into a lake; and whatsoever of the mud clave to the pole, this they collected and formed bricks thereof; and with these they made me. . . .

. . . And near to the corner where the labyrinth endeth is a pyramid forty fathoms high [40 fathoms = 73.78 m.], whereon great figures are graven. And there is a way into it under the ground. Such is this labyrinth. But the lake called the lake of Mœris, beside which this labyrinth is builded, affordeth a yet greater marvel. The circuit thereof measureth three thousand and six hundred stades [3,600 stades = 665 km.], *or threescore schœni, even as the seacoast of Egypt itself.* And the lake is longest from north to south, and fifty fathoms [50 fathoms = 92.35 m.] in depth where it is deepest. And it is plain that it is made with hands; for well nigh in the midst of the lake stand two pyramids, each of which riseth fifty fathoms above the waters, and the part beneath the waters is even so deep; and on both is a stone image seated on a throne. *Thus the pyramids are an hundred fathoms high* [100 fathoms = 184.71 m.]. *But an hundred fathoms are a stade of six plethra, because a fathom measureth six feet or four cubits, if a foot be four hands' breadth and a cubit six hands' breadth.* . . .

Manetho of Sebennytos (*c.* 280 B.C.)

In his *Epitome,* handed down by Syncellus, the oldest pyramids mentioned are those of Kochome (Cho, in the Armenian version of Eusebius), the work of Uenephes, fourth king of the First Dynasty. He goes on to say that Suphis (second king of the Fourth Dynasty) built the Great Pyramid, which Herodotus said had been built by Cheops.

Manetho reports that Queen Nitocris (sixth ruler of the Sixth Dynasty), "the noblest and loveliest woman of her time," built the third pyramid.

Diodorus Siculus (56 B.C.)

Book I, 63.4–64.14: The eighth king, Chemmis of
Memphis, ruled fifty years and constructed the largest of
the three pyramids, which are numbered among the
seven wonders of the world. These pyramids, which are
situated on the side of Egypt which is towards Libya,
are one hundred and twenty stades from Memphis and
forty-five from the Nile, and by the immensity of their
structures and the skill shown in their execution they fill
the beholder with wonder and astonishment. For the
largest is in the form of a square and has a base length on
each side of seven plethra [7 plethra = 246.26 m.] and a
height of over six plethra [6 plethra = 211.08 m.
(ridge)]; it also gradually tapers to the top, where each
side is six cubits long. The entire construction is of hard
stone, which is difficult to work but lasts for ever; for
though no fewer than a thousand years have elapsed, as
they say, to our lifetime, or, as some writers have it,
more than three thousand four hundred, the stones
remain to this day still preserving their original position
and the entire structure undecayed. It is said that the
stone was conveyed over a great distance from Arabia
and that the construction was effected by means of
mounds, since cranes had not yet been invented at that
time; and the most remarkable thing in the account is
that, though the constructions were on such a great
scale and the country round about them consists of
nothing but sand, not a trace remains either of any
mound or of the dressing of the stones, so that they do
not have the appearance of being the slow handiwork of
men but look like a sudden creation, as though they had
been made by some god and set down bodily in the
surrounding sand. Certain Egyptians would make a
marvel out of these things, saying that, inasmuch as the
mounds were built of salt and saltpetre, when the river
was let in it melted them down and completely effaced
them without the intervention of man's hand. However,
there is not a word of truth in this, but the entire material
for the mounds, raised as they were by the labour of
many hands, was returned by the same means to the
place from which it came; for three hundred and sixty
thousand men, as they say, were employed on the

undertaking, and the whole structure was scarcely completed in twenty years.

Upon the death of this king his brother Cephren succeeded to the throne and ruled fifty-six years; but some say that it was not the brother of Chemmis, but his son, named Chabryes, who took the throne. All writers, however, agree that it was the next ruler who, emulating the example of his predecessor, built the second pyramid, which was the equal of the one just mentioned in the skill displayed in its execution but far behind it in size, since its base length on each side is only a stade [1 stade = 211.08 m.]. And an inscription on the larger pyramid gives the sum of money expended on it, since the writing sets forth that on vegetables and purgatives for the workmen there were paid out over sixteen hundred talents. The smaller bears no inscription but has steps cut into one side. And though the two kings built the pyramids to serve as their tombs, in the event neither of them was buried in them; for the multitudes, because of the hardships which they had endured in the building of them and the many cruel and violent acts of these kings, were filled with anger against those who had caused their sufferings and openly threatened to tear their bodies asunder and cast them in despite out of the tombs. Consequently each ruler when dying enjoined upon his kinsmen to bury his body secretly in an unmarked place.

After these rulers Mycerinus, to whom some give the name Mencherinus, a son of the builder of the first pyramid, became king. He undertook the construction of a third pyramid, but died before the entire structure had been completed. The base length of each side he made three plethra [3 plethra = 105.54 m.], and for fifteen courses he built the walls of black stone like that found about Thebes, but the rest of it he filled out with stone like that found in the other pyramids. In size this structure falls behind those mentioned above, but far surpasses them in the skill displayed in its execution and the great cost of the stone; and on the north side of the pyramid is an inscription stating that its builder was Mycerinus. . . . There are also three more pyramids, each of which is one plethrum [1 plethrum = 35.18 m.]

long on each side and in general construction is like the others save in size; and these pyramids, they say, were built by the three kings named above for their wives.

It is generally agreed that these monuments far surpass all other constructions in Egypt, not only in their massiveness and cost but also in the skill displayed by their builders. And they say that the architects of the monuments are more deserving of admiration than the kings who furnished the means for their execution; for in bringing their plans to completion the former called upon their individual souls and their zeal for honour, but the latter only used the wealth which they had inherited and the grievous toil of other men. But with regard to the pyramids there is no complete agreement among either the inhabitants of the country or the historians; for according to some the kings mentioned above were their builders, according to others they were different kings; for instance, it is said that Armaeus built the largest, Amosis the second, and Inaros the third. And this last pyramid, some say, is the tomb of the courtesan Rhodopis, for some of the monarchs became her lovers, as the account goes, and out of their passion for her carried the building through to completion as a joint undertaking.

Strabo (c. 24 B.C.)

On proceeding forty stadia from the city, one comes to a kind of mountain-brow; on it are numerous pyramids, the tombs of kings, of which three are noteworthy; and two of these are even numbered among the Seven Wonders of the World, for they are a stadium in height, are quadrangular in shape, and their height is a little greater than the length of each of the sides; and one of them is only a little larger than the other. High up, approximately midway between the sides, it has a movable stone, and when this is raised up there is a sloping passage to the vault. Now these pyramids are near one another and on the same level; but farther on, at a greater height of the hill, is the third; which is much smaller than the two, though constructed at much greater expense; for from the foundations almost to the middle it is made of black stone, the stone from which mortars are made, being brought from a great distance, for it is brought from the mountains of Aethiopia; and because of its being hard and difficult to work into shape it rendered the undertaking very expensive. It is called "Tomb of the Courtesan," having been built by her lovers—the courtesan whom Sappho the Melic poetess calls Doricha, the beloved of Sappho's brother Charaxus, who was engaged in transporting Lesbian wine to Naucratis for sale, but others give her the name Rhodopis. They tell the fabulous story that, when she was bathing, an eagle snatched one of her sandals from her maid and carried it to Memphis; and while the king was administering justice in the open air, the eagle, when it arrived above his head, flung the sandal into his lap; and the king, stirred both by the beautiful shape of the sandal and by the strangeness of the occurrence, sent men in all directions into the country in quest of the woman who wore the sandal; and when she was found in the city of Naucratis, she was brought up to Memphis, became the wife of the king, and when she died was honoured with the above-mentioned tomb. [1]

Pliny the Elder (c. 20 A.D.):

In Egypt too are the pyramids, which must be mentioned, if only cursorily. They rank as a superfluous and foolish display of wealth on the part of the kings, since it is generally recorded that their motive for building them was to avoid providing funds for their successors or for rivals who wished to plot against them, or else to keep the common folk occupied. Much vanity was shown by these kings in regard to such enterprises, and the remains of several unfinished pyramids are still in existence. There is one in the nome of Arsinoe, and there are two in that of Memphis, not far from the labyrinth, a work which also will be described. Two more stand in a position once occupied by Lake Moeris, which is merely a vast excavation, but is nevertheless recorded by the Egyptians as one of their remarkable and memorable achievements. The points of these pyramids are said to tower above the surface of the water. The other three pyramids, the fame of which has reached every part of the world, are of course visible to travellers approaching by river from any direction. They stand on a rocky hill in the desert on the African side of the river between the city of Memphis and what, as we have already explained, is known as the Delta, at a point less than 4 miles from the Nile, and 7½ miles from Memphis. Close by is a village called Busiris, where there are people who are used to climbing these pyramids.

XVII. In front of them is the Sphinx, which deserves to be described even more than they, and yet the Egyptians have passed it over in silence. The inhabitants of the region regard it as a deity. They are of the opinion that a King Harmais is buried inside it and try to make out that it was brought to the spot: it is in fact carefully fashioned from the native rock. The face of the monstrous creature is painted with ruddle as a sign of reverence. The circumference of the head when measured across the forehead amounts to 102 feet, the length is 243 feet, and the height from the paunch to the top of the asp on its head is 61½ feet. [2]

The largest pyramid is made of stone from the Arabian quarries. It is said that 360,000 men took 20 years to build it. The time taken to build all three was 88 years and 4 months. The authors who have written about them, namely Herodotus, Euhemerus, Duris of Samos, Aristagoras, Dionysius, Artemidorus, Alexander Polyhistor, Butoridas, Antisthenes, Demetrius, Demoteles and Apion, are not at all agreed as to which kings were responsible for their construction, since chance, with the greatest justice, has caused those who inspired such a mighty display of vanity to be forgotten. Some of the writers mentioned record that 1600 talents were spent on radishes, garlic and onions alone. The largest pyramid covers an area of nearly 5 acres. Each of the four sides has an equal measurement from corner to corner of 783 feet; the height from ground-level to the pinnacle amounts to 725 feet, while the circumference of the pinnacle is 16½ feet. As for the second pyramid, each of its sides from corner to corner totals 757½ feet. The third is smaller than those already mentioned, but on the other hand is far more splendid, with its Ethiopian stone towering to a height of 363 feet along its sloping sides between the corners. No traces of the building operations survive. All around far and wide there is merely sand shaped like lentils, such as is found in most of Africa. The crucial problem is to know how the masonry was laid to such a great height. Some think that ramps of soda and salt were piled against the structure as it was raised; and that after its completion these were flooded and dissolved by water from the river. Others hold that bridges were built of mud bricks and that when the work was finished the bricks were allotted to individuals for building their own houses. For it is considered impossible that the Nile, flowing at a far lower level, could have flooded the site. Within the largest pyramid is a well 86 cubits deep, into which water from the river is supposed to have been brought by a channel. The method of measuring the height of the pyramids and of taking any similar measurement was devised by Thales of Miletus, the procedure being to measure the shadow at the hour at which its length is expected to be equal to the height of the body that is throwing it. Such are the wonders of the pyramids; and the last and greatest of these wonders, which forbids us to marvel at the wealth of kings, is that the smallest but most greatly admired of these pyramids was built by Rhodopis, a mere prostitute. She was once the fellow-slave and concubine of Aesop, the sage who composed the Fables; and our amazement is all the greater when we reflect that such wealth was acquired through prostitution.

Concerning the obelisk of Sesostris placed in Rome's Campus Martius.

The one in the Campus was put to use in a remarkable way by Augustus of Revered Memory so as to mark the sun's shadow and thereby the lengths of days and nights. A pavement was laid down for a distance appropriate to the height of the obelisk so that the shadow cast at noon on the shortest day of the year might exactly coincide with it. Bronze rods let into the pavement were meant to measure the shadow day by day as it gradually became shorter and then lengthened again. This device deserves to be carefully studied, and was contrived by the mathematician Novius Facundus. He placed on the pinnacle a gilt ball, at the top of which the shadow would be concentrated, for otherwise the shadow cast by the tip of the obelisk would have lacked definition. He is said to have understood the principle from observing the shadow cast by the human head. The readings thus given have for about thirty years past failed to correspond to the calendar, either because the course of the sun itself is anomalous and has been altered by some change in the behaviour of the heavens or because the whole earth has shifted slightly from its central position, a phenomenon which, I hear, has been detected also in other places. Or else earth-tremors in the city may have brought about a purely local displacement of the shaft or floods from the Tiber may have caused the mass to settle, even though the foundations are said to have been sunk to a depth equal to the height of the load they have to carry.[3]

Solinus (third century A.D.)

The pyramids of Egypt are raised towers, higher than any other man-made work; since they exceed the reach of their shadows, they cast no shadow on the ground.

Cassiodorus (c. 520 A.D.)

This author also reports the phenomenon of the Pyramid's consuming its own shadow: "the shadow, consuming itself, cannot be seen anywhere beyond the monument."

THE ARAB AUTHORS

The majority of the Arab authors are in agreement concerning the names of the kings who constructed the great pyramids of Giza. The names they give are as valid as Herodotus' Cheops, Kephren, and Mykerinos.

According to the Arab authors, the builder of the Great Pyramid was Surid. Now, the "Khnum-Khufu" cartouche could validly be read as "Soris-Khufu," with the sun god Khnum represented by the divine ram "Soris." Besides, Manetho assigns the name Soris to the first ruler of the Fourth Dynasty.

The builder of the second pyramid is called "*Herdjib*" which is in fact Kephren's first name: *wsr ib* ("powerful heart").

Mykerinos is correctly called "Minkaus" or "Kerures"—(Men) Kaura.

Maqrizi (born in Cairo in 1360 A.D., died *c.* 1442)

This Arab chronicler mostly restricts himself to reporting accounts by historians who preceded him.

Chapter 40 of his work *The Book of Warning* is devoted to the pyramids. I shall only extract the principal passages.

Formerly, the pyramids in Egypt were very numerous; there were a great number of them in the district of Abusir, some large, others small; some made of limestone and/or brick, but most made of stone; some stepped, others with a smooth surface. At Giza, opposite the town of Masr, there were many pyramids, all small, which were torn down, during the reign of the sultan Saleh el-Din Yussef ben Ayub, by Karakush [1240–50 A.D.], who used the materials thus obtained to build the citadel of the Mountain, the surrounding wall of Cairo and Masr, and the bridges of Giza.

The three largest pyramids are those which are still standing today opposite Masr. There is some disagreement as to the date of their construction, the names of those who built them, and the reason for building them. Many contradictory legends, most of them unfounded, surround the subject.

Maqrizi relates a dream had by the pharaoh Surid ben Sahluq, which the priests interpreted as presaging a flood, according to the account of Ibrahim Wassif Shah:

Then the king ordered that the pyramids be built and that they include passages that the Nile would penetrate to a set point, then draining off toward certain regions of the West and of Said.[4] He had the pyramids filled with talismans, wonders, riches, and idols; he had the bodies of the kings placed there, and, according to his orders, the priests traced on these monuments all the maxims of the sages; thus on every possible surface of the pyramids—ceilings, bases, sides—was written all the knowledge possessed by the Egyptians, and there the constellations were drawn, and there were inscribed the names of drugs and their useful and harmful properties, the science of talismans, of mathematics, of architecture —in short, all the branches of learning—and all this was shown very clearly for those who are acquainted with their writing and understand their language.

Having resolved to build the pyramids, the king had blocks cut, enormous slabs polished, and lead mined from the land to the West and from the boulders of the Aswan region . . .

[Upon arriving at the plateau of the pyramids], they set the slabs in place, piercing a hole in the middle of each; an iron bar was set vertically in this hole; then another slab, also pierced with a hole, into which the iron bar was inserted, was placed over the first; then molten lead was poured into the hole around the bar in order to bind the two slabs firmly; they continued in this manner until the pyramid was completed.

. . . Once the monuments were completed, the king had doorways carved in them 40 cubits underground. The doorway of the eastern pyramid is to the west and is located at a distance of 100 cubits from the pyramid's face; the doorway of the western pyramid is to the west and 100 cubits from the pyramid's face; the doorway of the colored[5] pyramid is to the south and is also 100 cubits from the pyramid's face. If one were to dig at this distance, one would find the doorway that permits access into the pyramid by way of an arched passage faced with stone.

For each of the pyramids, the king decided upon a height above the ground of 100 cubits,[6] equal to 500 of our modern cubits; the length of each of the faces was also 100 cubits, and the faces were designed to that the summit ended in 8 of our cubits.[7]

. . . Construction of the pyramids was begun upon a sunrise favored by the stars, a day chosen by common consent. Once the pyramids were completed, they were covered from top to bottom with a colored brocade,[8] and a festival was called in their honor, attended by all of Egypt's inhabitants.

The western pyramid was equipped with thirty storerooms of colored granite filled with all sorts of riches and various objects: statues made of precious stones, magnificent iron tools, rustproof weapons, malleable glass, extraordinary talismans, basic and compound drugs, deadly poisons.

In the eastern pyramid chambers were constructed in which were depicted the sky and the stars, and in which were amassed what Surid's ancestors had accomplished in the way of statues,[9] the perfumes that were burned in honor of the planets, the books concerning them, the chart of the fixed stars and the table of their revolutions in the course of time, the list of the events of past eras subject to their influence, and the moment at which it is necessary to examine them in order to know the future —in sum, everything concerning Egypt till the end of time; in addition, basins containing the magical water and other similar things were placed there.

In the painted pyramid were placed the bodies of priests enclosed in black granite coffins; there was enclosed with each priest a book outlining the wonders of the art he practiced, his acts and his life, what was accomplished in his time, and what had been and would be from the beginning to the very end of time.

On each face of the pyramids were depicted figures carrying out all sorts of tasks and grouped according to their importance and rank. These representations were accompanied by a description of the trades, of the tools necessary to them, and of all the information concerning them. No branch of learning was omitted; all were accounted for, in writing and drawing.

Also placed in the pyramid were the treasures of the planets, all that was given in offering to the stars, and the treasures of the priest, the whole amounting to a wealth beyond computation.

To each of these pyramids was assigned a guardian.

The western pyramid was placed under the guardianship of a granite mosaic statue; this statue was standing, holding something like a javelin in its hand, and wearing

a headdress in the form of a coiled viper. Whenever anyone approached the statue, the viper sprang at him,
wound about his neck, killed him, and resumed its
original position.

The guardian of the eastern pyramid was a statue of
black stone speckled with black and white, with glitter-
ing open eyes; it was seated on a throne and held a
javelin. Whenever anyone looked at it a terrifying voice
would emerge from the statue's side, making the on-
looker fall on his face; he would die there, unable to
rise.

The painted pyramid was watched over by a stone
statue of an eagle perched on a base of similar stone.
Whoever looked at it would be drawn to it and would
become stuck to it, unable to detach himself until dead.

All this having been accomplished, the pyramids were
surrounded by immaterial spirits; victims' throats were
slit in their honor, in a ceremony designed to protect
the spirits against anyone wishing to approach them,
except for initiates, who had performed the necessary
rites.

The Copts relate, moreover, that the spirit attached
to the pyramid of the North is a naked yellow devil
equipped with a mouthful of long teeth. The spirit of the
pyramid of the South is a woman who reveals her intimate parts; she is beautiful, but her mouth is also
equipped with long teeth; she charms the men who look
upon her, smiles at them, attracts them, and makes them
lose their minds. The spirit of the painted pyramid is an
old man who carries a censer in which perfumes are
burned.

Numerous people have repeatedly seen these spirits
circling the pyramid around midday and at sunset.

Maqrizi reports that, according to el-Masudi:

The calif Abdallah Al-Mamun ben Harun el-Rashid
ordered that the Great Pyramid be opened; and for him
was made the hole that is still gaping today; fire, vine-
gar, and levers were used for this purpose; blacksmiths

worked on it, spending a considerable amount of money. The thickness of the wall was approximately 20 cubits [9.20 meters]. . . .

Masudi (born in Baghdad, died in 956 A.D.)

In his historical encyclopedia, entitled *Meadows of Gold and Mines of Gems,* Masudi reports a conversation that Ahmad, son of Tulun, had with a Copt elder around 260 A.H. (874 A.D.).

. . . When questioned about the construction of the pyramids, he said, "They were the tombs of kings. When one of their kings died, his body was placed in a basin of stone, similar to what is called a *djaroun* in Egypt and Syria; the cover was sealed, then they began to build, having determined the height of the pyramid in advance. They placed the sarcophagus in the center of the structure and continued to raise the vault until it reached the height that you see.

"The door was placed under the pyramid itself, and one entered it through a vaulted, underground passage, which could be 100 or more cubits long; each pyramid had such a door and entry."

"But," he was asked, "how were the smooth pyramids built? How could the workers climb up and work? With the help of what machinery did they transport these enormous stones, a single one of which cannot be lifted now without incredible effort, if at all?"

The Copt answered: "They built the pyramids in superimposed layers, step-by-step, like a staircase; then they polished them by scraping them from the top to the bottom. This was the working procedure of these people who combined admirable strength and patience with religious respect for their kings."

He was asked why the inscriptions which cover the pyramids and the temples are indecipherable. He answered: "Since the learned men and those who used this writing have disappeared, and Egypt has been occupied by a succession of foreign peoples, the Greek alphabet and writing have prevailed. As the Copts became familiar with this writing, they used it and combined the letters with those of their own alphabet; from their contact with the Greeks, resulted a writing related both to Greek and ancient Copt, and thus they lost the understanding of the writing of their ancestors."

After relating the conversation with this 130-year-old Copt, Masudi adds:

The pyramids are very high and of remarkable construction: all kinds of inscriptions cover their surface, written in the characters of ancient nations and kingdoms that no longer exist. We don't know what sort of writing this is and what it means. Those who have studied the dimensions of the pyramids estimate their height to be 400 cubits or more; this was confirmed by those who climbed them. Their width is approximately equal to this number; their inscriptions relate to the sciences, to the properties of bodies, to magic and to the secrets of nature . . .

The physician Ali ben Radvan says:

I have reflected on the construction of the pyramids and I have come to the conclusion that a profound theoretical and practical knowledge of architecture and mechanics was required of those who traced the square outlines of their bases, carved the male and female stones, and coated the whole with a marine plaster in such a way as to raise the edifice as high as heavy weights could be lifted. The higher the edifice grew, the narrower it became . . . and at each course was placed a perfectly fitted stone, alternately male and female.[10] They continued thus as far as they could; then the top was truncated and the projecting edges, used in raising the materials, were trimmed, and, by completing this operation from top to bottom, they obtained a [smooth] block forming the pyramid.

The first pyramid, measured according to the cubit still used for construction in Egypt today, runs 400 cubits along the side, which gives, in black cubits (the length of which is 24 digits), 500 cubits,[11] and, since the base is square, the sides, as well as the angles, are equal. Two of these sides are parallel to the meridian; the other two are parallel to the east-west line, and each side measures 500 black cubits.

The apothem descending from the pyramid's summit to the middle of the base of the side measures 470 cubits and, if the pyramid were complete, would measure 500 cubits.

The pyramid's faces form four triangles; these four triangles are isosceles triangles, and if the pyramid were complete, each of their sides would measure 560 cubits and the four triangles would be joined at the top by a single point that would be the peak of the pyramid. These various dimensions give the height a value of 430 cubits; it is along this line that the pyramid's center of gravity is located.

Al Mamun, having opened a hole in this pyramid, there discovered a corridor that led, along a sloping passage, to a cubic chamber; on the floor was a marble coffin that is still there today, for no one has been able to remove it . . .

Ibn al-Nadim writes in his book entitled *The Index:*

These monuments—that is, the pyramids—have a length of 480 *hachémique* cubits and a width that is also 480 cubits. The edifice recedes as it rises from the base, and at the summit the dimensions are only 40 cubits; this was done intentionally and by design. In the middle of the plateau a beautiful chamber was built, inside of which a sort of mausoleum was set up. At the top of the tomb are two magnificent, perfectly dressed blocks, surmounted by two stone statues representing a man and a woman facing each other. The man holds in his hand a stone tablet covered with writing, and the woman a mirror and a gold tablet decorated with wonderful carvings. Between the two pedestals is a stone vessel sealed with a gold lid; lifting the lid, one perceives a sort of odorless dried resin in which has been placed a gold box enclosing a quantity of blood, which, upon exposure to the air, shows the coagulation peculiar to blood, then dries up. The tombs are sealed with stone lids that, when withdrawn, reveal, in one of the tombs, a man lying on his back, perfectly preserved and dried; his flesh, as well as his hair, is still visible. In the neighboring sarcophagus is the body of a woman in the same position and the same condition as the man.

This pavement is pierced by a man-sized passage that plunges like a tunnel; its vault is made of stone, and one finds there portraits and seated or standing statues, and a quantity of other things, the meaning of which is not known.

Abv Abdallah Mohammed ben Abd el-Rahim el-Hokm, in his book *A Gift of Hearts*, reports that:

The pyramids are square at the base and triangular on their faces, and that there are eighteen of them. Opposite Fostat, there are three pyramids; the main pyramid has a perimeter of 2,000 cubits, with each side measuring 500 cubits; its height is also 500 cubits. Each of its stones measures 30 cubits wide and 10 cubits high; the setting and size of these stones are perfect.

Near the town of the pharaoh of Joseph is found another pyramid even larger and more imposing, its perimeter measuring 3,000 cubits and its height 750. The stones with which it was built measure 50 cubits each.

In the vicinity of the town of the pharaoh of Moses is a pyramid that is larger still and even more extraordinary.

Finally, another pyramid, known as the pyramid of Medum, resembles a mountain and is composed of five levels.

Al Mamun opened up the largest of the pyramids located opposite Fostat, entered the corridor of this edifice, and penetrated a very large chamber with a square base and vaulted ceiling; *a well 10 cubits deep*[12] had been dug in the middle of the chamber. *This well was square,* and the men who descended in it found in each side a door leading to a vast hall full of dead bodies, each wrapped in a shroud longer than any hundred robes. The passage of time had affected these corpses, which had turned black; these bodies, which are no larger than our own, have lost none of their tissue or hair; no bodies of old or white-haired men were found; these bodies were still solid and no one was able to tear off a single limb, but they were extremely light, the passage of time having rendered them as weightless as dry straw. Thus, in this well were found four chambers full of corpses and enormous bats.

In the chamber deep within the pyramid's interior is a door leading to the monument's summit; the passage has no steps and measures nearly 5 spans wide. It is said that during the reign of Al Mamun a man who had penetrated it arrived at a small chamber where there was a statue of a man made of a green stone like *dahang*. This statue was brought before Al Mamun. It had a cover, which was removed, and they found within the body of a man wearing a cuirass made of gold incrusted with all kinds of jewels; across his chest lay a sword of inestimable value, and near his head was a red ruby the size of a hen's egg, which shone like a flame and was inscribed with characters that no one could read; this Al Mamun took for himself. The statue from which the dead man had been taken was left near the doorway of the king's palace in Cairo, where I saw it in the year 511 [1117 A.D.].

The Cadi el-Galil Abu Abdallah Mohammed ben Salamat el-Qodai reports:

Certain people, having cleared a tomb in the monastery of Abu-Hermes, found there a dead man enveloped in a shroud and bearing on his chest a document wrapped in cloth. Having removed it, they looked at the writing but were unable to understand any of it, as the document was written in the ancient language of the Egyptians. They tried to find someone who could read it to them, but in vain. They were told that at the monastery of Klimun in Fayum there was a monk familiar with this kind of writing. They went in search of this monk, very doubtful that he could explain it to them, but he read it, and this is what the text means:

"This book was written in the first year of the reign of the emperor Diocletian, and I have copied it from a book itself copied in the first year of the reign of the emperor Philip [324 B.C.]. This emperor had had it copied from gold leaves on which the writing was broken down letter by letter. The primitive book was translated for Philip by the two Copt brothers Eilu and Yertsa . . . The length of time elapsed until Philip's copy was 2,372 years. As for the person who had the copy made on gold leaves, in writing broken down letter by letter, as Philip found it, his time was separated from that of the original manuscript by 1,785 years. The copied book forecast the flood to the king Surid ben Sahluk, who decided to erect pyramids upon which would be carved the body of scientific knowledge.

"The person who translated the Copt book into Arabic calculated the dates up to Sunday the 1st of Thoth in the year 225 A.H. [840 A.D.], and the figure was as high as 4,321 solar years; he then calculated how many years had passed from the flood up to that time and got 1,741 years, 59 days, 13 hours, 51 seconds; and subtracting this number from the first, he got a remainder of 399 years, 205 days, 10 hours, 2 minutes, and 1 second, from which he knew that the book in question had been written exactly the same number of years, days, hours, minutes, and seconds before the flood.[13]

". . . The advent of the misfortune that was threatening the earth must have occurred at the moment when the Lion's Heart was located in the first minute of the Head of the Crayfish[14] . . .

". . . I then studied what had occurred after this catastrophe and what the world was to undergo by way of calamities, and I discovered that the planets were auguring that a new scourge, the complete opposite of the first, would descend from the sky.

"This scourge would be a fire that would set the entire world ablaze. Attempting to determine the era in which this catastrophe would occur, I found that it would happen when the Lion's Heart was located in the last minute of the fifteenth degree of Leo . . ."

. . . Such were the contents of the document.

And when Surid died, he was buried in the eastern pyramid, Huheit in the western pyramid, and Krus in the pyramid with the base of Aswan stone and the summet of Kaddan stone. These pyramids have entrances dug in subterranean vaults; the length of each passage is 150 cubits.

The door of the eastern pyramid opens toward the north, that of the vault of the western pyramid opens toward the south. And amassed in the pyramids was an indeterminable quantity of gold and emeralds.

. . . It is said that [Al Mamun's men] discovered, in certain parts of these pyramids, an arched portal with three doors giving onto three chambers. Each door was 10 cubits high by 5 wide; they were made of carved and perfectly fitted marble, and on the lintel an undecipherable inscription was traced in blue.

They spent three days trying to open these doors; finally they noticed, at a distance of about 10 cubits opposite the doors, three marble columns, each of which had a hole carved out toward the top. Each hole contained the statue of a different bird: the first column contained the image of a dove in green stone; the center column, the image of a vulture in yellow stone; the third column, the image of a cock in red stone.

They moved the vulture, and the door opposite it moved; they raised the vulture, and the door also rose; and it was so heavy that a hundred men could not have carried it. They removed the two other statues, and the two other doors rose.

They entered the central chamber, where they found three beds made of transparent, luminous stone, and, on these three beds, three bodies covered with three robes, and, near the head of each body, a book written in unfamiliar characters.

In the second chamber were arranged a number of stone shelves supporting stone baskets containing marvelously worked gold receptacles incrusted with jewels.

The third chamber also contained stones shelves and receptacles in which had been placed instruments of war and a great number of weapons. They measured one of the swords; it was at least 7 spans; one of the cuirasses measured 18 spans.[15]

Al Mamun had the entire contents of these chambers

removed; then, the birds having been put back in place, the three doors closed and regained their ancient position.[16]

The number of pyramids was as high, it is said, as eighteen, of which three are located opposite Giza. The largest of these has a perimeter of 2,000 cubits; it is square, and each of its sides measures 500 cubits. Al Mamun, having opened it, found, it is said, a stone cask sealed with a slab and filled with gold . . . It is also said that he found there a statue of a man made of a green stone similar to *dauat;* when the cover was removed, they found within the statue the body of a man wearing a gold cuirass decorated with jewels, and across his chest lay a long sword of incalculable value; near his head was found a red ruby as large as a hen's egg. Al Mamun took it, saying: "This is worth more than gold."[17]

Certain Egyptian chroniclers claim that the green statue in which this body was found remained standing near the palace of the king in the town of Masr up until 611 A.H.[18]

Ibn Khurradhbih, in his book *Marvels of Construction* writes:

The geometrists claim that the base of each of the two great pyramids measures 400 cubits, *in black cubits,* and that the platform of the summit forms a square 11 cubits along the side, in ordinary cubits . . .

What is most wondrous is the admirable arrangement of the superimposed stones; it could not be improved upon, to the extent that we were unable to insert a needle, or even a hair, between two stones. Spread between the stones is a blue clay, the nature and composition of which are not known; and on the surface of the stones are traced inscriptions in unfamiliar ancient characters; no one in Egypt has ever heard tell of anyone who could understand them. These inscriptions are so numerous and extensive that, if they were transferred to paper, they would cover ten thousand sheets.

I have read, in certain old Sabean books, that one of these pyramids was the tomb of Adamun and the other the tomb of Hermes; according to these books, these personages were great prophets and Adamun was the greatest.

Pilgrimages were made to the pyramids, and people flocked to them from the ends of the earth.

The king El-Aziz Othman ben Salah el-Din Yussef ben Ayub . . . was urged by ignorant courtiers to destroy the pyramids. He began with the small red pyramid. This was in 593 [1196 A.D.]. After much work and enormous expenditures, they had to give up in utter exhaustion, having been unable to complete the task; all they succeeded in doing was disfiguring the pyramid and providing proof of their powerlessness and of the inanity of their efforts. This was in 593.

Today, to look at the pile of stones torn from the pyramid, one would think it had been completely destroyed; but if one examines the pyramid itself, one comes away convinced that nothing was removed and that only a part of the sides had crumbled . . .

As quoted by Maqrizi, Ibn Afir states:

Our Egyptian elders always acknowledged that the pyramids had been built by Sheddad ben 'Ad; it is also this king who dug the grottos in which treasures were buried. The populace of that time believed in resurrection, and when an individual died, all his possessions were buried with him; if the dead person had been a workman, the tools of his trade were buried with him.

The Sabeans made pilgrimages to the pyramids.

Al-Biruni, in _The Chronology of Ancient Nations_ (tr. C. Edward Sachau [London: W. H. Allen, 1879]), says:

The Persians and the great mass of the Magians, deny the Deluge altogether. . . . They say, a partial deluge occurred in Syria and the west at the time of Tahmurath, but it did not extend over the whole of the then civilized world . . . ; it did not extend beyond the peak of Hulwan, and did not reach the empires of the east. Further, they relate, that the inhabitants of the west, when they were warned by their sages, constructed buildings of the kind of the two pyramids which have been built in Egypt, saying: "If the disaster comes from Heaven, we shall go into them; if it comes from the earth, we shall ascend above them." . . . People are of the opinion, that the traces of the water of the Deluge and the effects of the waves are still visible on these two pyramids half-way up, above which the water did not rise.

Maqrizi's chapter on "Pyramids" ends with verses composed by the *cadi* Fakhr ed-din el-Wahab el-Masri in 655 A.H. (1257 A.D.):

...Was it a pious man who had them erected to attest to his
    piety?
And did he construct the pyramids for one of his idols?
Or is this the work of a man who believed that the soul
    returns
To the body after having left it?
And did he build them to house his treasures and his corpse,
As a tomb designed to protect them from the flood?
Or are they observatories for watching the planets,
    Chosen by the observers for the excellence of the site?
Or do they represent planetary calculations
    Such as those once made by the Persians and the Greeks?
Or was there carved upon their faces
    A knowledge that the mind endeavors to grasp?
A maddening desire to comprehend their message
    Surges in the heart of the beholder.

Howard-Vyse (in *Operations Carried on at the Pyramids of Gizeh in 1837* [London: J. Fraser, 1840–42], vol. 2, p. 352) reports that according to Maqrizi:

The square of the base, and the height of the Great Pyramid, are five hundred cubits, each consisting of twenty-four inches.

Norden (in *Travels in Egypt and Nubia*) reports that:

The Sabeans and the Magi, says an Arab author, used to make pilgrimages to the pyramids; they went there from the remotest lands and lit torches from the mountain to the river—but these accounts may be fictitious.[19]

**In his opuscule, Andalusi says, in regard
to the character of the Egyptians:**

From the form of government of this people, it appears that they had a caste of scholars, and in particular architects and astronomers. This is shown by all that they have left by way of wondrous edifices, such as the pyramids and temples, the ruins of which dumbfound the most perspicacious mind and stupefy the most clairvoyant imagination. They represent the remains of an astonishing, puzzling endeavor . . .

It is claimed that the pyramids are the tombs of illustrious kings who wished thus to be honored after their deaths, as they had been honored during their lives, and to ensure that their memory would survive for centuries and through the ages.

When the calif Al Mamun visited Egypt, he ordered that one of the pyramids be opened; his men set upon one of those opposite Fostat; having met with extraordinary difficulties and greatly exhausted, they finally reached the pyramid's interior, which they found to be riddled with wells and steep ramps; the passage was hazardous. Finally, at the end, they came upon a cubic chamber measuring about 8 cubits along the side. In the middle of the chamber was a marble cask sealed with a lid, which they raised; and all they found in the cask was a corpse decomposed from the passage of centuries.

Al Mamun then ordered that no other pyramid be opened, since the expense of opening this hole had been, assuredly, extraordinarily great . . .

It is said that they were built by a king named Surid ben Sahluk ben Siriak. According to other sources, the personage who erected the pyramids located opposite Fostat was Sheddad ben Ad, who built them following a dream.

The Copts, who contest the Amalekite invasion of Egypt, attribute the construction of these monuments to Surid, also following a dream informing him that a calamity would descend from the sky; this refers to the flood . . .

We examined the faces of these pyramids; they are crossed by longitudinal lines forming narrow parallel bands completely covered with writing that, though it is clearly visible, no one now knows how to read; its meaning is no longer understood.

. . . It is said that Al Mamun had a man climb the Great Pyramid, equipped with a rope 1,000 royal cubits long (each royal cubit equals 1⅔ ordinary cubits). The perimeter of the base, each face being equal, was 400 cubits for each face. It took three hours of daylight for the man to climb the pyramid, and upon reaching the summit he found that the pyramid ended in a plateau with a surface equal to the space that would be occupied by eight kneeling camels.[20]

Abd-al-Latif (1162–1231)

From Silvestre de Sacy's translation in *Description de l'Egypte,* vol. 9, p. 468:

Of all the countries I have visited, or known by report of others, there are not any can compare with Egypt for the number of its ancient monuments.

The pyramids are one of its wonders: they have engaged the attention of a multitude of writers, who have given in their works the description and dimensions of their edifices. They are numerous, and are all of them situated on the same side of the river as Gizeh, on the same line as the ancient capital of Egypt, and are comprised within the space of two days' journey. At Boufir also there are many. Some of the pyramids are large, others small; some are formed of earth and brick, from the major part of stone: part of them are constructed so as to present steps, or stairs; mostly, however, they are of an exact pyramidial shape, with even surfaces.

Formerly there was a great number of pyramids, small, indeed, at Gizeh; but these were destroyed in the time of Salaheddin Yoofoof the son of Ayyout. Their ruin was effected by Karakouth, a Greek eunuch, one of the âmeers of the army of that prince, and a man of genius.

As to their pyramids, the object of so many recitals, to which I will advert; pyramids distinguished above the rest, and the superior size of which excites admiration, the number of them is three; and they stand in a line at Gizeh, in front of Fostat, at a short distance asunder, their angles pointing to each other, and towards the east. Two of these pyramids are of enormous dimensions. The poets who have described them, have given the reins to that enthusiasm they are so well calculated to inspire; they compare them to two immense breasts rising from the bosom of Egypt. They are very near to each other, and are built of white stone: the third, a fourth part less than the others, is of red granite marked with points, and so extremely hard, that iron with difficulty makes impression on it. The last appears small compared with the other two, but viewed at a short distance, and to the exclusion of these, it excites in the mind a singular oppression, and cannot be contemplated without painfully affecting the sight.

The shape chosen for the pyramids, and their solidity, are alike admirable. To their form is owing the advantage of their having resisted the attack of centuries; but resist, do I say, it seems as if even time itself stood only on defence against their everlasting monuments. In fact, after mature reflection on the structure of the pyramids, one is forced to acknowledge a combination of efforts of the most intelligent men, an exhaustion of the genius of the most subtle; that the most enlightened minds exercised with profusion, in favour of these edifices, all the talents they possessed; and that the most learned theory of geometry called forth the whole of its resources, to show in these wonders the utmost term of human ability. We may likewise affirm, that these structures hold discourse with us, even in the present day, respecting those who were their founders, teach us their history, in a manner intelligent to us, relate their progress in the sciences, and the excellence of their genius, and, in short, effectually describe their life and actions.

The most singularly remarkable fact presented by these edifices is the pyramidal form adopted in their structure, a form which commences with a square base, and finishes in a point. Now, one of the properties of this form is, that the center of gravity is the center of the building itself; so that it leans on itself, itself supports the whole pressure of its mass, all its parts bear respectively one upon the other, and it does not press on any external point.

Another admirable peculiarity is the disposition of the square of them, in such a manner that each of their angles fronts one of the four cardinal points. For, the violence of the wind is broken when cut by an angle, which would not be the case if it encountered a plane surface.

To return to the two pyramids. Those who have taken their dimensions pronounce the base of each to be four hundred cubits long, by as many broad, and their perpendicular height likewise four hundred cubits; the cubit used in the mensuration being the black cubit.[21] Their pyramidal shape is truncated above, and presents at the summit a level of ten cubits square. Of the following fact I was myself an eyewitness. When I visited them, we had an archer in our company, who shot an arrow in the direction of the perpendicular height of one of these pyramids, and another in that of its breadth, at its base, and the arrow fell at about the middle of the space. We were told that in a neighboring village there were people accustomed to mount to the summit of the pyramids, and who effected it without difficulty. We sent for one of these men, who for a trifle ascended one of the pyramids in the same manner as, and even quicker than, we should a staircase, and without taking off his shoes, or his dress, which was very wide. I desired him, on attaining the summit, to measure with his turban, which corresponded with that of the level, to be eleven cubits of the measure.[22]

A man whom I saw, skilled in the art of measuring, ascribed to the pyramid a perpendicular height of about three hundred and seventeen cubits, and to each of the sides of the four triangular planes, which incline to this perpendicular, four hundred and sixty cubits.[23] I think there must be some error in these measures, and that, if the latter be exact, the perpendicular height must be four hundred cubits; but, if heaven favor my intention, I will myself ascertain the truth.

One of these pyramids is opened, and has an entrance by which the interior may be penetrated. This opening leads to narrow passages, to conduits extending to a great depth, to wells, and precipices, according to the testimony of individuals bold enough to enter; for many, excited by deliberate cupidity, and by chimerical expectations, have ventured into the interior of this building. They explore its deepest cavities, and finally arrive at a spot beyond which it is impossible to advance. As for the passage the most frequented, and that which is commonly followed, it is by a glacis which leads towards the upper part of the pyramid where a square chamber is seen containing a sarcophagus of stone.

The opening by which the pyramid is now entered, is not the door formed at the period of its erection, but a hole evacuated with great trouble, and directed by chance, the making of which is ascribed to the Calif Mamoun. The major part of our company entered this opening, and ascended to the chamber of the upper part of the pyramid: on their return they detailed the wonderful things they had seen; that the passage was so full of bats and their ordure as to be almost closed; that the bats were as large as pigeons, and that in the upper openings were seen, and windows, designed apparently for the admission of air and light. On the second visit, I myself, with several others, entered the interior conduit, and penetrated about two-thirds of its length; but, losing my senses, owing to the terror I experienced in the ascent, I returned half dead.

These pyramids are built of large stones from ten to twenty cubits long, by a breadth and thickness of from two to three: but most especially worthy of admiration is the extreme nicety with which these stones are fashioned and disposed, one above the other. The courses fit so exactly, that not even a needle or a single hair can be thrust between the joints. They are cemented together by a mortar, which forms a layer of the thickness of a leaf of paper. With the composition of this mortar I am totally unacquainted. The stones are covered with writing, in that ancient character of which the meaning is now unknown. I have met with no one in Egypt, who either knew it himself, or had ever heard of any person by whom it was comprehended. So numerous are these inscriptions, that, were these only to be copied which are found on the surface of these two pyramids, they would fill ten thousand pages.

In some of the books of the ancient Sabeans, I have read, that, of these two pyramids, one is the sepulchre of Agathodaimon, the other of Hermes. These, according to this authority, were two great prophets; but Agathodaimon is the more ancient, and the greater of the two. They further assert that these two pyramids were resorted to by pilgrims from all countries of the earth.

On this subject I have treated at large in my great work, and have related what others have said of these buildings; to that therefore I refer the reader felicitous of more minute details, confining myself in this to the representation of that alone of which I have myself been witness.

Upon the succession of Malik-Alaziz Othman Ben-Yoofoof [24] to the throne of his father, he suffered himself to be prevailed upon by certain persons belonging to his court, men who were strangers to common sense, to demolish these pyramids; they began with the red pyramid, the last and least considerable of the three.

Hither the Sultan dispatched sappers, miners, and carriers, under the conduct of some of the principal officers and amurs of his court, with orders for its destruction. Accordingly they pitched their camp near the pyramid, where they collected from every quarter a vast number of workmen, who were maintained at a prodigious expense. Here they remained the space of eight months, occupied wholly in putting into effect the commission with which they were instructed, removing every day, after oppressive labour, and almost utter exhaustion of the strength of those employed, at most but two or three stones. Some were appointed with wedges and levers to force them forward, while others, with cords and cables pulled from the bottom. When at length one of them fell, it occasioned a tremendous noise, which resounded at a vast distance; shook the very earth, and made the mountains tremble. In its fall it buried itself in the sand, and it required extraordinary efforts to disengage it; after which notches were wrought for receiving wedges. By means of these the stones were split into several pieces, each of which employed a wagon for its transport to the foot of the mountain, situated a short distance thence, where it was left.

After remaining long encamped on this spot, and expending all their pecuniary means, as their toil and fatigue continually increased, while on the contrary their resolution diminished daily, and their strength became exhausted, those of the commission were forced shamefully to abandon the undertaking. So far from obtaining the promised success and accomplishing their design, all they did was to spoil the pyramid, and exhibit a manifest proof of their inability and weakness. This occurrence took place in the year 593 of the hejra [beginning November 1196 a.c.]. Now, when the mass of stones collected by this demolition is contemplated, one feels disposed to consider the pyramid ruined to its foundation; but on looking, on the other hand, at the pyramid, it seems as if it had suffered no injury, a part of its case on one side only having been detached.

Witnessing one day the extreme difficulty experienced in dragging down a single stone, I addressed one of the foremen who superintended the work, and questioned him whether, if a thousand pieces of gold were given him to replace one of these stones in the place it was in before, he thought himself competent to the undertaking; his answer was, that were he offered that sum many times told, he should never be able to accomplish the task, and this he affirmed with an oath.

In front of the pyramids, on the eastern bank of the Nile, is seen a number of immense and very deep excavations, communicating one with the other, of which several are of three stories. The name by which they are known is the town.[25] A man on horseback, with his lance erect, may enter them, and make excursions for a day together without having traveled the whole, so numerous and vast are they, and of such great extent. It is easy in these to recognize the quarries whence the stone was drawn which served for the structure of the pyramids. As for the quarries whence the red granite was taken, they are said to be situate at Kolzom and at Ofwan.[26]

Near these pyramids are yet visible the remains of ancient gigantic edifices, and a number of subterranean cavities of solid structure; and seldom is any part of them found without inscriptions in the ancient, but now unknown character.

At little more than an arrow's flight from these pyramids, is a colorful figure of a head and neck projecting from the earth. The name of this figure is Aboo'lhaud, and the body to which the head pertains, is said to be buried under the earth. To judge from the dimensions of the head or those of the body, its length must be more than seventy cubits.[27] On the face is a reddish tint, and a red varnish as bright as if fresh put on. The face is remarkably handsome, and the mouth expresses much grace and beauty. One might fancy it smiling gracefully.

A sensible man enquiring of me what of all I had seen in Egypt had most excited my admiration. I answered the nicety of proportion in the Sphinx. In fact, between the different parts of this head, the nose, for example, the eyes and the ears, the same proportion is remarked, as is observed by nature in her works. Thus the nose of a child is suitable to its stature, and proportioned to the rest of its frame, while, if it belonged to the face of a full grown man, it would be reckoned a deformity; thus also the nose of a grown man on the visage of a child would equally be a disfigurement. The same holds good with respect to all the other members; there are none but should have a certain form and dimension, in order to bear relations to such and such a face; and where these proportions are not observed, the face is spoiled. Hence the wonder, that in a face of such colossal size, the sculptor should have been able to preserve the exact proportion of every part, seeing that nature presented him with no model of a similar colossus, or any at all comparable.

Ben Abd al-Rahman reports that:

The well is square, 10 cubits deep, with four doors leading to as many rooms, in which mummies were placed; this well is located in the center of a room that is square at the bottom and round on top.[28] In this room was a door leading to the top of the pyramid, by way of a stepless passage 5 achbar [spithames] wide. Al Mamun's men climbed it and reached a small suite in which was found the statue of a man, made of a green stone like an emerald; it was hollow and contained a human body, covered with a thin sheet of gold set with a great quantity of jewels. Upon his chest was the hilt of a priceless sword and upon his head was a ruby as large as a hen's egg, which shone like a flame . . . I myself saw the statue from which the corpse was removed; it was near the royal palace of Fostat in 511 [611] A.H.[29]

Abu'l Faraj recounts a journey made to Egypt by Denis de Telmahre, Jacobite patriarch of Antioch, in 214 A.H. (820 A.D.), during the reign of Al Mamun, among that prince's party:

We saw these edifices in Egypt; they are not, as is commonly held, the granaries of Joseph, but rather amazing mausoleums, raised over the tombs of the ancient kings. They are oblique—that is, having an inclined plane—and solid, not hollow and empty. We looked into a 50-cubit-deep[30] opening that had been made in one of these edifices and ascertained that the masonry consists of ashlars arranged in layers. Along the base they [the edifices] measure 500 cubits wide, by an equal length, measured in cubits[31] . . . and their height is 250 cubits. The stones used in building them measure from 4 to 10 cubits; these are all dressed stones; from a distance these edifices look like large mountains.

Groff and Abbas Pasha

After the Arab authors' accounts, it is interesting to quote in its entirety a paper William Groff read to the Institut d'Egypte on January 8, 1897. It is difficult to doubt the reality of the phenomena observed by Groff. Groff's interpretation, however, is within the realm of possibility, no more.

About two weeks ago, I happened to spend the night in the desert in the company of our vice-president, Dr.

Abbas Pasha; we were near the pyramids of Giza. At around 8:00 P.M., I noticed a light which seemed to be slowly circling the third pyramid at about half its height; it was like a small flame, or rather—as a Bedouin put it—like a falling star. It seemed to me as if the light circled the pyramid three times, then disappeared.

I watched the pyramid carefully for a good portion of the night. At around eleven o'clock, I again saw a light. This time, it was a pale bluish color; it rose slowly, almost in a straight line, and once it had reached a certain height above the pyramid's summit, it disappeared.

In the desert that evening and night the air was very clear, the temperature cold; there was very little wind. The whitish zodiacal light was still visible at around 10:30; one could even make out stars of the fifth magnitude. In the morning, at daybreak, the rising sun appeared a dazzling green.

Having spent the night in the desert, near the pyramids, numerous times, I had often noticed lights around these pyramids, at first without seeking to determine their origin; then I became curious and did some research, which seemed to indicate that these lights, though rarely seen, occasionally appear about five hours after sunset.

The light (or lights) that I saw at 8:00 P.M. were on the north and east sides of the pyramid; the light I saw appear and rise at 11:00 was on the north side.

Some research and a strictly provisional study led me to suspect that these lights derive from emanations leaving the pyramid's interior. The air inside the pyramid is hotter than the desert air; this creates drafts, which sweep along with them the emanations which are or become luminous.

These lights have been sighted in the past, with varying frequency, and have given rise to certain legends and traditions.

According to Maqrizi, after the pyramids were built, each was assigned a guardian, and the pyramids were surrounded with immaterial spirits. The Copts still relate that the spirit attached to the northern pyramid is a yellow devil; the spirit of the southern pyramid is a beautiful naked woman who charms men, lures them, and causes them to lose their minds; the spirit of the painted pyramid is an old man who carries a censer filled with burning incense. Many people have, repeatedly, seen these spirits circling the pyramids at around midday and sunset.

The third pyramid was built by Man-Kau-Ra, fourth king of the Fourth Dynasty. The pyramid of Menkaura, left unfinished, was completed by Nitocris (Rhodopis) at the end of the Sixth Dynasty. It was at the very center of this pyramid, above the chamber in which the pious Mykerinos had lain for over six centuries, that she was entombed.

When seeking to understand "the past as it was," one must be careful not to take legends too seriously, because they tend to pursue will-o'-the-wisps, mysterious luminous apparitions, sparks emanating from Nitocris' sepulcher, their pale glow conjuring up the phantom of the queen herself.

THE WESTERN TRAVELERS OF THE EIGHTEENTH AND NINETEENTH CENTURIES

Among the accounts of the pre–eighteenth-century Western travelers, only that of Baron d'Anglure (1395) is of any interest, because he claims to have witnessed the demolition of the second pyramid's facing. He notes, moreover, that according to his dragoman:

> the excoriation and uncovering of these granaries was begun over a thousand years ago, and they are still only half-uncovered. . . .

Maillet
France's consul general in Egypt from 1692 to 1708, Benoît de Maillet was the first Frenchman to record the Great Pyramid's approximate measurements. In *Description de l'Egypte* (Paris: Chez Genneau et Rollin, 1735) he formulated some rather strange hypotheses concerning the subject.

According to him, all the Pyramid's passages had been *completely* plugged with blocks that had been stored in the

Grand Gallery. These blocks had been set in place with a hard cement that joined them so firmly they seemed to be part of the edifice.

The despoilers, using powerful machines and hot water (which, when poured down the Descending Passage, softened the cement), were able to free the blocks and pull them out. Maillet states that this work was carried out "without mutilating the passage walls, which have retained their original polish."[32]

Maillet notes that the sarcophagus in the King's Chamber is broken along the side; no trace of the cover was found. He mentions two facing holes 3½ feet (1.14 meters) above the floor.

The south hole was 1 foot (0.328 meter) wide and 8 inches (0.22 meter) high, whereas the north hole, *perfectly round,* was wide enough so that one could insert one's two fists in it, and expanded to a diameter of 1 foot (0.325 meter) as it inclined toward the Pyramid's base.

I think that anyone would conclude that they were conceived for no other purpose than the provisioning of those who had to remain in the tomb. The first served to bring in air and as a duct for the conveyance of food and other necessary objects. They were undoubtedly provisioned with the help of a long box proportioned to the duct's diameter; this box was attached to a long rope with which they could pull the box toward them, and another rope was left hanging outside the pyramid so that people could pull the box to the outside. It is probably in this manner that they were able to meet their needs long enough so that some of them could remain alive.

I would imagine that upon entering, each of them was provided with a coffin in which he would be placed; and that, successively, they performed this last pious duty of placing each man in his coffin, except for the last man, who was without help.

The second duct was used for carrying out their excrement, which fell into a large hole dug for this purpose. It was my intention to examine the outside of the Pyramid in order to see where this duct ended, and perhaps find new proof for my claims; but this investigation aroused suspicion among the country's government —they may have thought I was searching for hidden treasure.

However, others may examine the place and find full proof of the use to which it was to be put; as for myself, I find this to be a pointless argument, for it is impossible to imagine any other function that could be ascribed to it. . . .

This is all I shall quote from Maillet's absurd ramblings. His spirit, now in Amenti, must still be trying to solve the puzzle of removing the excrement of the volunteers of death through an *ascending* duct, thus inverting the laws of gravity!

According to Maillet, all of the Great Pyramid's passages were closed off along their entire length by blocks temporarily stored in the Grand Gallery.[33] This would have required over one hundred blocks[34] 2 meters long with a section of over 1 square meter, each block weighing nearly 6 metric tons. Even assuming that such storage was possible, by means of stacking, *before* the gallery was completed, the distribution of these blocks in the various passages was impossible because the section of the passages—in which a man could not stand erect—was obviously the same as that of the blocks. The friction coefficient would not have allowed them to slide down a 26-degree slope, and certainly not across the Horizontal Passage to the Queen's Chamber. Norden quite rightly refuted Maillet's assertions, and Petrie even proved that the three granite blocks obstructing the Ascending Passage could not have fit on the landing located at the Grand Gallery's entrance.

Nevertheless, my congratulations to the old consul general for having dared to descend the Pyramid's "well," though apparently without having the pleasure of meeting Maat, the goddess of truth. The richness of his imagination also merits admiration: it beats, by far, all the Arabic records in the field.

There is, however, one significant detail in Maillet's account—the fact that in his time the "well" was obstructed at a depth of 133 feet (43.20 meters) by sand and pebbles from the excavation of the "grotto" located at the level of the bedrock. Thus this excavation occurred prior to 1700 A.D.

Pococke

There are very few details worth noting in Richard Pococke's report on the pyramids (1737), for he merely confirms Maillet's and Greaves's statements.

Concerning the platform, he mentions that Greaves found a length of 13 feet (3.96 meters), that there are nine blocks at the top (two being missing at the corners), and that the two uppermost layers are not perfect. He found no signs that a statue had been affixed in the center.

He writes:

The upper tiers of stones not being entire, I measured two steps below the top, and it was twenty-six feet on the north side, and thirty on the west; so that either the pyramid is not square, or it inclines with a greater angle to the west and east than to the north and south. The number of steps have been related very differently; from two hundred and seven, Greaves's number, to two hundred and sixty, the number of Albert Lewenstein; but as Maillet, who also was very exact, counted two hundred and eight, it is probable the number of the steps is two hundred and seven, or eight, tho' I counted them two hundred and twelve.[35]

Frederick Louis Norden[36]

The pyramids are not situated in plains; but upon the rock, that is at the foot of the high mountains, which accompany the Nile in its course, and which make the separation betwixt Egypt and Libya. They have been all raised with the same intention; that is to say, to serve for sepultures; but their architecture, as well in the inside as without, is extremely different, with regard to the distribution, the materials, and the grandeur.

Some of them are open; others ruined; and the greatest part of them are closed; but there is none, but what has been damaged in some of their parts.

The most northern of these great pyramids is the only

one that is open; and as it is that which we meet with the first, I shall begin my description with it: after which I shall examine what occurs the most remarkable in the others.

One does not perceive the least mark, to prove that it has been coated by marble; for tho' certain travellers have conjectured so, by seeing the summit of the second pyramid coated with granite,[37] there is so little appearance of this, that we find not in the steps the least remains of granite or of marble, and which it would not have been possible to take away in such a manner that none of it should have continued. It is true, that about this pyramid, and about some others, we perceive a great quantity of little pieces of granite, and of white marble; but that does not appear to me to be a proof, that the pyramids have been coated by them. Such sort of materials had been employed in the inside, and in some temples, on the outside: thus it is more natural to presume, that these remains are owing rather to the cutting of stones for employing them, or to the ruin of temples, than to the detached pieces of marble from the coating of the pyramids.

After describing the Pyramid's various rather slippery passages and the difficulty of climbing and descending them, Norden mentions the sarcophagus:

A well-hollowed piece, which rings like a bell when hit with a key.

He adds that before coming back down from the King's Chamber, they would usually shoot off a gun a few times.

When you are in this saloon, you commonly make some discharges of a pistol, to give yourself the pleasure of hearing a noise, that resembles thunder. . . .

As soon as you are got out of the pyramid, you dress yourself; wrap yourself up well; and drink a good glass full of strong liquor; which preserves you from the pleurisy, that the sudden change from an extremely hot air to a more temperate, might occasion. Afterwards, when you have regained your natural heat, you mount up to the top of the pyramid, in order to have a prospect from thence of the country round about, which is charming to behold. You there perceive, as well as at the entrance, and in the chambers, the names of abundance of persons, that have visited, at different times, this pyramid, and who were willing to transmit to posterity the memory of their travels.

THE FRENCH EXPEDITION TO EGYPT

With the French Expedition to Egypt (1799–1801), the Great Pyramid became the subject of the first serious studies, in particular those of Coutelle and Jomard. The results of their investigation were published in various volumes of the *Description de l'Egypte,* particularly Volume 9. The most important extracts from this work are reproduced here.

Coutelle

In *Observations sur les pyramids de Ghizeh (Description de l'Egypte,* vol. 9, pp. 261–94), Coutelle mentions the results of Jomard's measurements: base, 227.32 meters; height above the course carved in the bedrock, 137.218 meters. According to Coutelle, the Great Pyramid's entrance is located on the north face, 14.489 meters above the base, at the level of the fifteenth course. Behind this entrance is a narrow, sloping passage 1.110 meters high and wide.

THE GALLERIES

The first gallery, 22.363 meters long [38] to where it now ends [in 1801 A.D.], wasn't really closed off except at its entrance. . . . If the first passage had been closed off along its entire length, there would be signs that the stones had been torn out along the sides and the ceiling; these have remained, on the contrary, perfectly smooth.

The second gallery, or Ascending Passage, whose slope is 27 degrees,[39] is 33.134 meters long and has the same height and width as the first gallery. It [the second gallery] is still closed off at its entrance by a large granite block having the same dimensions as the passage. The difficulty of breaking through such a hard rock in so small a space meant conceiving and executing a plan to proceed by breaking through the softer stones forming the mass on the right side of this passage, parallel with it; this attempt was successful. In getting around this obstacle, one enters the second passage[40]; reaching the end, one finds oneself on a sort of landing.

The entrance to the well is to the right. Here, transecting the plane of the great Ascending Passage, begins the Horizontal Passage, equal in height and width to the two other passages traversed; it is 38.791 meters long and leads to the lower chamber,[41] which is covered by discharging stones arranged in the shape of a roof. This chamber, commonly referred to as the "Queen's Chamber," measures 5.793 meters long by 5.022 meters wide, with a height of 6.307 meters at the entrance; it is constructed of limestone similar to the type used in the galleries, and taken from the same quarries.

The excavation one notices to the left upon entering does not indicate any particular construction; it is simply where the Arabs tore up stones while searching for reputed treasures.

From the outer entrance of the Horizontal Passage or the landing that precedes it, one climbs back up onto the extension of the second passage, in a gallery 40.508 meters long, 8.121 meters high, and 2.091 meters wide. On each side is a banquette 571 millimeters high and 501 millimeters wide. The sunken ramp between the banquettes is the same width as the three other galleries and has the same slope as the second gallery. Each banquette contains *twenty-eight* holes placed equidistantly along its length; they measure 325 by 162 millimeters, and their vertical depth ranges from 162 to 216 millimeters.

The lateral walls of this gallery, formed by eight corbeled courses, form a kind of arch ending in a ceiling having the same width as the sunken ramp between the two banquettes. It is constructed of the same type of stone as that found in the previous galleries. Wax drippings from torches, smoke, and the effect of visitors rubbing their hands along the walls have given the galleries a sheen and hue that have led many travelers to believe that the galleries were constructed of granite.

Having reached the top of this gallery, on a landing that is 1.557 meters deep and has the same height and width as the gallery, one passes through an opening

1.049 meters wide and 2.955 meters deep. Along its sides the vestibule contains three grooves that were apparently meant to hold granite blocks destined to close off the entrance to the sepulchral chamber.

In the middle, opposite the gallery and along its axis, an opening 1.047 meters wide, 1.110 meters high, and 2.563 meters long provides access to the sepulchral chamber, known as the "King's Chamber," the chamber toward which all the building operations and the entire pyramid itself seems to have been directed.

This chamber, as well as the entire area starting from the entrance to the vestibule, is constructed of large, perfectly dressed and polished granite blocks. Its dimensions are: height, 5.858 meters; length along the north side, 10.467 meters; south side, 10.472 meters; length along the west side, 5.235 meters; east side, 5.200 meters. The south side overhangs by 18 millimeters, which reduced the ceiling's width accordingly. The largest dimension of this chamber is that of east-west.

The granite sarcophagus lying north-south at the west end of this chamber measures 2.301 meters long by 1.002 meters wide and 1.137 meters high; its thickness is 6 inches.[42] The lid, which was probably broken (no fragments have been found), must have been 162 to 217 millimeters thick, judging from the proportions of whole sarcophagi I have found elsewhere in Egypt.

Before entering the vestibule, we noticed an opening at the top of the Grand Gallery, in the wall to the left, but we did not know where it might lead. . . . We had scarcely entered a passage 731 millimeters high and 650 millimeters wide when a swarm of bats descended on us, trying to get out. For a long time we were forced to lie flat on a layer of dust and bat dung, as we were deafened by the whirring of their winged paws and suffocated by the pungent odor that they leave in the places they inhabit. We were obliged to shield our faces in order to protect ourselves from their claws, and to cover our lamps, one of which soon went out nonetheless. We finally succeeded in crawling a distance of 8.385 meters and reached a space where no light had penetrated for many centuries.

We were then right above the sepulchral chamber;

but the space, as long and wide as that chamber, is only
1.002 meters high. The granite stones forming the ceiling
as well as the four walls have only been dressed, not
polished; and the stones forming the floor (and consequently the ceiling of the sepulchral chamber) are rough
on this side and of varying heights, from 54 to 135 millimeters. The floor is entirely covered over with a layer
of bat dung which is perfectly level along its entire surface; its thickness ranges from 14 centimeters on top of
the highest stones to over 28 centimeters on top of the
lowest stones, so that the total coating is about 21 centimeters thick along the entire floor, as well as in the
passage.

There can be no doubt as to the reason for building
this double ceiling: it was installed solely to create a
relieving mechanism, similar to the one at the Pyramid's
entrance, so that the sacred chamber would not collapse
under the weight above it.

This precaution was not entirely pointless: many
stones in this second ceiling are cracked not far from
their bearings, and the granite blocks supporting them
are split along the edges from the weight of the relieving
stones placed at the edge of this ceiling and the weight
of the mass above it.

THE WELL

The well, whose opening is found on the landing at the
entrance to the Horizontal Gallery, particularly attracted our attention. We were interested in discovering
what motive there could have been for making such an
irregularly shaped excavation in the bedrock and over-
coming the difficulties inherent in so arduous a task as
breaking up and carrying out fragments of a hard stone
to a depth of about 65 meters in a space as narrow as
596 by 650 millimeters. A few months before beginning
my research I had already descended into the well with
Mr. Alibert, by means of a rope attached to a piece of
wood placed across the upper part. I was carrying—
along with a lamp—a compass, a thermometer, and
instruments for measuring depth and slope; but I had
not been able to calculate the length of rope necessary
for an unknown depth. The part of the well that should

have been the easiest to descend, since it is carved in the form of steps along a slope less steep than that of the rest of the well, was obstructed by a granite block and two large limestone blocks that left a width of only 271 millimeters (and a somewhat larger breadth) in which to pass. Having overcome this difficulty and reached the end of my rope, I still had not reached the bottom. However, it was difficult to deliberate with my feet precariously lodged in small irregular holes 30 or 40 millimeters deep, one hand occupied, and a lamp in my mouth; moreover, I found myself in a nearly perpendicular shaft, surrounded by air that, hardly circulating at all, grew each instant less suitable for breathing. The difficulty of the endeavor increased my desire to succeed: I did not waver.

With my back pressed against the upper part, one hand gripping one of the sides, and with my feet wedged in the small notches below, I ventured to descend. The goal I proposed to reach might still have been far below; the space might have suddenly enlarged; if I had lost the point of support sustaining me, I would have been hurled to the bottom with no way of climbing back up—assuming I were in any condition to do so. It was luck, and not some impossible calculation, that came to my aid; I had only 14.5 meters more to descend, and the shaft remained the same size.[43]

I reached the end, but not at the point where the workers had stopped. The bottom was filled with dirt and pebbles; I filled up one of my pockets with them and then took all the measurements I needed. But my lamp was already growing dim, my breathing labored; the Réaumur thermometer registered 25 degrees, and, although dressed in simple cloth pants and jacket, I was drenched with sweat.

In order to climb back up, I used the same method I had used in descending; once I had grabbed on to the rope and headed for the entrance, still 33 meters distant, it seemed as if the rest were downhill.

While descending, I had stopped at a sort of grotto found above the steep part of the well; that is, in the second vertical part. This excavation had been made by removing pebbles, bits of which still remained stuck to the arch; there were more underfoot. I rested there [and] compared the pebbles I was carrying with these pebbles and ascertained that the pebbles at the bottom of the well derived from the excavation of this grotto.

I then formulated the plan of removing the pebbles from the well and putting them back where they had come from. It seemed quite likely that once the grotto had been filled in, I would not be far from the point where the workers had stopped, and that I might discover the reason for so arduous a task. I suppose that while digging the well they encountered a mass of pebbles and dirt, about 4 feet [1.40 meters] thick, between two courses of stone. In order to prevent a cave-in, they built a wall around the four sides, using quarry stones about 8 inches [0.216 meters] thick. The first people to descend the well broke into this wall in the hope of finding something valuable hidden behind it. They threw the dirt and pebbles that they removed down the well, filling it to a height proportional to the quantity removed. This explains the excavation, at the end of which is found the stone course that apparently corresponds to the Pyramid's base.

We observed that whereas the outer facing is very carefully drafted and the courses are perfectly horizontal, the inner courses are made up of irregular blocks, just as they came from the quarry, and that the spaces resulting from these incongruities were filled in with pebbles and a crude mortar made of stone chips; it is possible that in order to economize on stones, the builders intentionally left spaces between the courses and filled them in with pebbles mixed with dirt; this would not affect the solidity of a mass as enormous as the Great Pyramid.

One of our first projects was to descend to the grotto and to place one of our Turks at the bottom [of the well] and another at the entrance with an interpreter. I'd had some small buckets 22 centimeters wide and 40 centimeters deep made; the worker crouched at the bottom was to fill one, which would be raised and emptied in the grotto as the other bucket was being lowered.

After climbing back up, we remained in the well a

while in order to position our workers and distribute tasks. We had brought in several lamps and absorbed a large quantity of oxygen. A little while later the interpreter, pale and trembling, came to inform us that the lamp at the bottom had gone out by itself, and that the workers had climbed up full of fear, saying that the devil was in the well but was in league with the French, since the lamps had burned as long as we were there. We raised their wages by a couple of *parats* and made it clear that they would have to go back as soon as the lamps began to burn higher. On the following days they were able to work for about four hours in the morning and three in the evening, after a four- or five-hour rest to allow a change of air.

Occasionally one of us would go to see the workers, and we had already cleared 16 to 17 meters, still in the limestone bedrock and along the same width. We had progressed to over 16 meters below the level of the Nile[44] when military operations recalling the members of our party to their various corps forced us to suspend work.

As my main concern here is the material aspect of the monuments, I will not discuss the various opinions held concerning the extraordinary excavation. Everything leads one to believe that it was carried out before the construction of the Pyramid was completed. Indeed, it is difficult to imagine how the workers could possibly have cut through hard rock in so narrow a space and removed debris to a depth of over 65 meters, or how they could have transported the debris to the outside by way of galleries difficult to traverse because of their narrow dimensions and steep slope. The number of men and quantity of lamps that would have been necessary would have soon used up so much oxygen that it would have been impossible to work for more than a few hours without a change of air.

THE GREAT PYRAMID'S DIMENSIONS

While we were busy with these operations, others were working at the northeast angle of this Pyramid in order to discover its true base. At a distance of approximately 2.75 meters from the core, or apparent base, we found the part of the bedrock in which the cornerstone of the facing had been imbedded. This stone is still perfectly dressed and is sunk 207 millimeters in a space 3.90 by 3.40 meters.

The line along which the first course lies is still complete and extends, under the debris, all the way to the northwest angle, at the same distance [from the core] and on the same level. This line, measured with the most scrupulous accuracy, is 232.747 meters long.

The vertical height, measured most carefully course by course, is—including the two ruined steps of the summit—139.117 meters; and, omitting the two uppermost steps, which equal 1.117 meters, exactly 138 meters. The lower step, carved in the bedrock, is divided into two parts which together equal 1.849 meters.

The 203 courses, including the visible part of the course carved in the bedrock, add up to—according to my measurements—138.598 meters. The part that we uncovered in order to reach the bedrock, or the base of the socket on which the first course was placed, measures 0.519 meter.

The height of the core, from the base of the socket up to the two ruined steps of the upper plateau, is thus 139.117 meters altogether, as I said earlier. Adding to this what has been torn down, the total height of the Pyramid and its socle must have been about 146 meters, which is over twice the height of the towers of Notre Dame in Paris. [Coutelle gives the platform's side as 9.96 meters.]

What proves that nothing was overlooked in making these monuments indestructible is the fact that it is difficult to draft with greater accuracy, to establish straighter lines or more perfect joints than those in the Great Pyramid's internal construction and in the part of the second pyramid's facing that has been preserved. In the latter, each stone in the four ridges is imbedded in the next stone. The lower stone, hollowed by 54 millimeters, holds a corresponding projection of the stone above it, so that each ridge is connected along its entire height; and despite the fact that the facing has been removed from at least four-fifths of the lower part, the facing that remains has not undergone the slightest displacement, the least dilapidation.[45]

The three faces that are struck by the sun have taken on a sort of reddish-brown tint; they have a certain luster when the sun illumines them. This shiny reddish-brown tint has led those who have not examined the pyramid up close to believe that it was coated with a type of cement. The north face has retained a slightly dusty grayish tint; it is covered with lichens in many places.[46]

It is very likely that the stones forming the facing were left rough and square on the outside; then, after the construction had been completed, the angles were removed, starting from the top. Each tier thus served as a scaffold and ladder for mounting and descending, for placing machines, for lifting stones, and for the final trimming.[47]

Jomard

I have amply quoted from the careful study made by Colonel Coutelle, one of the eminent members of the French Expedition to Egypt. In his memoirs concerning the pyramids, his colleague Jomard recounts the writings of the ancient and Arabic authors. As I have already provided these, I will merely analyze this scholar's commentaries.

Jomard starts off by criticizing Herodotus in regard to the Great Pyramid's causeway, of which he could find no trace. He writes:

> It is thus an absolutely unwarranted supposition, as I see it, that a causeway 10 orgyias wide and 2 to 3 leagues long should have been built from the Arabian mountain or from the Nile to the Libyan mountain.

But his criticism is ill founded because significant vestiges of the causeway exist to this day; proceeding east-northeast, the causeway passes through the Arab village of Kars el-Haram, where enormous aligned blocks are still to be found.

Jomard then criticizes Herodotus' assertion concerning the existence of a tomb surrounded by the waters of the Nile, brought in by way of an underground canal. Jomard found nothing in the Pyramid to indicate its existence. He should have reserved judgment, however, since he wasn't even aware of the presence of the Subterranean Chamber (known as the "unfinished chamber") because the Descending Passage and the well that could have led him to it were obstructed at the time. Even now, we cannot dismiss Herodotus' claims peremptorily: a surprise is still possible. There is a chance, moreover, that the pyramid of Sesostris I at Lisht may have been laid out and rendered inviolable in the same manner that Herodotus describes in relation to the Great Pyramid.

Jomard's criticisms concerning the dimensions provided by the Greek historian are exaggerated; besides, he himself makes a mistake in regard to the value of the plethron, as well as that of the Egyptian cubit and the foot used by Pliny. Herodotus' plethron is the Greek plethron of 30.78 meters, and Pliny's foot is the Roman foot of 0.2955 meter. However, it is obvious that the Greek traveler, unlike Pliny, had no great concern for accuracy and that the figures he provides are only "round" numbers.

Another petty criticism of Jomard's concerns the three other pyramids, including that of Cheops' daughter, "that standeth in the midst of the three in front of the great pyramid." Jomard finds Herodotus' text too vague to enable one to locate this pyramid without error. But Herodotus' text is clear: the three pyramids are those situated to the east of the Great Pyramid along the edge of the plateau. The discovery of a votive stella from Cheops to his daughter (now at the Cairo Museum) leaves no doubt in this matter.

Jomard does adopt Herodotus' erroneous view that Rhodopis ("the rosy-cheeked") was a courtesan during the reign of Amosis (Twenty-sixth Dynasty). But obviously this Rhodopis is none other than Queen Nitocris (Sixth Dynasty), who was described as "fair-skinned with red cheeks"—"the noblest and loveliest woman of her time; she had a fair complexion," according to Manetho. It is not impossible that this queen should have chosen for a tomb the chamber surmounting Mykerinos' granite cave, a chamber in which was found the sarcophagus that had been used in the transferral of the divine *ka* upon the king's death, the same sarcophagus in which his mummy was to be placed.

After recounting the texts of the Arab authors, Jomard adds:

> Leaving aside the study of the methods that Calif Al Mamun employed to penetrate the Great Pyramid, I will point out that he was forced to pierce a wall about 20 cubits, or 9 meters, thick; thus it must be assumed that the passage, or the descending gallery, had been filled in toward its upper end. It is difficult to concede that the mummy of a man, wrapped in gold, with precious stones covered with inscriptions, should have been found in the Pyramid. This part of the account could not apply to the hollow stone in the King's Chamber (that which is commonly referred to as the sarcophagus), for it is only 2.14 meters long; the stone statue, or chest shaped like a human body and containing an average-size man, could not have fit in this narrow space.

This remark of Jomard's is judicious; the length and width of the sarcophagus could, just barely, hold a human body placed in a single thin wooden coffin. Tutankhamen's sarcophagus, which measures 2.75 meters long and 1.50 meters high, contained three coffins, as did the sarcophagi of Psusennes and Sesonchis at Tanis.

In my opinion—and I will come back to this later—the sarcophagus in the King's Chamber never served as Cheops' sepulcher; it was used solely by his successor, Kephren, who was placed in it *live* for the isiac ceremony of the transferral of the divine *ka*.

On the subject of the sarcophagus in the King's Chamber, Jomard further writes:

> Could this cask, or hollow granite prism, with its extreme simplicity and narrow dimensions . . . be compared to the sarcophagi of the royal tombs of Thebes, and did it ever share their destination? Was this cask a tomb or a simulacrum? [Should we] renounce Herodotus' assertion, which states in precise, certain terms that the site of the king's sepulcher was an island surrounded by a canal and contrived in the underground passages dug in the hill of the pyramids? And did not Diodorus

say that neither of the two kings who had the great pyramids built was buried in them, that their bodies were buried in unmarked places?

Thus we see that Jomard, while doubting the veracity of Herodotus' assertions, invalidates his original opinion concerning the subterranean sepulchral chamber.

As for the Great Pyramid's platform, Jomard reports the various measurements given by the travelers: Diodorus Siculus, 6 cubits (2.77 meters);[48] Pliny, 16½ feet (4.30 meters);[49] Abd-al-Latif (1200), 11 cubits (5.20 meters); Greaves (1628), 5.01 meters; Lambert (1638), 4.048 meters; Monconys (1647), 16 feet (5.20 meters); Father Fulgence Meyer (1690), 5.40 meters; Pococke (1737), 7.92 meters; Jomard (1800), 30 feet 6 inches (9.91 meters).

Since this increase in the platform's side through the ages is obviously the result of the progressive destruction of the upper courses, Jomard deduced that there must have been nine more courses between the uppermost course of 1800 and the level of the platform during Diodorus Siculus' time, which would bring the total number of courses to 210, not counting the socle carved in the bedrock.

Concerning the twenty-eight slots in each of the two banquettes of the Grand Gallery, Jomard writes, very fittingly, that:

> We are not at all clear on the origin or use, the usefulness or purpose, of the Pyramid's various galleries and passages; but do we know any more about the well, or about the twenty-eight slots or little holes artfully cut along the high-ceilinged ascending gallery, or about other mysterious aspects of the system followed in the construction? . . . Some have thought that they (the twenty-eight slots) served to facilitate the transportation of the cask or sarcophagus from the bottom of the gallery to the top, then into the King's Chamber. But if this explanation is correct, what was the purpose of the perfect finished work evident in all these prismatic holes, and why were they placed at the back of the banquettes, where the ropes could easily be cut by the banquettes' sharp edges, instead of on the side, or better yet, on the passage's floor?

THE MYSTERIES OF THE GREAT PYRAMIDS

THE GREAT PYRAMID'S DESTINATION

. . . Here a thought naturally occurs to attentive minds. That the pyramids in general are related—either in reality or through analogy—to the tombs cannot be denied, and I have certainly not suggested the contrary. . . . Given this fact, if one were to discover traits relating to astronomical science in the pyramids, should it come as any surprise?

. . . How amazing would it be, after all I have just said, if the pyramids should offer, not material representations, as at Thebes, but indications relating to science, and proof that celestial observations had been made during the construction. And if this proof should be found (as it incontestably has been), would it be possible to maintain that no scientific goal played any part in this construction, and that its sole object was to serve as the sepulcher of a king?

. . . Whatever the case, if we agree that the idea of the pyramid includes the idea of the tomb, is it reasonable to conclude that no other intention presided over the erection of these great monuments? I do not think so. How is it possible to assume, for example, in a nation as religious as Egypt, that religion and its mysteries played no part in the goal envisioned in erecting the pyramids?

Now, who can deny the Great Pyramid's precise orientation and the difficulty of tracing so extensive a meridian correctly? . . . It was difficult to carry out this operation (and it would still be today) so as not to deviate more than a few degree minutes along a length of 716 feet 6 inches.

. . . People have wondered how the Egyptians went about orienting their pyramids; this is a question indeed deserving of an answer. It is possible that they used the rising and setting positions of a star, or of the sun at the solstice and even the equinox. However, the unevenness of the earth would not permit absolute precision in the observation of solstitial or equinoctial shadows. How is it, then, that the Great Pyramid is correctly oriented to within a few minutes?

. . . Proclus, who was familiar with Egyptian astronomy, says that it is possible to trace a meridian by means of corresponding shadows; perhaps he alludes to the observation of solstitial or equinoctial shadows. According to the same Proclus, the pyramids were used in determining the length of the year. If the Egyptians used a method based on observations of the rising and setting positions of a star such as Sirius or Canopus, they must have traced on the ground an alignment from the star as it rose and another as it set, and marked off these lines at an equal distance from the observation point; the line perpendicular to the line joining the two points would be a meridian. The precision would be greater if one were to extend the two directions observed, and measure off an equal distance along these extensions; one would thus have four points forming a square with correctly oriented sides. Lastly, the Egyptians may have determined the desired direction from the passage of a star along the site's meridian.

. . . Thus it is unreasonable to claim that the idea of a tomb played no part in the erection of the pyramids in general; I maintain that the great pyramids were subject, in their construction, to certain conditions that science seized upon and set down there, perhaps even intentionally hiding important data that are only now being discovered through scientific inquiry.

. . . In these monuments, the funerary function was not—by a long shot—the primary objective; it has not even been proved that any king was ever placed there after his death.

Concluding his long and penetrating study, Jomard writes:

These pyramids, to which the modern and ancient worlds have assigned so many diverse purposes— vanity, according to some, superstition, according to others—and hailed as among the wonders of the world, were perhaps used as tombs, but as the tombs of princes who wished or permitted that they should attest to posterity the wisdom of scholarly Egypt. They have served their purpose, for they have preserved for us a reliable model of the size of the terrestrial globe and the invaluable concept of the invariability of the pole. . . . There is, moreover, no reason to reject the idea that mysteries were celebrated in such edifices, or that initiations were performed in the lower chambers.

Jomard is quite right, as opposed to Lauer, who rashly insists "that the archeological discoveries that have accumulated since that time have reduced these assertions of Jomard's to naught." Jomard, who was a first-rate scholar, was correct about the Great Pyramid's astronomical, geodesic, and isiac destination—it was simultaneously the *solar temple* of the god *Khnum* and the *tomb* of King *Cheops*, whose royal mummy probably still lies in the crypt described by Herodotus, which I hope remains inviolate.

Gerard de Nerval

The following extracts are from *The Women of Cairo— Scenes of Life in the Orient*, George Routledge & Sons, Ltd., London.

THE PYRAMIDS

I had determined to visit the pyramids before I left, and I went to see the Consul-General to ask his advice about this expedition . . .

The branch of the Nile between Roddah and Ghizeh is so wide that it takes about half an hour to make the crossing. . . .

The nearer one comes to them, the smaller these great monsters seem. This is the result of perspective which is doubtless due to the fact that their breadth is equal to their height. However, when you reach their feet, and stand in the very shadow of these mountains made by men's hands, there is nothing for it but to admire and marvel. In order to reach the apex of the first pyramid, you have to climb a staircase of which each step is about a yard high. As you go higher, these steps diminish slightly, the last steps being reduced by a third at most.

A tribe of Arabs has taken upon itself the duty of protecting travellers, and acting as guides to those who wish to climb the principal pyramid. As soon as they see a stranger coming in the direction of their domain, they gallop to meet him, firing their pistols in the air to assure him that they are at his service, and ready to defend him against the attacks of any thievish Bedouins who might chance to come upon the scene.

To-day this suggestion makes travellers smile, for they have been reassured upon this point beforehand, but in the last century they really were held up by a band of pseudo-brigands, who, after frightening and robbing them, surrendered to the protecting tribe, which then expected a handsome reward for the perils and wounds encountered in what was only a pretended fight. The police of the king of Egypt supervised these deceitful practices. Today it is possible to place complete trust in the Arab guardians of the only wonder of the world that time has preserved for us.

Four men were appointed to guide and support me during the climb. At first, I did not understand how it could be possible to climb steps of which the first alone came up as high as my chest. But, in a twinkling, two of the Arabs had jumped up on that gigantic ridge, and each had seized an arm. The other two pushed me under the shoulders, and all four, at each movement of this performance, chanted in unison the Arabic verse which ends with the ancient refrain: *Eleyson!*

In this way I counted two hundred and seven steps, and I hardly took more than a quarter of an hour to reach the platform. The moment the visitor stops to take breath, little girls, whose bodies are scarcely hidden by a blue shift, stand upon the step above his own and hold out at the level of his mouth little water jugs, whose ice-cold water cools him for an instant.

Nothing could seem more fantastic than these young Bedouin girls climbing about like monkeys with their little bare feet. They know every crack and cranny in the enormous stones. When you reach the top, you give them a backsheesh and a kiss, then you are lifted by the four Arabs and borne in triumph to the four points of the horizon. The flat platform on the top of this pyramid covers about a hundred square metres. Irregular blocks show that it has only been formed by the destruction of a point, doubtless like that of the second pyramid, which has been preserved intact, and may be seen a little distance away with its granite facing. The three pyramids, of Cheops, Chephren and Mycerinus, were all once adorned with that reddish envelope which was still to be seen in Herodotus's day. Little by little it has been stripped from them, as palaces needed to be built at Cairo for the caliphs and soldars.

From the top of this platform, the view, as you may imagine, is very fine. To the East, the Nile stretches from the end of the Delta to beyond Saccarah, where there are eleven pyramids smaller than those of Ghizeh. To the West, the range of the Libyan mountains forms what look like waves on the dusty horizon. The forest of palm-trees which occupies the place of the ancient Memphis stretches southwards like a green shadow. Cairo, upon the arid range of Mokatam, raises its domes and minarets at the entrance to the Syrian desert. All this is so well known that I need waste no time upon a description of it. But, when one sets bounds upon one's admiration, and looks at the stones which form the platform, there is something to be seen which may well compensate for any excess of enthusiasm. Every Englishman who has ventured upon this climb has, as a matter of course, inscribed his name upon the stones. Some have even thought fit to favour the public with their addresses, and a blacking merchant of Piccadilly has covered one whole block with an account of the merits of his invention, which are guaranteed by an "improved patent . . ."

I beg the reader's pardon for discussing a subject as well known as the pyramids. Still, the little I learned about them escaped the notice of most of the renowned scholars who, beginning with Maillet, consul of Louis XIV, have climbed this heroic ladder, the summit of which served me momentarily as a pedestal.

I am afraid I must admit that Napoleon himself only saw the pyramids from the plain. Certainly, he would not have compromised his dignity by allowing himself to be hoisted in the arms of four Arabs, like a parcel passed from hand to hand, and he must have contented himself with answering by a salutation from below the *forty centuries* which, according to his calculations, looked down upon him at the head of our glorious army.

When I had gazed all round the surrounding landscape, and read attentively the modern inscriptions which are preparing tortures for the scholars of the future, I was preparing to go down again, when a fair gentleman, well built, with a high colour, and admirably gloved, scaled, as I had done a short time before, the last step of the quadruple staircase, and greeted me with a very stiff salute, which was due to me as the first comer. I took him for an English gentleman. He recognised me as a Frenchman without any hesitation.

I very quickly regretted that I had judged him so lightly. An Englishman would not have greeted me, seeing that upon the platform of the pyramid of Cheops there was no one present to introduce us to one another.

"Sir," said the stranger to me with a slight German accent, "I am glad to find some civilised person here. I am an officer in the Guards of His Majesty the King of Prussia. I have obtained permission to join M. Lepsius's expedition, and as that expedition spent some weeks here, I have to find out what I can by paying visits to everything it must have seen." At the end of this speech, he gave me his card, with an invitation to go and see him if I should ever pass through Potsdam.

"You know," he added, seeing that I was about to go down again, "it is customary to take a collation here. These good fellows expect to share our modest provisions, and . . . if you feel like it, I shall be glad to offer you a share in a pie which one of my Arabs is carrying."

It does not take long for travellers to become acquainted, and, especially in Egypt at the top of the Great Pyramid, any European soon recognises another as a *Frank,* in other words as a compatriot. At such a distance, the map of our little Europe loses its colours. I except, however, the English, for they live upon an island apart.

The Prussian's conversation during the meal pleased me very much. He had letters with him which gave the latest news of M. Lepsius's expedition. At that moment it was exploring the neighbourhood of Lake Moeris and the subterranean cities of the old labyrinth. The Berlin scholars had discovered whole towns buried under the sands, built of brick, an underground Pompeii and Herculaneum which had never seen the light, which perhaps went back to the days of the Troglodytes. I could not help admitting that it was a noble ambition on the part of these learned Prussians to have followed in the footsteps of our own Institut d'Égypte, whose excellent work they could do no more than hope to complete.

This meal on the pyramid of Cheops is a matter of obligation for tourists, like that which is customary on the capital of Pompey's pillar at Alexandria. I was glad to have a learned and amiable companion to remind me of the fact. The little Bedouin girls had kept enough water, in their jars of porous earth, to give us refreshment, and then to make grog with the help of a bottle of brandy which was carried by one of the Arabs in the Prussian's train.

However, the sun had become too hot for us to remain long on the platform. The pure, healthy air which one breathes at that height had allowed us to go some time without noticing the fact.

We decided then to leave the platform, and go into the pyramid itself through an entrance about a third of the way up. We were taken down a hundred and thirty steps by an inverse process to that which had brought us up. Two of the four Arabs held us by the shoulders from the top of each course, and delivered us into the outstretched arms of their companions below. There is a certain element of danger in this descent, and more than one traveller has broken his skull or his limbs in making it. However, we reached the entrance to the pyramid in safety.

It is a kind of grotto with marble walls, and a triangular vaulted roof, above which there is a broad stone which, in a French inscription, relates the arrival of our soldiers at this monument; it is the visiting card of the Army of Egypt, carved in a block of marble sixteen feet wide. I was reading it with due respect when the Prussian officer pointed out another inscription beneath it. This was in hieroglyphs, and, strangely enough, freshly carved.[50]

"It was wrong," I told him, "to clean and restore this inscription."

"But don't you understand it?" he responded.

"I've sworn never to understand hieroglyphs . . . I've

read too many explanations of them. I started out with Sanchuniathon; I went on to Father Kircher's *Oedipus Aegyptiacus;* and I ended up with Champollion's grammar, after having read the observations of Warlurtau and Baron de Pauw. What disillusioned me about all these opinions was a pamphlet by Abbé Affre (who had not yet become the archbishop of Paris), which, after discussing the meaning of the Rosetta inscription, claimed that the scholars of Europe had agreed on a fictitious explanation of the hieroglyphs so that they could establish throughout Europe chairs in hieroglyphics good for, as a rule, stipends of six thousand francs . . ."

"Or fifteen hundred thalers," the officer added judiciously. "It's about the same amount in my country. But let us not joke about this: you have the grammar, we the alphabet, and I am going to read you this inscription as easily as a schoolboy reads Greek when he knows the letters, except that I shall hesitate more over the meaning of the words."

The officer did indeed know the meaning of these modern hieroglyphs, inscribed according to the system of Champollion; he began to read, recording the syllables one by one in his notebook. "It states," he said, "that the scientific expedition sent by the King of Prussia under the direction of Lepsius has visited the pyramids of Ghizeh, and hopes to solve with the same good fortune the other problems of its mission."[51]

I immediately regretted my hieroglyphic skepticism, thinking of the ordeals and dangers braved by these scholars, who were at this very moment exploring the ruins of the Labyrinth.

We had crossed the threshold, when twenty bearded Arabs, their girdles bristling with pistols and daggers, rose from the ground where they had just been taking a siesta. One of our guides, who seemed to be in charge, said:

"See how terrible they are. Look at their pistols and their muskets!"

"Do they mean to rob us?"

"On the contrary! They are here to defend you if the desert tribes should make an attack."

"But surely they don't exist any longer since Mohammed Ali came into power."

"Oh, there are still evil men, over there, behind the mountains. . . . However, for a *colonnate*, the brave fellows you see there will defend you against all attack."

The Prussian officer inspected their weapons, but did not appear to form a very high opinion of their powers of destruction. But it was only a question of five shillings or so for me, or a thaler and a half for the Prussian. We agreed, shared the expense, and told each other that we had not been swindled.

"It often happens," said the guide, "that hostile tribes make an incursion here, especially when they suspect the presence of rich strangers."

"Come now!" I told him. "It's proverbial, and everyone accepts it!" I then recalled that Napoleon himself, while visiting the interior of the pyramids accompanied by the wife of one of his colonels, was exposed to peril, provided by his guide. The Bedouins, arriving unexpectedly, he said, had dispersed Napoleon's escort and blocked up the pyramid's entrance (which was scarcely a meter and a half high and wide) with huge stones. A cavalry troop which happened to be passing by rescued him from danger.

Certainly there is nothing impossible about it, and it would be a sad business to find oneself captured and imprisoned inside the Great Pyramid. The *colonnate* (Spanish piastre) which we gave our guards at least gave us the assurance that *they* could not, in fairness, play this trick on us.

But there was never any suggestion that these good fellows would have even dreamed of such a thing. The activity of their preparations; eight torches lighted in the twinkling of an eye; the charming attention of providing us with little girls to go before and carry water for us—it was all most reassuring.

The first thing to do was to bend the head and the back, and set the feet cleverly in two marble grooves, one on either side of the way down. Between the two grooves, there is a kind of abyss as wide as the distance between the legs, and we had to be very careful not to fall into it. We went forward, step by step, placing our feet left and right as best we could, with a little assistance from the torchbearers, and so descended, bent almost double for about a hundred and fifty yards.[52]

After that, there was no more danger of falling into the enormous fissure which we saw between our feet, and instead we had the discomfort of having to go on all fours through a passage partly obstructed by sand and ashes. The Arabs only clean this passage for a further *colonnate*, which is usually paid by rich and corpulent people.

After crawling on hands and knees for some time beneath this vault, we rose at the entrance to a new gallery which was hardly any higher than the one before it. After two hundred yards' more climbing, we came to a sort of cross-roads, with a deep dark well right in the middle, and this we had to go round to come to the staircase leading to the King's Chamber.

When we reached it, the Arabs fired their pistols and lighted branches to frighten away, they said, the bats and snakes. Snakes would never inhabit such recesses. As for the bats, they are there, and they make their presence known by shrieking and fluttering around the torches.

The chamber, with a shelving ridged roof,[53] is seventeen feet long and sixteen wide. It is difficult to understand how this little space—intended to hold tombs or some kind of chapel or temple—happens to be the principal retreat contrived in the stone ruins surrounding it.

Two or three other similar chambers have been discovered since that time.[54] Their granite walls are blackened by smoke from torches. No trace of a tomb can be seen anywhere, except for a porphyry cask eight feet long which could indeed have served to enclose a pharaoh's remains. However, according to tradition, even the very earliest excavations in the pyramids turned up nothing more than some ox bones.

What amazes the traveller, in the midst of these funereal surroundings, is that one must breath hot air permeated with bituminous odors. Moreover, one sees nothing but passages and walls (no hieroglyphs or sculptures), smoke-covered ceilings, vaults, and debris.

We had returned to the entrance, quite disenchanted with this arduous journey, and we were wondering what this immense edifice might represent.

"It is obvious," the Prussian officer told me, "that there are no tombs there. What would have been the point of constructing such enormous buildings in order possibly to preserve a king's coffin? It is obvious that such a large amount of stones, transported from Upper Egypt, could not have been gathered and set in place during the lifetime of a single man. And what would it signify, then, this desire of a sovereign to be set apart in a tomb seven hundred feet high, when we see nearly all the dynasties of Egyptian kings tucked modestly in hypogea and subterranean temples?

"We would do better to trust the opinion of the ancient Greeks, who, closer than we are to the priests and institutions of Egypt, saw the pyramids solely as religious monuments consecrated to initiations."

On our way back from a voyage of discovery which had not proved very impressive, we had to rest at the entrance to the marble grotto, and we wondered what this strange passage along which we had come might have meant, with its marble rails, with an abyss between them, ending in a crossways, in the middle of which was that mysterious well of which we could not see the bottom.

The Prussian officer, ransacking his memory, gave me a reasonably logical explanation of its purpose. No one is so strong on the mysteries of antiquity as a German. According to his version, this was the purpose of the low, railed gallery which we had gone down and climbed again so painfully. The man who was to undergo the ordeal of initiation was seated in a chariot, which descended the steep slope by the force of gravity. When he reached the centre of the pyramid, the neophyte was received by priests who showed him the well and told him to cast himself into it. The neophyte, of course, hesitated, and this was regarded as a sign of prudence. Then he was brought a kind of helmet with a lighted lamp upon it, and with this he had to descend into the well, in which there were iron bars for him to set his feet upon.

Down and down he went, lighted to some extent by the lamp he carried on his head; then, about a hundred feet down, came to the entrance of a passage closed by a grating which immediately opened before him. Three men appeared at that instant, wearing bronze masks that represented the countenance of Anubis, the dog god. It was essential that he should not be disturbed by their threats, but should go forward and hurl them to the ground. Then on again for another league till he reached a place which seemed like a dark thick forest.

The moment he set foot in the principal avenue, the whole place blazed with light, producing an effect like that of a great fire. It was no more than fireworks and pitch burning in iron cages. The neophyte had to pass through the forest, though he might suffer a few burns, and usually succeeded in doing so.

On the other side there was a river, and across this he had to swim. When he had hardly reached the middle, he was stopped and thrown back by a tremendous stirring of the water caused by two gigantic wheels. Just as his strength was on the point of giving out, there appeared before him an iron ladder which seemed to offer the only means of escape from a watery grave. But this was the third stage in the ordeal. As the neophyte placed a foot upon each rung the one he had just left fell into the water. This nerve-racking situation was made still worse by a frightful wind which tossed about the ladder and the unfortunate man upon it. Just as his strength was really at an end, he was expected to have presence of mind enough to grasp two steel rings which came down to him, and by these he had to hang until he saw a door open, which by a supreme effort he succeeded in doing.

This was the last of the four elementary tests. The initiate then reached the temple, passed round the statue of Isis, and was welcomed and congratulated by the priests.

With such memories as these we tried to repopulate this imposing solitude. The Arabs around us had gone to sleep again, waiting until the evening breeze had come to cool the air before they left the marble grotto, and we contributed different ideas of our own to the facts which tradition really confirmed. Those strange initiatory ceremonies, so often described by the Greek authors, who may, indeed, have seen them performed, were astonishingly interesting to us, for the stories fitted in perfectly with the arrangement of the place.

"How delightful it would be," I said to the German, "to have Mozart's *Magic Flute* performed here. Why does not some rich man take it into his head to have such a performance? At very little expense all these passages could be swept out, and all that would then be needed would be to bring out the Italian company from the Cairo theatre, with appropriate costumes. Imagine the thunderous voice of Zarastro resounding from the Hall of the Pharaohs, or the Queen of the Night appearing on the threshold of the room they call the Queen's Chamber, and sending forth those marvellous trills to peal through the darkness of the roof. Imagine the strains of the magic flute echoing through these long corridors, the grimaces and the fright of Papayeno, forced, as he followed in the footsteps of his master the initiate, to confront the threefold Anubis, then the blazing forest, the gloomy river stirred by the iron wheels, then that strange ladder of which, as he mounted, each step fell and dropped into the water with a sinister splash."

ON THE ISIAC TRADITION

"It would be difficult," said the officer, "to do all that in the very heart of the pyramids. I told you that the initiate, when he left the well, went along a passage for about a league. That subterranean way took him at last to a temple at the gates of Memphis, whose site you saw from the top of the platform. But when, after successfully emerging from these first ordeals, he looked upon the light of day again, the statue of Isis was still veiled from him; there was a final trial for him to undergo, one of a purely moral kind, of which he had been given no warning, and the purpose of which he did not know. The priests had borne him along in triumph, as one who had become one of themselves; choirs and instruments had celebrated his victory. He had still to purify himself by a fast of forty-one days, before he might look upon the Great Goddess, the widow of Osiris. Each day, that fast came to an end at sunset, and he was allowed to renew his strength with a few ounces of bread and a little water from the Nile. During this long penance, the neophyte was allowed to converse, at certain hours, with the priests and priestesses whose whole life was spent in the subterranean cities. He had the right to question any of them, and observe the customs of this mystic people who had given up the external world, and whose great numbers astounded Semiramis the Victorious, who, when she was laying the foundations of the Egyptian Babylon (the old Cairo), witnessed the collapse of the roof of one of these cities of the dead which were still inhabited by the living."

"And what happened to the initiate after his forty-one day fast?"

"There were still eighteen days of retreat in which he had to maintain complete silence. He was allowed only to read and write. Then he was put through an examination in which all the actions of his life were analysed and criticised. This lasted for another twelve days; then he was made to sleep for nine more days behind the statue of Isis, after he had implored the goddess to appear to him and inspire him with wisdom in his dreams. At last, after about three months, the trials were completed. The neophyte's aspiration towards divinity, encouraged by his reading, instruction and fasting, aroused in him such a pitch of religious enthusiasm that he was at last worthy to see the sacred veils of the goddess fall before him. Then, his astonishment reached its height as he saw that cold statue come to life, and its features suddenly take the form of those of the woman he loved the most, or the ideal which he had formed for himself of the most perfect beauty.

"The moment he stretched out his arms to take her, she vanished in a cloud of perfume. The priests entered with great ceremony and the initiate was proclaimed like unto the gods. Then, taking his place at the banquet of the Sages, he was allowed to taste the most delicate food, and intoxicate himself with the earthly ambrosia, which was never lacking at these feasts. He had but one regret, that he had had but one instant to admire the divine apparition which had deigned to smile upon him.

But this he was to enjoy in his dreams. A long sleep, doubtless induced by the lotus juice which had been pressed into his cup during the feast, enabled the priests to carry him to some leagues from Memphis, to the shores of that famous lake which still bears the name Karoun (Caron). There, still asleep, he was set upon a small boat and taken to the province of Fayoum, a delightful oasis, which, even to this day, is the country of roses. There was a deep valley, partly surrounded by mountains, and partly cut off from the rest of the world by precipices made by men's hands. Here the priests had brought together all the wealth of nature. Trees from India and the Yemen mingled their lush foliage and their strange blossoms with the richest vegetation of the land of Egypt.

"Tame animals supplied the element of life in this wonderful scene, and the initiate, set down asleep upon the turf, found himself at his awakening in a world which seemed the very perfection of created nature. He rose, and breathed the pure morning air, born again in the warmth of the sun which for so long he had not seen. He heard the cadenced song of the birds, admired the perfumed blossoms, the calm surface of waters bordered by papyrus and starred with red lotuses, with the pink flamingo and the ibis bending gracefully at their edge. But there was still something lacking to make this solitude live. A woman, an innocent virgin, so young that she seemed to spring from the pure dream of a morning, so beautiful that when he looked more closely upon her, he thought he recognised the glorious features of Isis, glimpsed as through a cloud. Such was the divine creature who was to be the mate and the reward of the triumphant initiate."

Although it is a pity that Gerard de Nerval did not divulge the Prussian officer's name, there seems to be no reason to doubt the validity of their curious encounter on top of the Great Pyramid. I leave it to the reader to decide whether the gift of lush imagination is reserved to the Arabs, or whether Nordic mists give rise to phantasmagorias as romantic as those fomented by the sun's intense heat. We will soon be encountering flights of fancy of a different sort but just as preposterous.

In my opinion, the two speakers were probably Freemasons. (It is well known that Mozart composed his *Magic Flute* after his initiation into this order.) The Prussian officer simply "transposed" into the eerie setting of the Great Pyramid the four trials by the elements (earth, water, air, fire) that he had undergone.[55] Let us not forget that at this time the Romantic Era was in full flower and that the *Revue des deux mondes*, in which Gerard de Nerval's letters appeared, had to cater to its readers' somewhat morbid imaginations.

There is only one item of interest in all this. As at the time of the Old Guard's Expedition to Egypt (1801), the only access to the Pyramid was the Descending Passage, which was obstructed a little below the Ascending Passage. In order to reach the latter it was necessary to climb up the narrow hole that the despoilers had dug around the three granite blocks plugging the entrance to this passage. This was also the case during Norden's time (1737).

THE ENGLISH ARCHAEOLOGISTS

Having read the works of Howard-Vyse, Perring, and Caviglia concerning the Giza Plateau, I am amazed to find the Sphinx and pyramids still standing.

After the plunderers and religious fanatics of all sects came the Egyptologists of the Howard-Vyse ilk, prepared to use every method of destruction in order to reach the sepulchral chambers. In all the pyramids of Giza Howard-Vyse used gunpowder in order to force passages that quite often proved useless. He had a hole 25½ feet (8 meters) deep dug in the Sphinx's shoulder, and another 27 feet (8.20 meters) deep dug in its back, which fortunately (but to his deep regret), he was unable to continue because the Arab workers ruined the drills through negligence. Nevertheless, these Egyptologists' accounts of their work are significant because they mention the state of the Great Pyramid upon their arrival, as well as the results of their investigations.

I provide here the most important passages from Howard-Vyse's journal (*Operations Carried on at the Pyramids of Gizeh*), noting the dates on which they were recorded.

Howard-Vyse

State of the Great Pyramid at Gizeh in November 1837. The inclined passage from the entrance to the subterraneous apartment, that apartment itself, and the unfinished passage proceeding to the southward from it, were open, although much encumbered with stones and rubbish; as were the forced and upper passages leading to the King's and Queen's Chambers. These two chambers, together with Davison's, and the communication, or well, descending from the great upper passage to that of the subterraneous apartment, were also open.[56] In the floor of the subterraneous apartment, an excavation had been made to the depth of a few feet; some stones had also been removed from behind the wall at the southeastern corner of Davison's Chamber: one of the blocks composing the pavement had been taken up near the north-western corner of the King's Chamber, and an excavation had been carried on beneath the Sarcophagus: this last, however, was almost entirely filled up with rubbish. The mouth of the southern Air Channel had been partially enlarged, and an excavation of a few feet had been made near the portcullis, along the course of the northern Air Channel. In the Queen's Chamber a considerable passage had been forced into the solid masonry, from the niche on the eastern side. There was also a large hollow near the granite blocks at the commencement of the ascending passage, which was supposed to have been the forced entrance made by the Caliphs. These were the only excavations of any consequence. On the exterior of the Pyramid a vast heap of stones and rubbish, 50 feet in height, extended from the base to the entrance of the inclined passage.

On February 23, 1836, Caviglia informs Howard-Vyse:

that he had made the excavation in the Subterraneous Chamber; that to the south of Davison's Chamber, and the one also along the Northern Air Channel; and that he had attempted to force the mouth of the Southern Air Channel in the King's Chamber.

Howard-Vyse notes:

It is to be remembered that Greaves, who travelled in 1638, describes the mouth of the Southern Air Channel to have been then partially forced, and blackened with smoke. He likewise alludes to excavations near the sarcophagus; but he neither mentions the Subterraneous Chamber, Davison's Chamber, nor the passage leading to it.

February 12, 1837:

Mr. Perring discovered the mouth of the northern air-channel.

February 22:

The excavation for a southern entrance in the Great Pyramid was begun at the distance of twenty-four feet westwards from the centre, and carried on to the depth of thirty feet, which was a work of considerable difficulty and labour, and was not finished till the 29th of May. The stones were very large, and the half of each of them was keyed in under the upper layer, besides which, many of them were in slanting directions, although in horizontal courses.

March 29:

In examining the ground to the northward of the Great Pyramid, I observed a line of rock projecting above the sand, which appeared to have been scalped down, and might, therefore, I considered, have contained an entrance to the subterraneous passage mentioned by Herodotus. It was parallel to the building, and about a hundred yards from it. But, upon removing the sand to the depth of six or seven feet, it was found to be in its natural state, and the work was given up.

April 5:

The entrance of the forced passage made by the Caliphs on the exterior of the northern front of the

Great Pyramid, was uncovered. It was in the centre, of considerable size, and appeared to have been effected by fire.

May 9:

Several pieces of broken pottery, a quantity of red stucco, or mortar composed of pounded granite, and of a red stone (some of which was found near it), were dug out near the base of the northern front of the Great Pyramid. This red stone is still used for the same purpose in Egypt.

May 21, 1838:

The exact level of the mouth of the northern Air-channel, on the exterior of the pyramid, was carried round to the southern front, the centre of which was also marked, and a reward of one hundred piastres offered to Abd el Ardi if he could find the mouth of the southern Channel. It was soon discovered in the same relative position as the northern.

The length of the southern channel is 174 feet 3 inches (53.04 m.) and the length of the northern channel is 233 feet (71.02 m.).

In May 1837, the base of the pyramid was 146 feet 5 inches (44.50 m.) above the level of the Nile; and, if we allow 20 or 30 feet for the elevation of the riverbed, the total would be only 176 feet (53.64 m.). A passage similar to the one in the second pyramid, sloping 36 degrees at a distance of 40 feet (12.20 m.) from the base, should arrive to a depth of 220 feet (67 m.) beneath the centre of the pyramid.

The ground of the underground chamber which is now open is more than 100 feet (30.48 m.) under the base.

According to Howard-Vyse,[57] the Great Pyramid's coordinates are:

Lat. 29° 59′ 12″ N; Long. 28° 8′ E

I directed, when I left Egypt in 1837, that a shaft should

be sunk in the floor of the subterraneous chamber, to the depth of fifty feet. This operation was attended with difficulty, from the want of a free circulation of air; but, in September 1838, it had penetrated thirty-eight feet through the solid rock, without any appearance of a chamber.

Two of the blocks were in their original position, nearly in the centre of the pyramid;

They were quite perfect, the joints were scarcely perceptible, and not wider than the thickness of silver paper; and such is the tenacity of the cement with which they are held together, that a fragment of one, that has been destroyed, remained firmly fixed in its original alignment, notwithstanding the lapse of time and the violence, to which it had been exposed.

Petrie

I provide here long extracts from Petrie's major work, *The Pyramids and Temples of Gizeh,* (London: Field & Tuer, 1883), which is considered to be authoritative in the field.

THE GREAT PYRAMID'S EXTERIOR

Since the time of the first discovery of some of the sockets in 1801,[58] it has always been supposed that they defined the original extent of the Pyramid, and various observers have measured from corner to corner of them, and thereby obtained a dimension which was—without further inquiry—put down as the length of the base of the Pyramid. Hence it was concluded that the distances of the socket corners were equal to the lengths of the Pyramid sides upon the pavement.

Therefore, when reducing my observations, after the first winter, I found that the casing on the North side (the only site of it then known) lay about 30 inches inside the line joining the sockets, I searched again and again for any flaw in the calculations. But there were certain check measures, beside the regular checked triangulation, which agreed in the same story . . .

The mean value of the casing on the platform is 230.348 m. (±0.127 m.) and, the mean angle being very near 51° 52′ (±2′), the height of the pyramid was 146.710

m. (±0.178 m.). The pyramid rests on a base with the mean value of 231.789 m.[59]

INFRASTRUCTURE OF THE GREAT PYRAMID
according to Petrie

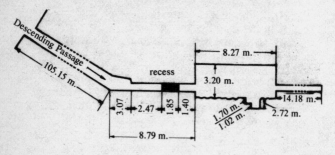

According to Petrie, the casing blocks at the top of the Pyramid must have had an average horizontal thickness of 1.575 meters (±0.203 meter), while their thickness at the base was 2.743 meters (±0.203 meter).

At the corners, however, the casing was thinner, averaging but 33.7 (difference of core plane and casing on pavement); and this is explained by the faces of the core masonry being very distinctly hollowed. This hollowing is a striking feature; and beside the general curve of the face, each side has a sort of groove specially down the middle of the face, showing that there must have been a sudden increase of the casing thickness down the mid-line. The whole of the hollowing was estimated at 37 on the N. face; and adding this to the casing thickness at the corners, we have 70.7, which just agrees with the result from the top (71 ± 5), and the remaining stones (62 ± 8). The object of such an extra thickness down the mid-line of each face might be to put a specially fine line of casing, carefully adjusted to the required angle on each side; and then afterwards setting all the remainder by reference to that line and the base.[60]

DIMENSIONS OF THE DESCENDING PASSAGE
AND SUBTERRANEAN CHAMBER

Petrie gives the following measurements for the Descending Passage and the Subterranean Chamber:

Width of the Descending Passage: from 0.686 to 0.762 m.; height, from 0.667 to 0.749 m.

Length of the Descending Passage from the original entrance: 105.15 m.

Length of the horizontal landing to the Horizontal Passage's entrance: 3.07 m.

Length of the Horizontal Passage: 5.72 m.

Distance from the Passage's entrance to the recess: 2.47 m.

Length of the recess: 1.85 m.

Recess: length, 1.85 m.; width, 0.97 m.; height, from 1 to 1.22 m.

Section of the passage: height, 0.91 m.; width, 0.80 m.

Since the floor of the Subterranean Chamber is very uneven, its height varies from 3.0 to 3.20 m. Its dimensions are the following: east side, 8.27 m.; west side, 8.37 m.; north side, 14.06 m.; south side, 14.40 m.[61]

Difference in level at the Horizontal Passage's exit: 0.70 m.

Length of the southern blind passage: 14.18 m.; its section: 0.742 by 0.762 m.

The large chamber is most clearly unfinished,[62] both in the dressing of the walls, and more especially in the excavation for the floor. The walls have an average irregularity estimated at ±.7, and projecting lumps of rock are left untouched in some parts. The roof is more irregular, estimated average variation ±3. The floor is most irregular, at the W. end it rises at the highest to only 10 inches from the roof; and over all the western half of the chamber it is irregularly trenched with the cuttings made by workmen to dislodge blocks of the rock.

It is, in fact, an interesting specimen of quarrying, but unfortunately now completely choked up, by Perring having stowed away there all the pieces of limestone taken out of his shaft in the floor.

The best worked floor surface is just around the square shaft, 198 below the roof, and about 40 below the main part of the floor, which is 155 below roof on a knob of rock beside the shaft. The square shaft is not parallel to the chamber, but is placed nearly diagonally.

The approaches to the well are in bad condition. This cavity is really composed of two superimposed square wells; the upper, about two meters on each side is driven to a depth of 1.70 m., while the lower and smaller well measures 1.50 m. on each side, and according to Vyse, is 1 m. deep. Perring's round well, next to the smaller square well, is 11.60 m. deep.

The southern passage is very rough, apparently merely a first drift-way, only just large enough to work in, intended to be afterwards enlarged, and smoothed; its sides wind 6 or 8 inches in and out.

THE ASCENDING PASSAGE

Petrie gives the three granite blocks obstructing this passage a total length of 4.53 meters, and a section 1.201 meters high perpendicularly (or 1.32 meters high vertically) and 1.057 meters wide. The passage's angle with the horizontal is 26° 12′ 50″; its total length up to the Grand Gallery is 39.29 meters. Its width is constant and equals 2 cubits (1.05 meters); its height perpendicular to the incline varies from 1.11 to 1.245 meters.

It has often been said that the Queen's Chamber was intended to contain the blocks for plugging the ascending passage, until they were required to be let down. But there is an absolute impossibility in this theory; the blocks are 47.3 × 41.6 in section, while the Queen's Chamber passage is but 46.2 × 40.6, or too small in both dimensions to allow the blocks to pass. Hence the blocks must have stood in the gallery until they were wanted, since they could never be got upwards through the ascending passage, as that is but 38.2 at the lower end, and the existing plugs are 41.6 wide above that. Neither could the plugs be brought up the well shaft, as that is but 28. square; nor out of the King's Chamber, as the passage is but 43.6 high. The total length of plug-blocks would be about 203 inches, or very probably 206 inches, or 10 cubits, like so many lengths marked out in that passage. Now, the flat part of the Queen's Chamber passage floor within the gallery, on which blocks might be placed, is but 176 long; and the whole distance, from the N. wall of the gallery to the vertical cut down, is but 199.4: so in no way could 203 inches of blocks stand on the horizontal floor, and certainly any passage through the gallery door would be impossible, to say nothing of the difficulty of pushing such blocks along a rough floor, so as to tip them down the passage. Thus the plug-blocks cannot have stood in any place except on the sloping floor of the gallery.

For them, then, to be slid down the passage, it was necessary that the opening to the Queen's Chamber should be completely covered with a continuous floor. The traces of this floor may still be seen, in the holes for beams of stone, across the passage; and in fragments of stone and cement still sticking on the floor of the Queen's Chamber passage at that point. It is certain, then, that the Queen's Chamber was closed and concealed before the ascending passage was closed.

But we are met then by an extraordinary idea, that all access to the King's Chamber after its completion must have been by climbing over the plug-blocks, as they lay in the gallery, or by walking up the ramps on either side of them. Yet, as the blocks cannot physically have been lying in any other place before they were let down, we are shut up to this view.[63]

The Queen's Chamber

According to Petrie, the Grand Gallery's north landing is located 21.80 meters above the Pyramid's socle; its length is 4.47 meters. The passage leading to the Queen's Chamber is 38.70 meters long; the section of this passage is 1.173 by 1.031 meters. An 0.50-meter difference in level is found 33.20 meters from its start; the level of the chamber's floor is located 21.21 meters above the Pyramid's socle.

It appears that the ridge of the roof of the Queen's Chamber falls exactly along the Pyramid's north-south axis. The chamber's dimensions are the following: length, 5.75 meters;

width, 5.22 meters; height of the north and south walls, 4.69 meters; ridge, 6.22 meters. These values correspond to exactly 9, 10, 11, and 12 cubits, respectively.

The niche located in the east wall must have contained the diorite statue of Cheops (his "double"), as the Queen's Chamber was the Pyramid's *serdab*. Apparently Petrie was the first to discover the middle chamber's true destination. However, he was not certain of this, for he writes:

> It may be an open question whether the Queen's Chamber was not the sepulcher of Khnumu-Khufu (section 113), the co-regent of Khufu. Edrisi, in his accurate and observant account of the Pyramid (1236 A.D.), mentions an empty vessel in the Queen's Chamber; and that this was not a confused notion of the coffer now known, is proved by his saying that in the King's Chamber "an empty vessel is seen here similar to the former."

Since no fragment of a sarcophagus has been found amid the great quantity of stones removed from the floor and the niche (debris that has been thrown into various holes outside the Pyramid), there is very little hope of learning any more on this subject. Though Caviglia found no sarcophagus while clearing the chamber, fragments might easily have gone unnoticed.

The two ducts stemming from the chamber are similar to the so-called ventilation ducts of the King's Chamber, but each of the ducts in the Queen's Chamber was sealed with an unperforated plaque. They were discovered by Dixon on August 14, 1872. The opening of the north duct is 0.218 meter high and 0.203 meter wide; the duct runs horizontally for 1.93 meters before turning upward.

THE WELL

The remarkable shaft, or "well," that leads away from the lower end of the gallery down to the subterranean passage, was fully measured about its mouth; but it appears to be so rough and so evidently utilitarian (for the exit of workmen) that it is not worth while to publish more complete measures than those of Prof. Smyth. As, however, the position of its mouth has been supposed to have a meaning, it should be stated that the opening is from 21.8 to 49.0 horizontally from N. wall of gallery on floor, 21.8 to 48.7 near its top, and 21.9 to 48.9 by the sloping distance reduced.

The shaft, or "well," leading from the N. end of the gallery down to the subterranean parts, was either not contemplated at first, or else was forgotten in the course of building; the proof of this is that it has been cut through the masonry after the courses were completed. On examining the shaft, it is found to be irregularly tortuous through the masonry, and without any arrangement of the blocks to suit it; while in more than one place a corner of a block may be seen left in the irregular curved side of the shaft, all the rest of the block having disappeared in cutting the shaft. This is a conclusive point, since it would never have been so built at first. A similar feature is at the mouth of the passage, in the gallery. Here the sides of the mouth are very well cut, quite as good work as the dressing of the gallery walls; but on the S. side there is a vertical joint in the gallery side, only 5.3 inches from the mouth. Now, great care is always taken in the Pyramid to put large stones at a corner, and it is quite inconceivable that a Pyramid builder would put a mere slip 5.3 thick beside the opening to a passage. It evidently shows that the passage mouth was cut out after the building was finished in that part. It is clear, then, that the whole of this shaft is an additional feature to the first plan.[64]

THE GRAND GALLERY

Petrie gives the following measurements for the Grand Gallery:

From the north wall to the "incision" (entrance to the passage to the Queen's Chamber): 5.670 m.

From the north wall to the far end of the ramp ("Great Step"): 46.10 m.

From the north wall to the south wall: 47.84 m.

Height of the landing of the "Great Step" above the Pyramid's socle: 42.80 m.

Height of the "Great Step": 0.889 m.

Width of the "Great Step" or upper platform: 3 cubits = 1.55 m.

Average width of the banquettes: 1 cubit = 0.52 m.
Vertical height of the ramps or banquettes: 0.58 m.
Width of the floor of the middle passage between the
banquettes: 2 cubits = 1.05 m.

The holes cut in the ramps or benches, along the sides
of the gallery (see section of them in Pl. ix), the blocks
inserted in the wall over each, and the rough chopping
out of a groove across each block—all these features are
as yet inexplicable. One remarkable point is that the
holes are alternately long and short, on both sides of the
gallery; the mean of the long holes is 23.32, with an
average variation of .73, and the mean of the short holes
is 20.51, with average variation .40. Thus the horizontal
length of a long hole is equal to the sloping length of a
short hole, both being one cubit.

THE ANTECHAMBER
Level above the Pyramid's socle: 43 m.
Length of the passage, starting from the south wall of
the gallery: 1.32 m.
North-south length of the Antechamber: 2.972 m.
Length of the passage leading to the King's Chamber:
2.565 m.
East-west width of the Antechamber: 1.651 m.
Height of the Antechamber: 3.798 m.

The granite leaf which stretches across the chamber,
resting in grooves cut in the granite wainscots, must be
somewhat less in width than the breadth between the
grooves, i.e., 48.46 to 48.76. The thickness of the two
stones that form it was gauged by means of plumb-lines
at 33 points; it varies from 15.16 to 16.20, but the details
are scarcely worth printing. This leaf is not simply a flat
slab of granite, but on both its upper and lower parts it
has a projection on its N. side, about 1 inch thick, where
it is included in the side grooves. The edge of this projection down the W. side has been marked out by a saw
cut.

This boss, of which so much has been made by theorists, is merely a very rough projection, like innumerable
others that may be seen; left originally for the purpose

of lifting the blocks. When a building was finished these bosses were knocked away (I picked up a loose one among waste heaps at Gizeh) and the part was dressed down and polished like the rest of the stone. Remains of another boss may be seen on a block in the passage to the King's Chamber; remains of 15 or 16 others in the King's Chamber; 5 others complete in the spaces above that. The E. to W. breadth of the leaf between its side ledges in the grooves, varies from 40.6 to 41.2 at different heights up the middles of the ledges; but furthermore, the edges are not square, and we may say that 40 to 42 will about represent its irregularity. Yet this was another so-called "standard of measure" of the theorists. The top of the upper block of the leaf is a mere natural surface of the granite boulder out of which it was cut, utterly rough and irregular. It varies from 51.24 to 59.0, and perhaps more, below the ceiling.

THE KING'S CHAMBER

Level above the Pyramid's socle: 43 m.
Average length: 10.476 m.
Average width: 5.241 m.
Average height: 5.844 m.

From twelve measurements made of the chamber's walls, Petrie derived the value of the cubit: 0.52367 meter, a value that should be considered the closest to that of the cubit in use during the Fourth Dynasty.

Sarcophagus
Exterior length: 2.271 m.
Exterior width: 0.778 m.
Interior length: 1.983 m.
Interior width: 0.683 m.
Depth: 0.874 m.

THE VENTILATION DUCTS

The north duct was forced and opened like a passage, except along the west side of the bottom. Both ducts are blocked by sand.

The north duct climbs at an angle of 31° 33', the south duct at an angle of 45° 13' 40".

METRIC RELATIONSHIPS EXISTING
IN THE GREAT PYRAMID

1. Examining the validity of the various theories put forth concerning the Great Pyramid, Petrie writes, on the subject of the slope:

> For the whole form the π proportion (height is the radius of a circle = circumference of Pyramid) has been very generally accepted of late years, and is a relation strongly confirmed by the presence of the numbers 7 and 22 in the number of cubits in height and base respectively; 7:22 being one of the best known approximations to π.

The Pyramid's profile is thus determined by the ratio:

$$\frac{\text{height}}{\frac{1}{2}\text{ base}} = \frac{14}{11} = \tan \alpha$$

2. Once the shape and size were thus fixed, the floor of the edifice's main chamber, the King's Chamber, was placed at a level such that the area of the Pyramid's horizontal section at that height is equal to half the area of its base; in which case

a. The diagonal of this square section (ED) equals the length of the base (AB);

b. The length (CD) of the face equals half the diagonal of the base.

3. The Queen's Chamber was placed at half the height of the "King's Chamber."

4. Since the King's Chamber measures 20 cubits long by 10 cubits wide, its height equals half the diagonal of the rectangle of the base, or $5\sqrt{5}$ cubits.

Thus the triangles obtained by cutting the chamber along the planes passing through the diagonals of the east and west faces are sacred triangles such as AD'B. According to Petrie, the floor of the King's Chamber is therefore found at a distance of $\frac{h\sqrt{2}}{2}$ from the Pyramid's summit, or $h\left(1 - \frac{\sqrt{2}}{2}\right)$ above the socle. Since the Pyramid's height above its socle equals 146.56 meters, the King's Chamber should be located

THE DIMENSIONS OF THE KING'S CHAMBER
IN ANCIENT CUBITS
according to Petrie

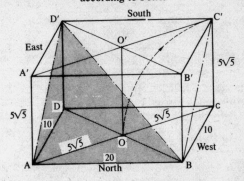

MEDIAN SECTION
OF THE GREAT PYRAMID

If S is the surface of the Great Pyramid's base and S' the surface of its horizontal section at the level of the King's Chamber, we have, according to Petrie:

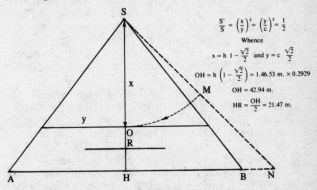

$$\frac{S'}{S} = \left(\frac{x}{y}\right)^2 = \left(\frac{y}{c}\right)^2 = \frac{1}{2}$$

Whence

$$x = h\,\left(1 - \frac{\sqrt{2}}{2}\right) \quad \text{and} \quad y = c\,\frac{\sqrt{2}}{2}$$

$$OH = h\left(1 - \frac{\sqrt{2}}{2}\right) = 1.46.53 \text{ m.} \times 0.2929$$

OH = 42.94 m.

$$HR = \frac{OH}{2} = 21.47 \text{ m.}$$

The position of the King's Chamber (O) in relation to the Pyramid's summit (S) is equal to half the hypotenuse of an isosceles triangle having as its sides the Pyramid's height.

42.94 meters above the socle, which is consistent with the measurements.

The Queen's Chamber (the *serdab*), located at half this height, is thus located 21.47 meters above the socle.

THE DOOR OF THE BLUNTED PYRAMID AT DAHSHUR (SOUTHERN PYRAMID)

The greater part of its casing still remains. The casing blocks are very deep from back to front, about 80 inches; though only 20 inches high, and about 60 wide. The angles are respectively 54° 14' 46" and 42° 59' 26" for the bottom and for the top of the casing.

On either side of the passage is a hole in the wall; now very rounded and cavernous, owing to weathering; but apparently about 3 or 4 inches in diameter, and 5 or 6 deep, originally. These two holes are just opposite one to the other, the centres being about 13 inside the Pyramid, and 6 above the passage roof.

Above these holes, the wall, having been recut, rises more perpendicularly toward the Pyramid's exterior.

The possibility of the Pyramids having had movable doors has been quite overlooked in modern times, owing to the general belief that the passages were plugged up. Of course, if a passage was filled up solid there could not have been any door to it; but as we have seen that there is no evidence of such plugging, doors may have existed. And as we shall further see that there is very substantial evidence of the former existence of doors, we have, therefore, equally valid proofs of the non-existence of any plugging.

The traces of a stone flap door, or turning block, in the mouth of the South Pyramid of Dahshur, have been already described (section 109), as well as the signs of a wooden door behind that. Such a formation of the passage mouth is unmistakable in its purpose; but after drawing conclusions from that doorway, it was a most satisfactory proof of the generality of such doors, to observe the following passage from Strabo on the Great Pyramid. "The Greater (Pyramid), a little way up one side, has a stone that may be taken out (εξαιρεσιμον, *exemptilem*), which being raised up ('αρθεντον, *sublato*) there is a sloping passage to the foundations." This sentence is most singularly descriptive of opening a flap door; first, the stone is taken out, or lifted outwards from the face and then, being thus raised up, the passage is opened. The two different words exactly express the change in the apparent motion, first outwards and then upwards; and they show remarkable accuracy and precision in their use. Besides this description, there is another statement that the Pyramids of Gizeh had doors, in an Arabic MS., quoted by Vyse; this was written in 850 A.D., and, therefore, only twenty or thirty years after Mamun had forced his way into the Great Pyramid, and thus re-discovered the real entrance.

The mechanical proofs of the existence of a door to the Great Pyramid are of some weight, though only circumstantial, and not direct evidence like that of the above authors. No one can doubt that the entrance must have been closed, and closed so as not to attract attention at the time when the Arabs made their forced passage, about a hundred feet long, through the solid masonry. Moreover, it is certain that the entrance was not covered then by rubbish: (1) because the Arabic hole is some way below it, and the ground-level at the time of the forcing is seen plainly in the rubbish heap; (2) because the rubbish heap, which is even now much below the original doorway, is composed of broken casing, and the casing was not yet broken up at the time of forcing the passage. Therefore the doorway must have been so finely closed that the various accidental chippings and weathering on all the general surface of the casing completely masked any wear or cracks that there might be around the entrance; and so invisible was the door then, that, standing on the heap from which they forced their hole, the Arabs could not see anything to excite their suspicion on the surface only 35 feet above them; they, therefore, plunged into the task of tearing out the stone piecemeal, in hopes of meeting with something in the inside. Yet we know from Strabo that the Romans had free access to the passage, though he says that it was kept a secret in his time. . . .

To sum up. A self-replacing door, which left no external mark, is absolutely required by the fact of the Arabs having forced a passage.[65] Only a flap door, or a diagonal-sliding portcullis slab, can satisfy this requirement. A flap door is unequivocally shown to have been used at Dahshur. And Strabo's description of the entrance agrees with such a door, and with no other. Such is the evidence for the closing of the Pyramids by doors; equally proving also the absence of any plugging up of the entrance passages.

NOTES

1. *The Geography of Strabo* [Trans. by H. L. Jones] (New York: G. P. Putnam's Sons), vol. VIII, pp. 84–95.
2. Pliny the Elder, Natural History, Book 36, pp. 59–65.
3. Ibid., pp. 57–59.
4. This passage is but a distorted recollection of Herodotus' texts concerning, on the one hand, Cheops' subterranean sepulcher and on the other, the subterranean channel of the lake of Moeris. (Cf. Herodotus, II, 149.)
5. The third pyramid, that of Mykerinos, the lower third of which was constructed of Aswan granite.
6. It is obvious that this unit of measurement was not the cubit but the orgyia. The measurement of 500 cubits is correct, "cubit" meaning the *baladi* cubit, which is simply the Lagid Dynasty or Greek cubit of 0.462 m.
7. This text confirms other texts, particularly that of Pliny: the Great Pyramid never ended in a point, with a pyramidion, like the Twelfth Dynasty pyramids of Seostris and Ammanene.
8. There is no doubt that the manuscript's text has been altered: the word *brocade* was misinterpreted; the Arabic term must have been makra, which designates a type of red hematite still used by quarriers. Like the Sphinx, the Great Pyramid has been painted red. I will return to this subject later.
9. This phrase is incomprehensible; in my opinion, it is necessary to reconstruct it as follows: "in which were amassed the statues that had been done of Surid's forebears." The Pyramid's Grand Gallery was, in fact, *the gallery of King Cheops' ancestors*.
10. Indeed, one can see, in the casing blocks of the second pyramid that are still in place, mortises that must have corresponded either to tenons carved in the block directly below or to other mortises designed to hold metal rods that would ensure the stability of the casing.
11. The translation must be faulty or the text inverted. Abd-al-Latif gives 400 black cubits of 30 digits, this cubit being one-

fifth longer than the normal cubit of 24 digits. Thus 400 black cubits equal 500 normal cubits.

The figures given are accurate:

500 black cubits = 0.557 m. × 400 = 230.80 m.
500 baladi cubits = 0.4618 m. × 500 = 230.90 m.

The other figures, corresponding to the apothem, the ridges, and the height, are erroneous.

12. The description does not correspond to the Great Pyramid's interior layout. The square hole mentioned seems to be that of the Subterranean Chamber, but the latter is not arched.

13. According to Louis Mathieur Langles, as quoted by Jonard (*Description de l'Egypte*, Paris, French Government, 1809–22, vol. 9, p. 461), the time elapsed since the flood was 1,471 years (not 1,741).

14. The Arabic calculation for the date of the onset of the flood is based on this shifting of the "Lion's Heart" (Regulus) at the summer solstice, in the first minute of Cancer, which in fact gives a time lapse of about 400 years.

Silvestre de Sacy, the translator of the Arabic texts for *Description de l'Egypte*, notes that this entire passage seems incorrect in the Egyptian Museum's text and does not lend itself to a precise interpretation.

However, there may be some basis of truth in this account. According to the data, the original manuscript dates from: 1785 + 2372 + 324 = 4481 B.C.

In this case, there would have elapsed between the date of the original manuscript and the translation of the Coptic text into Arabic (225 A.H. = 840 A.C.), there would have elapsed 4481 + 840 = 5,321 years.

But the Egyptian Museum's papyrus gives 4,321 solar years; that is, one millennium less. It is thus probable that an error was made by either the copyist or the translator. According to my chronological reconstruction, the original manuscript would date from the year 7 of the reign of Rathures, sixth king of the Fifth Dynasty (4481 B.C.), and the first copy of gold leaf from the reign of one of the Fourteenth Dynasty kings (2696 B.C.).

Since, according to the Christian chroniclers, the flood occurred in 2242 A.M. (in the chronology of Athothis), or 3316 B.C., the original papyrus must have been written 1,165 years before the cataclysm.

15. Span: the distance from the end of the thumb to the end of the little finger, with the hand stretched out (22 to 24 centimeters) 7 spans = 1.54 to 1.68 m.; 18 spans = 3.96 to 4.32 m.

16. The preceding description does not correspond to what we know about the three great pyramids; but that does not prove its unfeasibility. We could attribute it to the Arabic Oriental

imagination and view these accounts as nonsense; however, the discoveries of this century, especially that of the tomb of Tutankhamen, should arouse in us a certain caution.

17. Rodai gives the Pyramid's true measurement in ordinary or *baladi* cubits. The discovery of the coffin made of green stone seems likely; since the interior width of the cask in the King's Chamber measures 0.674 meters and the breadth of an average man is 0.50 meters, the thickness of the body-shaped coffin wall added to the thickness of the gold plate could not have exceeded 8 centimeters, which is possible.

18. From May 13, 1214 to May 1, 1215 A.D.

19. I do not know from which Arab author Norden derived the information concerning the Sabeans' pilgrimage to the Great Pyramid. Neither have I been able to find, in Maqrizi, the passage cited by Howard-Vyse, but I am certain that this statue was simply a gnomon.

20. The text is not very comprehensible. The 400 cubits assigned to each of the Pyramid's faces ascribe to the cubit a value of 0.578 meter, which is that of Al Mamun's black cubit and not that of the royal or lithic cubit. But how are we to interpret the text concerning the value of this cubit as equaling $1^2/_5$ cubits?

There is, in my opinion, only one possible interpretation: that the royal cubit exceeds by two-fifths *of its own value* the value of the ordinary or *baladi* cubit. In this case the ratio of the royal cubit's value to that of the *baladi* cubit is 5:3. Since the ordinary cubit equals 0.462 meter, the royal cubit equals 0.771 meter (the lithic cubit.)

The Great Pyramid's base (measuring 231.40 meters) thus has a value of, respectively:

500 *baladi*, or Lagid Dynasty cubits of 0.462 m.;
400 Al Mamun's black cubits of 0.578 m.;
300 royal or lithic cubits of 0.771 m.

21. According to the text, the black cubit equals 0.578 meter; the side of the platform, 5.78 meters.

22. The cubit in question is the exact cubit of 24 digits (0.462 meter); the side of the platform thus measures 5.08 meters.

23. It is Abd-al-Latif who is mistaken; since the cubit equals 0.462 meter, the result is $0.462 \times 317 = 146.454$ meters, which is the Great Pyramid's exact height, and $0.462 \times 460 = 212.52$ meters, which is obviously the length of the ridge up to the platform. The same dimensions are given by Bakui in *Description de l'Egypte*, vol. 9, p. 462.

24. 1200–1218; probably Saladin's brother rather than son.

25. These are the Turah quarries, and the description is not exaggerated. In 1931 numerous high mounds of rubble from the cutting of the pyramids' blocks were still visible; today they have

disappeared, the limestone rubble having been transformed into cement at a large factory located nearby.

26. Suez and Aswan.

27. Obviously, it is difficult for Abd-al-Latif to ascertain the length of the Sphinx's body, which was totally covered with sand. Only Pliny has given its exact length: 243 Roman feet (71.82 meters). Therefore the Sphinx unquestionably had been cleared of sand prior to his time.

28. The text seems to suggest that the chamber in question is the Great Pyramid's Subterranean Chamber. It is nothing of the kind, for the "well," which I myself have descended and which was originally square, has no door; besides, the Subterranean Chamber does not have a rounded ceiling.

29. 1117 or 1214 A.D.; Codai says 211 A.H.

30. This specification is significant because it means that since the Descending Passage was only 50 cubits (23.10 meters) long during the reign of Al Mamun, in 829 A.D. it was already obstructed right below the Ascending Passage.

31. Undoubtedly this is the exact Arabic cubit of 0.462 meter.

32. It is true that the walls of the Descending Passage show no signs of serious damage, which would certainly have been the case had the Descending Passage been sealed with cemented blocks. Maillet's hot water—obviously ineffectual—can only be taken as a joke; the same is true of his hypotheses concerning the blocks stored in the Grand Gallery and the use of the so-called "ventilation" ducts—one was, he believed, for the provisioning of the "volunteers of death," the other was a sewage pipe.

33. What is hardest to believe is that Lauer, *Les Problems* (p. 32) should support Maillet's preposterous theories; it is to be hoped that this author will without delay resume studying the Great Pyramid, with which he seems to be insufficiently familiar.

34. Maillet, unaware of the existence of the Subterranean Chamber, omitted from his calculations the 86 supplementary meters of the Descending Passage.

35. There are 203 courses at present.

36. *Travels in Egypt and Nubia* (London: L. Davis & Reymers, 1757), pp. 104–116.

37. The upper facing—still in place—of the pyramid of Kephren is constructed not of granite but of Turah limestone; however, since this facing was painted with red ochre, it is not surprising that Norden, like most travelers, should have mistaken it for granite. Only the bottom two courses were actually covered with granite.

38. 21.15 meters down the plumb line of the Ascending Passage, which is obstructed by three granite blocks. Thus, in 1801, the Descending Passage was obstructed by debris from the tunnel

dug around the granite blocks. This tunnel was certainly not made by Al Mamun, but it alerted his stonemasons to the position of the Ascending Passage so that they were able to determine the location of the hole currently being used as an entrance. In my opinion, this tunnel was made long before Al Mamun came along; it must date from the Seventh, Eighth, or Ninth Dynasty. I will explain the reasons for this belief elsewhere.

39. Actually 26° 34′, corresponding to tan ½.

40. "Al Mamun's" hole was not cleared until 1917. The members of the Commission d'Egypte Expedition were unaware of its existence.

41. Coutelle and Gratien le Père were unable to reach the Subterranean Chamber, known as the "unfinished chamber," because the Descending Passage and the "well" were obstructed by debris from excavations. The length of 22.363 meters is that of the Descending Passage down to the point where it was broken into beneath the level of the three granite blocks closing off the Ascending Passage.

42. That is, 0.162 meter. (It is actually 0.154 meter.)

43. The "well's" vertical depth, from the level of the Grand Gallery's lower landing (the level of the floor of the Queen's Chamber) down to where the "well" opens on the west wall of the Descending Passage, is 48.10 meters. Its real length is 57.50 meters. In order to appreciate Coutelle's exploit fully, one has to attempt the descent oneself; it is, even today, not at all easy or without risk.

In fact, I myself, along with one of my colleagues at the Lycée du Cairo, experienced the same misfortune as Colonel Coutelle. Having attached the end of a 50-meter-long rope to the "well's" entrance, we proceeded to descend; soon our flashlights could no longer pierce the thick cloud of dust raised by our descent. As we came to the end of the rope, our feet searched in vain for the floor at the bottom of the "well." We had to seek, by feeling about with our toes, notches capable of supporting our weight, and to thusly descend 8 meters before finding solid ground beneath our feet. We left the Pyramid looking like baker's apprentices, covered from head to foot with a layer of dust several millimeters thick, and it took us several hours to clear out our nostrils and bronchial passages.

44. Here Colonel Coutelle makes a mistake. According to the Survey of Egypt, the altitude of the Pyramid's plateau is 59.60 meters above the Mediterranean, and the Nile's average bed is 10 meters, the average water level being 12.25 meters and high water 20.63 meters. The bottom of the well is located 26.70

meters beneath the Pyramid's plateau; the floor of the Subterranean Chamber 30.70 meters. Consequently, the bottom of the well and the floor of the Subterranean Chamber are located, respectively, 22.90 and 18.90 meters *above* the *present* level of the Nile.

Taking into account the average alluvion coefficient of 0.130 meter per century, it can be estimated that the bed of the Nile in Cheops' time was 8.50 meters lower than it is at present. The Subterranean Chamber, known as the "abandoned chamber," was thus 27.60 meters *above* the bed of the Nile and 25.15 meters above the average flood level in Cheops' time.

If the subterranean burial chamber mentioned by Herodotus exists, its ceiling would have to be 58.10 meters below the Great Pyramid's plateau; that is, about 27.40 meters below the Subterranean Chamber known to us at present. (See the diagram of the levels of the Great Pyramid, p. 7.)

45. This mode of construction, using tenons and mortises, is not peculiar to the angle stones but was applied to all the facing blocks.

46. Coutelle is wrong; the second pyramid's facing, like that of the first, was covered with a layer of cement made of crushed granite and red ochre.

47. Here Coutelle adopts Herodotus' assertions, however, he is certain that the size of the angle blocks, as well as that of the blocks making up the facing's lower courses, was determined *before* they were set in place. This size was an especially delicate matter, for on it alone depended the Pyramid's slope and height, which were connected to the dimensions of the terrestrial globe.

48. It is possible that Diodorus' cubit might be the *lithic cubit* equal to 0.77 meter, which would give the platform's side a length of 4.62 meters; otherwise, a copyist's error should be assumed.

49. Pliny gives 16½ feet; that is, 4.88 meters, as the foot Pliny refers to is the Roman foot of 0.2955 meter (Jomard wrongly assigns it a value of 0.2771 meter).

50. This inscription is completely invisible at present (1970).

51. The Prussian officer's knowledge of hieroglyphics must have been rather slim, and if Gerard de Nerval had known the inscription's true meaning, he would surely not have missed this opportunity to poke fun at it in his fashion.

52. The Descending Passage, with a width of 1.06 meters (2 cubits), does in fact contain on each side, down to where it meets the Ascending Passage, two banquettes 0.18 meter (⅓ cubit) wide and about 0.52 meter (1 cubit) high. The corridor between the two banquettes thus has a width of 0.70 meter. At the plumb line

of the Ascending Passage, the Descending Passage contains three horizontal steps; the length of the Descending Passage down to this point is 20 meters.

53. Gerard de Nerval seems to be confusing the King's Chamber and the Queen's Chamber; it is the latter that has a ridged roof.

54. Here the author is alluding to the relieving chambers, located above the King's Chamber, discovered by Howard-Vyse in 1837.

55. Edouard Schuré, in his work, *The Great Initiaics* (Philadelphia, David McKay, 1922), has, on the subject of Hermes, borrowed a great deal from Gerard de Nerval; in fact, certain passages are nearly identical. Just as amusing is Paul Brunton's *A Search in Secret Egypt* (London, Rider, 1936), in which the author recalls a hallucinatory night he spent in the Great Pyramid.

56. The clearing of the Descending Passage (which reestablishes communication with the Subterranean Chamber, known as the "unfinished chamber," whose existence was unknown at the time) and the unplugging of the "well" were carried out under Caviglia in 1836.

57. Colonel H. H. Howard-Vyse, *Operations Carried On at the Pyramids at Gizeh in 1837*, J. Fraser, London, 1840.

58. In January 1801 Coutelle and Le Père discovered the two sockets of the two angle blocks of the north face; carved in the bedrock, they measure 3.90 and 3.40 meters along the sides and 0.207 meter deep.

59. Petrie notes the dimensions of the Great Pyramid's bases (given here in meters):

	NORTH	EAST	SOUTH	WEST	Averages
Base upon the socle	230.363	230.320	230.365	230.342	230.3475
Base of the socle upon the bedrock	231.896	231.922	231.747	231.628	231.798
Survey (1925), base upon the socle	230.253	230.391	230.454	230.357	230.366
Survey (1881), base upon the socle	231.900	231.925	231.747	231.628	231.800

My own measurements for the north base are:

Base upon the socle 230.253

Edge of the socle 231.093

Base of the socle upon the bedrock 231.393

60. The explanation is not very clear; Petrie's idea seems to be that *only* the *core* of the Pyramid had been hollowed toward the center of its faces, that this hollowing was corrected by making the facing blocks overly thick. Therefore, once the facing had been completed, the faces would have been perfectly flat. That is not how I see it; the still-visible remains of the facing adjoining

the bedrock show a hollowing of not only the core but also the facing itself. I will take up this question again when providing the astronomical reason for the hollowing of the Pyramid's faces.

61. According to my measurements, the Subterranean Chamber is 14 by 8.23 by 3.48 meters.

62. This chamber was *not* an unfinished, abandoned chamber; it was used as the setting for the first degree of isiac initiation. I will return to this subject later.

63. I disagree with Petrie; it was absolutely impossible to slide the three blocks (whose section was equal to—indeed, greater than—that of the passage) over a distance of 39 meters; the friction coefficient would have moreover unquestionably prevented such an undertaking.

64. The perforation of the "well," after the breakthrough, is limited to the part transecting the Pyramid's core down to the "grotto," which is at the level of the plateau. Hewn in the bedrock, the shaft beneath the grotto was excavated after the Descending Passage had been completed and before work on the Subterranean Chamber was begun. This shaft must have been used to accommodate descending workers, since the Descending Passage was actually reserved for the re-ascent of workers carrying stone-cutting debris. I will return to this question later.

65. I disagree with Petrie. Al Mamun's stonemasons certainly must have discovered the Descending Passage and penetrated the Pyramid's interior, passing under the three granite blocks; they thus rediscovered the millennarian internal opening that had been obstructed during the reign of Ramesses II by means of a few rows of blocks and the replacement of the facing.

It is obvious that Al Mamun's dignity as a pasha would have prevented him from crawling on his belly to enter the Pyramid's interior; so he ordered that the tunnel be reopened, which merely required that 9 meters of limestone be perforated.

CHAPTER 3

THE PYRAMIDAL EPIDEMIC

While certain Arab authors have given us accounts of the pyramids that are full of phantasmagoric legends, one has to admit that some Western authors have greatly outdone them. In fact, Arabic mysticism seems rather mild compared to that of our pseudoscientific Western dreamers. If the Prussian officer, in his conversation with Gerard de Nerval, opened the way to the isiac mysteries, what are we to think of the fantastic speculations of Smyth, Moreux, Lagrange, Davidson, et al.?

THE GREAT PYRAMID'S
IMAGINARY DESTINATION

For a hundred years a great many Europeans, particularly the English and the Germans, have been enthralled by the Great Pyramid and have given free rein to their overheated imaginations. These authors seem to be suffering from a mysterious ailment: acute pyramiditis. At first sporadic, the disease soon spread to such an extent that it is now epidemic. The sickness assumes two different forms: biblical and pseudoscientific. In either case the patient becomes a fantasist.

The biblical fantasists, such as Morton Edgar, believe the Great Pyramid is a "bible in stone" that reveals past and future events to clairvoyants. They assume each part of the edifice has significant dimensions, which can be expressed in *pyramidal* cubits, palms, inches, or digits. The pyramidal cubit—presumed to be sacred—equals one ten-millionth of the earth's polar radius; that is, 0.635660 meter. Using this as a basis, it is possible to devise mysterious numerical combinations (through addition, subtraction, multiplication, and division) that will permit the Truth to emerge at last from the depths of the Pyramid.

According to the enlightened, the lower chamber corresponds to chaos, the start of the Ascending Passage to the Hebrews' exodus from Egypt, and the Grand Gallery's entrance to the crucifixion of Jesus Christ. The Queen's Chamber would correspond to June 18, 1918, while the entrance to the King's Chamber would correspond to September 16, 1936. This is the prophetic date that Georges Barbarin gave in a famous article published in *Paris-Soir* on September 15 of the same year—on that memorable day in 1936 humanity was supposed to enter the age of enlightenment!

The biblical fantasists seize on one fact to prove their contentions: that the Descending Passage is at an angle of 26° 33' with the horizontal. If, they say, one traces this angle on a map from the parallel on which the Pyramid is located, one gets the exact direction of Bethlehem! Better still, taking a thousandth of the distance between the Pyramid and Bethlehem, expressed in sacred cubits, one gets the number 2138, and this is highly significant, they claim, because Christ was born 2,138 years after the erection of the monument! With this claim the biblical fantasists prove only their own ignorance of Egyptian chronology, since the erection of the Pyramid dates from 4800 B.C. But one single remark should suffice to controvert their morbid speculations definitively. The ancient Egyptians expressed slopes trigonometrically, using what we call the cotangent—which is the simplest method possible. Now, the angle 26° 33' 54" corresponds exactly to cotangent 2. In plain language, this means that the stonemason cutting through the bedrock would break through 1 cubit deep vertically when he had gone 2 cubits horizontally. The level gauge that the worker used is so simple a child could easily reconstruct one.

The *pseudoscientific fantasists,* such as the renowned astronomer Charles Piazzi Smyth and his emulators, Father Théophile Moreux, Charles Lagrange, and David Davidson, are more dangerous, because they claim to be able to prove—by means of *a priori* reasoning based on false data—that various astonishing mathematical relationships are contained in the Great Pyramid.

Smyth, having tortured all of the Pyramid's dimensions (which are inaccurate to begin with), discovers that the monument is not only a geodesic landmark, but also an astrological clock, as well as a central bureau of weights and measures, a model of the solar system (in terms of weight, volume, and density), a map of the Nile including a flooding schedule, etc.—in all, the Great Pyramid contains twenty-two relationships, each one stranger than the last, which numerous subsequent collaborators have copiously supplemented.

Moreux proposes the following dilemma:

> Either the builders of this monument, which is unique in the world, possessed a science as advanced as our own, which is absurd and hard to imagine; or, as guardians of a tradition dating back to the beginning of time, they wished to set in stone the insights imparted by revelation to the spirit of the first man.

One of the most haunting relationships has to do with the "coffer" in the King's Chamber, which was definitely not a sarcophagus but a unit of volume and weight. Because its volume equals 69,000 cubic pyramidal inches, the weight of water at 20° C. that would fill it would be the same as that of 12,500 cubic pyramidal inches of a substance having as its density the average density of the earth; i.e., 5.52. The "coffer" is thus thought to be the universal standard of mass, of which 1/2500th would be the English pound of 453.59 grams. That's all it takes for the fantasists to deduce the Egypto-Hebraic descent of proud Albion!

But all this is mere crackpot imagination. With many difficulties, because it is in a sorry state, I was able to recon-

Ivory figurine of King Cheops (Cairo Museum). No other statuette or statue of this king is known to exist. It was discovered at Abydos. The king's meditative attitude differs from the haughty expression shown by his son, Kephren; however, it gives an impression of great deliberation. According to Manetho, Cheops was a scholar who had contempt for the gods; he was the author of a widely renowned work, the *Sacred Book*, still popular under the Lagid Dynasty. (*Hassia*)

The great pyramids of Giza, seen from the south. (*Author's collection*)

The Turah quarries branched out underground at a depth of several kilometers. Fifty years ago, large 20-meter-high mounds composed of the stone-cutting debris from the pyramids' blocks were still being worked by a major cement factory located nearby. (*Author's collection*)

The pyramidal mountain overlooking the Valley of the Kings (Thebes). It is likely that this pyramidal mountain, like the Sphinx, was carved out by hand under the predynastic rulers. Excavations might unearth some great surprises. (*Author's collection*)

The entrance to the Great Pyramid on its north face. The entrance to "Al Mamun's" hole (on the right) is found at the fifth course, whereas the real entrance, that of the Descending Passage, is found in the middle of the fifteenth course. (*Author's collection*)

The Great Pyramid's "eye," sometimes called the "sign of the horizon." (*Author's collection*)

The *serdab* of Kagemni of Mereruka at Saqqara. (*Author's collection*)

Opposite page: The Great Pyramid's *serdab*, known as the "Queen's Chamber." King Cheops' "double," a statue probably made of basalt, stood in the four-corbeled niche. Traces of a table for offerings or of a stairway are clearly visible on the floor. There can be no doubt that this niche was set up almost exactly like that of the *serdab* of Kagemni of Mereruka, high priest of the pyramid of Teti at Saqqara (Fifth Dynasty). (*Author's collection*)

Opposite page: The King's Chamber and its granite sarcophagus. The walls, ceiling, and floor are also constructed of Aswan granite. (*Author's collection*)

Vestiges of the causeway described by Herodotus. In the background is the east face of the Great Pyramid. (*Author's collection*)

Partial view of the two upper plug blocks. The despoilers' tunnel passing under the blocks in order to connect with the Descending Passage (not visible in the photograph) is to the left, below the stairway carved in the stone; this stairway is very recent (1925). The uppermost block has been partly broken. (*Collection of Professor Zaba, Czechoslovakian Institute of Egyptology, Prague*)

The soul (*ba*), in the form of a kite, flutters about the mummified body (*tchet*) of the deceased. (*Author's collection*)

Above: One of the mysterious letters found on the ceiling of the Subterranean Chamber. (*Author's collection*) Below: The carved rock found in front of the north face of the pyramid of Kephren, with the hieroglyphic inscription mentioning the work carried out by the superintendent of construction, Mai, "Grandee of the Temple of Maat," under Ramesses II. Note the mysterious symbol, similar to the one sculpted in the ceiling of the Great Pyramid's Subterranean Chamber. (*Author's collection*)

The colossi and the northern pyramid in Tula, Mexico. (*Roger-Viollet*)

Opposite page, top: Symbols sculpted on the back of the first-period statues of Easter Island, according to Francis Mazière. It is impossible not to be struck by the resemblance between the Atlantean statues found at the pyramid of Tula and the Moai of Easter Island: both show the same hairstyle (*pukao*) and long ears, and their backs bear the same circle (solar symbol or shield). (*Author's sketch*)

Opposite page, bottom: Ornament of a central drum of one of the colossi of Tula, Mexico. (*Roger-Viollet*)

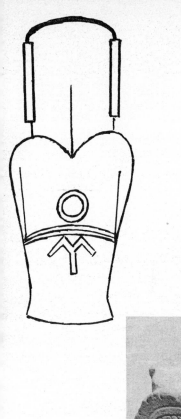

Facing blocks of the pyramid of Tula. The arrangement of the facing blocks is comparable to that of the Egyptian pyramids. (*Author's collection*)

Casing stones that have remained in place along the bottom of the Great Pyramid's north face. Note that these stones are set on a socle exactly 1 cubit (0.524 meter) thick. (*Author's collection*)

Three infrared photographs of the Great Pyramid's south face taken at fifteen-second intervals at 6:00 P.M. (the hour of the Pyramid) on March 21, 1934, the day of the spring equinox; they demonstrate beyond a doubt the phenomenon of the flash. (*Author's collection*)

The royal prince Rahotep, high priest of Ra at the temple of Heliopolis, and his wife, Nefrit, "Honored by the King" (*Cairo Museum*). The statues were found at Medum and date from the beginning of the Fourth Dynasty. The position of Rahotep's right hand, "in the manner of the Master," indicates that he was an advanced initiate. This is also true of Nefrit, whose right hand emerges from her peplum; she must have been a high priestess of Isis. (*Author's collection*)

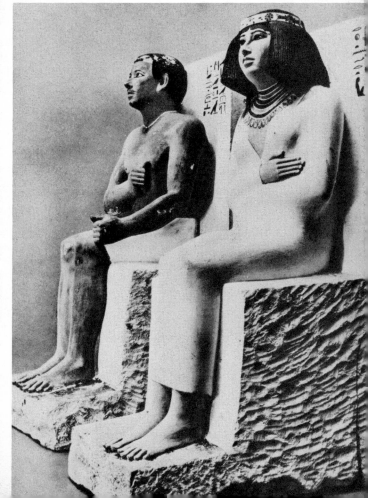

An extraordinary aerial photograph taken by the Royal Air Force at exactly 6:00 P.M. (the true time of the Pyramid) on the day of the equinox. Clearly visible on the south face of the Great Pyramid (above) is the phenomenon of the flash I have described. (*Author's collection*)

struct the "coffer" standard exactly. Its true internal and external dimensions sufficed to invalidate all of Smyth's and Moreux's calculations. It is just a sarcophagus like so many others (similar to that of Unas, for example), a sarcophagus with an automatically closing dovetailed lid. When the sarcophagus was closed, three metallic rods lodged in holes in the cover fell into three corresponding but shallower holes in the cask. A strange standard of volume and weights, this "coffer" with its sliding lid and automatic unpickable lock!

Davidson

In *The Hidden Truth in Myth and Ritual and in the Common Culture Pattern of Ancient Metrology* (Leeds: Davidson, 1934), David Davidson synthesizes the reveries of Edgar and Moreux. He is the inventor of the "displacement factor"—irrefutable proof, in his view, of the merits of his theories.

And of what does this mysterious as well as divine "displacement factor" (the value of which is 7.27 meters, or 286.1 pyramidal inches) consist? According to Davidson, the perimeter of the Great Pyramid's base, expressed in pyramidal inches, should correspond exactly to one hundred times the value of the tropical year of 365.242 days; thus it would equal 36,524.2 pyramidal inches.

Now, this perimeter, according to the Survey of Egypt, measures 921.455 meters, or 36,277.8 English inches, or 36,238.1 pyramidal inches. There is thus a difference of 286.1 pyramidal inches.[1] Davidson's explanation for this mistake (an explanation that, in his opinion, is irrefutable) is quite simple: After having set the first courses of the Pyramid in place, the ancient Egyptians realized they had made a mistake. Under the psychic directives of the Great Architect of the Universe, they corrected this mistake by shifting the Descending Passage's entrance 7.27 meters (286.1 pyramidal inches) east of the Pyramid's meridian.

Once the question is conceived in a religious—that is, Masonic—light, any refutation of the interpretation of the displacement factor may seem invalid to ardent mystics of the numerous "pyramidal" societies. However, the reader will bear with me in my attempt to refute such an absurd notion with reason.

First of all, attempting to determine the value of the

Pyramid's perimeter to the nearest tenth of an inch (2 millimeters) is absurdly pretentious. Given the present state of the Pyramid, the measurements obtained by the Survey, Petrie, and myself ought to include an uncertainty along the order of ±20 centimeters.

But the decisive argument proving the inanity of Davidson's explanation is that the Descending Passage was carved in the bedrock *before* the first course of the Pyramid had been set in place. The slightest correction of position was thus impossible. Moreover, the displacement of the Descending Passage was anticipated and was included in the original construction plan.

The essential, *necessary* reason for the eastward displacement of the Descending Passage is that, since the north face was hollowed along the monument's meridian, it was necessary to move the entrance in order to avoid flooding during rainfall. It is a mistake—and apparently a popular one—to believe that it never rains in Middle Egypt; violent storms are recorded there every year. Given the immense surface of the Pyramid's face, the hollow, acting as a gutter, could drain over 200 cubic meters of water, which would have poured down the Descending Passage. I will discuss this matter later at greater length.

But Davidson's imagination doesn't end there. He writes:

Scholars, who refer to the Great Pyramid as a pagan monument or temple, would therefore do well to understand that it enshrines an accurate system of astronomical chronology; that that system is proved to be the time-basis of the science of our visible creation; that the representation thus given is expressed in terms of modern science; and that modern science, as thus expressed, dates from the days of Kepler and Newton, and was unknown forty-six centuries ago when the Great Pyramid was built. Surely due reflection on a work that reveals such accurate foreknowledge of the ways and the idiomatic means of expression in modern thought should enlighten all but the most purblind of adversaries, and should reveal to them the operation of the all-controlling mind of the Grand Geometrician of Creation, and the purpose of the Great Architect of the Universe.

Seeking to enlighten his "blind" adversaries, Davidson sets down what the Great Pyramid reveals:

> The three forms of the year (Solar, Sidereal, and Anomalistic); the Law of Variation in the Elements of the Planetary Orbits; the Law of Variation in the Obliquity of the Ecliptic; the Law of Variation in the Gravitational "Constant" on the earth's surface; the Periodic Law of Seasonal Variations and Earthquake Frequency; the proportionate distribution of land and sea; the mathematical form of the earth; the Mean Sun Distance; the Law of Gravitation as it affects motion in the Earth's Orbit; the general astronomical Laws of Precessional Variation, and of the change in the Longitude of Perihelion, and the various astronomical Laws defining and governing the Pyramid's General and Special Systems of Chronology.

The divine rectification of the Pyramid builders' error (the *displacement factor*) is also shown, according to Davidson, as well as the date (year, month, and day) of Christ's birth and of the Last Supper—among other spiritual events.

The most unexpected result of these tortuous pseudoscientific speculations is that of the Judeo-Egyptian ancestry of proud Albion! It has been seriously proposed that if the English inch differs from the pyramidal inch by only 11/10,000ths of its value, it is obviously because the English people are of Egypto-Hebraic stock!

And leave it to Davidson to call upon supplementary proof drawn from biblical texts. Here he is quoting L. A. Waddell's *Phoenician Origins of Britons, Scots, and Anglo-Saxons* (1924):

> In relating the traditions concerning origins, Sanchoniathon[2] states that there "was one Elioun, called Hypsistus (*i.e., the Most High*); and his wife Beruth (Hebrew, *Berith* or *Brith*—Covenant), and they dwelt about Byblos, in Phœnicia. These were contemporary with 'Sydyk' (*i.e., the Righteous One*).
>
> "Kronus (or Saturn), whom the Phœnicians call Israel, and who after his death was deified . . . when he was king, had by a nymph of the country called *Ano-*

bret, an only son, who on that account is styled *Jeoud;* for, so the Phœnicians still call an only son; and when great danger from war beset the land, he adorned the Altar, and invested this son with the emblems of royalty and sacrificed him."

Sanchoniathon's and Philo Byblius' accounts were not taken seriously until the discovery, in 1930, of the tablets of Ras Shamra, which seem to confirm these accounts.

Connecting these writings with verses from the Bible (Gen. 14:18–20 and Hebr. 7:1–3),[3] Waddell concludes:

All this simply means that the *Only Son,* Jeoud,— the *Only Son* of the Most High—was to be of the seed of Israel, the seed of the people symbolised by the Israel-woman of Revelation, the Covenant One, or *Brit-ana,* called *Ano-Bret,* by inversion in the account by Sanchoniathon.

Thence the Hebraic-Phoenician origin of certain ancient tribes of Great Britain and also of the inhabitants of French Brittany.

Whether this ancestry of the "Britons" is possible, I do not know; however, it is a *certain* fact that *the pyramidal inch is an absurd notion,* and that the Great Pyramid, despite all the farfetched calculations made by the biblical fantasists, was the work of Cheops, who reigned from 4829 to 4766 B.C., whereas Abraham was born at Ur in Chaldea around 1967 B.C.—there is here a considerable time gap of 2,830 years.

Lagrange

Before we have done with the biblical fantasists, we should review the book by Charles Lagrange (instructor at the Military Academy, astronomer at the Observatory, and member of the Royal Academy of Belgium) entitled *The Great Pyramid, by Modern Science, an Independent Witness to the Literal Chronology of the Hebrew Bible & British Israel Identity, in Accordance with Brück's "Law of the Life of Nations": With a New Interpretation of the Time Prophecies of Daniel and St. John* (London: Burnet, 1894).

The work is based on (a) the alleged chronological law of

the Belgian genius R. Brück, which defines a cycle of 518 years from organization to decadence in the life of peoples; (b) biblical data; (c) the measurements of the Great Pyramid made by Smyth (1865) and Petrie (1883).

Lagrange claims to prove scientifically:

(1.) That the Pyramid is a monument of Hebrew origin;

(2.) That this marvellous stone book records the fundamental truths of astronomy and physics with a precision equal to that of modern science, and discloses these truths by means of a unit of measurement derived from the terrestrial globe;

(3.) That the chronology of the Bible, taking for argument the spiritual dispensations of Moses and of Christ, is itself accurately inscribed in the Pyramid by the diagram of the interior passages, traced in a plane meridian; the ordinate of this is a function of time. In any case the *form* of the diagram symbolises in a remarkable manner the dispensation in question, and its *dimensions* (by proportioning the lengths to time) agree with the dates of the Biblical chronology as well as could be hoped, seeing that the latter are a little uncertain at the present day.

The interest here at stake is, therefore, not simply that of a curious speculation; it is nothing less than to show by external proofs, having the force of numbers, the Divine Inspiration of the Scriptures; to decide, with this same force, upon their true interpretation; lastly, to establish on an immutable scientific basis all the history of humanity with its chronology; to establish also the reality of a rapidly-approaching end, announced during long centuries by the prophets, and which that history is on the point of attaining.

Thus the sole possible interpretation of the facts is, that the Great Pyramid and the Bible are both works of divine inspiration. If the immutable book of stone, in which are written simultaneously the main truths of the most advanced science of to-day, and in which the spiritual truths of the Bible are symbolised—if the Pyramid, I say, has been sealed and fixed at the beginning of time, it is in order that, being understood in these latter days—the days of scientific external facts—it may render the most powerful external evidence to these eternal truths, which are unacknowledged and yet alone are essential.

The units of length necessary in order to decode the message contained in the "stone Bible" are: the Pyramid (or pyramidal) inch (p.i.) = 1/500,000,000 the polar diameter of the earth = 0.0254264 meter; and the Pyramid cubit (p.c.) = 1/100,000,000 the polar *radius* = 0.635660 meter. Once these units have been defined, the following truths can be deciphered in the Great Pyramid:

1st. The perimeter of the base in Pyramid inches, divided by 100, equals the number of mean days in the year [i.e., the length of the tropical year, or 365.242 days].

According to this, the length of the side of the base is, in fact, 9.131.05 Pyramid inches

$$\left(\frac{4 \times 9.131.05}{100} = 365.242\right).\ \dots$$

Without going into a superfluous critique of Lagrange's views, let me simply mention that the 9.131.05 pyramidal inches he attributes to the perimeter correspond to a value of 232.41 meters for the base; now, the base of the socle on the bedrock has a value of 231.40 meters, whereas the real base upon the socle measures only 230.253 meters (±0.10 meter).

2nd. The height of the Pyramid is the radius of a circumference equal to the perimeter of the square base.

That is to say that the inclination of the sides of the Pyramid to the horizon has for its tangent $\frac{\pi}{4}$ or that this inclination equals 51° 51′ 14.3″.

Of all the claims that Lagrange makes, this relationship is the only one that seems likely.

3rd. The base representing the orbit of the earth . . . it follows, in the symbolism, that the height must represent the distance of the sun from the earth (the sun, placed at the summit of the Pyramid, the centre of the world, radiates therefore on all the circumference of the terrestrial orbit along the four faces of the Pyramid).

Now, in reality the distance of the sun from the earth is indeed equal to a thousand million times the height of the Pyramid.

The equatorial radius of the earth is equal to 250,836,007 Pyramid inches; one value of the radius vector of the orbit, equal to $5,813.01 \times 1,000,000,000$, gives for the sun's parallax an angle of $8.904''$, which is included amongst the best determinations of this parallax.

4th. The plane of the base of the Pyramid represents the plane of the ecliptic; the perimeter of the square represents the terrestrial orbit.

The intersection of the equator and of the ecliptic, then, makes the tour of the horizon in the plane of the base during the length of time occupied by the precession of the equinoxes.

The symbolic representation of the revolution of the equinox by the system of the two diagonals of the square is, therefore, a natural idea. It is also natural that the lengths of these diagonals should represent the duration of that revolution. This is exactly what takes place:—

The sum of the diagnoals in Pyramid inches equals in years the duration of the revolution of the equinoxes. This sum equals in reality 25,827, a number included amongst the best computations (Laplace: 25,816; Bessel: 25,868; Nyrén: 25,824). (There is no room here to discuss the variations which the epochs introduce.)

5th. The weight of the earth is equal to a thousand million of millions of that of the Pyramid.

The unit of weight is indifferent. Taking as a unit the Pyramid ton (the weight of a volume of water equal to that of the granite *coffer* which is to be found in the King's Chamber), we have, indeed:

Weight of the earth = 5,273,000,000,000,000,000,000 and

Weight of the Pyramid = 5,273,834.

6th. Just as the exterior of the Pyramid has special relation to the astronomical movements of the earth, so the interior (characterised by the central chamber called the King's Chamber, where we find the granite coffer, the standard of measure) makes known more especially the data relating to the terrestrial globe considered in itself. The weight of the Pyramid has already measured the weight of the earth; its density, given separately by the measurements of the central chamber and of the coffer, is 5.7; that is to say, the most exact of the values hitherto deduced from the theory of attraction; the unit of length, the Pyramid cubit, which is derived from the globe and which serves for all the measurements, is found to be actually given in its true size (by the eccentricity of the axis of the niche [in the Queen's Chamber]), and is no longer solely deduced by calculation.

7th. The orientation of the passages determines, by an astronomical calculation, the date of the construction of the monument. It is that at which the meridian of the Pyramid passed at the same time over the polar star α Draconis in the north, and the Pleiades in the south.

This date is −2170, according to the calculation of Piazzi Smyth, in 1866, in "Life and Work."[4] The astronomical circumstance just mentioned is remarkable; but it becomes especially so as indicating an intentional epoch for the construction by the fact that at the same time that α Draconis and the Pleiades were on the meridian, the equinoctial point was to be found there also; this cannot occur again before the 26,000 years have passed which complete the revolution of the equinox.

8th. The relation between the metrology of the Great Pyramid and that of the Bible rests on the following fundamental datum:

The Pyramidal cubit is not the same as the Egyptian cubit; the latter is only $^4/_5$ of the former.

The Pyramidal cubit is found to be none other than the Sacred Cubit of the Hebrews, such as it was determined two centuries ago by Newton.

That being so, relations probably exist between the metric data of the Bible and those of the Pyramid, data which are characterised on both sides by multiples of 5 and 10.

Now, these relations exist; they are direct and simple. They establish, by the medium of the Pyramid, that the metric data of the Bible, from the Deluge to the construction of the Temple, far from being arbitrary, are founded on a profound knowledge of the constants of terrestrial physics.

We have the following theorems:

The volume of Noah's Ark is equal to 100,000 times the volume of the granite coffer.

The weight of Noah's Ark (by the water it draws, Gen., VII., 20), is equal to $1/100$ of that of the Pyramid, or $1/10^{17}$ of that of the earth.

The volume of the ark of the Covenant is equal to that of the coffer.

The volume of the Sea of Brass in Solomon's Temple is equal to fifty times that of the coffer.

9th. Such intimate bonds render probable the supposition, that even the prophetic character of the Bible may be met with again in the Pyramid. Now, if we consider as a diagram, of which the ordinate is a function of time (reckoned on the floor of the passages) the very simple system of the ascending and descending interior passages, traced in a meridian plane, at the rate of one Pyramid inch for one year, it symbolises, in a manner, which at first sight agrees with the chronology of the Hebrew text, the Mosaic and Christian dispensations.

. . . A particular fact . . . will show the reader . . . the undeniable reality. This fact, in some respect the reason, hitherto hidden, which explains the entire development of history, is, that there exists a relation of descent between the Anglo-Saxons and the Ten Tribes of Israel—those tribes all traces of whom have been lost since shortly after their dispersion (-758, according to our literal chronology), and whose destiny, in spite of the numerous researches of which it has been the subject, has remained an historical enigma.

. . . This view rests upon the following facts:

1st. The English inch and the Pyramid inch are practically identical: the second is equal to the first multiplied by 1.001.

2nd. The sides of the Great Step [at the end of the Grand Gallery] are formed by a combination of the Hebrew and English units of measure, namely—the sacred cubit and the yard. . . .

In conclusion: In this work it is demonstrated, by external proofs having the force of numbers:

1st. That the literal chronology of the Hebrew text of the Bible is strictly exact. . . .

2nd. That the Anglo-Saxons are the descendants of the Ten Tribes of Israel.

3rd. That the Reformation is based upon the true Christian principle, and virtually continues the Apostolic Church, whilst Roman Catholicism is emphatically condemned by Scripture.

Very judiciously, Lagrange, of his own accord, ends with these words: "The system of ideas which has just been perused was conceived and developed in a very short time. . . ." Indeed, the Belgian astronomer-professor's proposals do seem to lack "maturity," to say the least!

All such nonsense is indeed regrettable, for it tends to cast doubt on more serious views concerning the scientific knowledge of the ancient Egyptians.

NOTES

1. One pyramidal inch = 1.0011 English inch = 0.0254264 meter.
2. According to Davidson, Eusebius states that Sanchoniathon flourished before the Trojan War and that his writings were translated into Greek by Philo of Byblos. The name Sanchoniathon is plainly Egyptian and might have meant "the living temple of Aton." He might have been one of the priests of the religion of Aton, which Amenophis IV (1395–1363 B.C.) wished to make universal. We know that Akhnaton had temples built to his god, Aton, in most of the neighboring countries, and certainly in Byblos, a city that was in constant contact with Egypt during his reign.
3. Genesis 14:18-20. "And Melchizedek king of Salem brought forth bread and wine; and he was the priest of the most high God. And he blessed him, and said, Blessed be Abram of the most high God, possessor of heaven and earth; And Blessed be the most high God, which hath delivered thine enemies into thy hand. . . ."

    Hebrews 7:1-3: "For this Melchizedek, king of Salem, priest of the most high God, who met Abraham returning from the slaughter of the kings, and blessed him; . . . first being by interpretation King of righteousness, and after that also King of Salem, which is King of peace; Without father, without mother, without descent, having neither beginning of days, nor end of life, but made like unto the Son of God; abideth a priest continually."
4. Charles Piazzi Smyth, *Life and Work at the Great Pyramid:* Edmunton & Douglas, 1867.

CHAPTER 4

THE MODERN AUTHORS

The two principal modern Egyptologists concerned with the Egyptian pyramids are Ludwig Borchardt and Jean Philippe Lauer. More recently, Julien Bruchet, of the Ancient Architecture Department of the Centre National de la Recherche Scientifique, published *Nouvelle recherches sur la Grande Pyramide* (Aix-en-Provence: La Pensée Universitaire, 1965).

As Lauer's work, *Le Problème des pyramides d'Egypte,* is considered to be authoritative in the field, I will take the liberty of subjecting it to a critique that, though not hostile, will be distinctly objective, thus occasionally severe. For I intend to refute the spiritual tendencies of many of our contemporary Egyptologists, who—still imbued, it would seem, with musty biblical notions—are convinced that the Egyptians of the early dynasties were, in terms of scientific knowledge, very nearly Neolithic. They find Berossus, who dares to claim that there existed in Assurbanipal's library manuscripts dating back 200,000 years, a source of amusement!

Courting their derision, I am among those who take Berossus and Manetho seriously, leaving to the future the task of settling the question. For I am firmly convinced that future discoveries will prove that the entire Egyptian chronology currently accepted as dogma was intentionally established by veritable forgers in order to serve the biblical cause.

Borchardt

In his work *Gegen die Zahlenmystik an des Grossen Pyramide bei Gise* (Berlin: Behrend, 1922), Borchardt severely criticizes the "pyramidal epidemic" that, having arisen in England with Smyth, contaminated Germany, Belgium, and France. He points out that the Pyramid is only part of the funerary complex comprising the reception temple or valley portal, the causeway or covered ramp, the funerary temple, and the pyramidal tomb.

Borchardt criticizes Lepsius' theory, according to which each pyramid was added to and enlarged during the course of the pharaoh's life, up to his death, just as a tree grows, forming a new layer each year; then the whole was covered with masonry. There was thus no way of knowing, at the start of construction, the building's ultimate dimensions. According to Borchardt, Lepsius' theory is inaccurate; the only part of it worth retaining is that this method of construction—"mantling"—is the principle behind the construction of the pyramids. There is absolutely no proof that each pyramid grew *continuously* throughout the king's reign.

Neither does Borchardt accept Petrie's thesis, which is that the Great Pyramid's plan was *absolutely* fixed from the time work was begun. He believes, on the contrary, that the plan was modified in the course of construction. According to him, the Great Pyramid wasn't built in a single spurt. At first it was to include a funerary chamber carved in the bedrock; this was left unfinished. The original plan was modified, and the new funerary chamber was to be located in the masonry core already begun. But before this second plan was carried out, before the floor of this second funerary chamber was completed, a third plan was adopted. The King's Chamber was then built. (He also believed this to have been the case with the pyramids of Kephren and Mykerinos.)

According to Borchardt, in order to avoid any confusion, one ought to identify the various chambers of the Great Pyramid as follows: the Subterranean Chamber—the unfinished chamber in the bedrock; the Queen's Chamber—the abandoned or reconsecrated chamber; the King's Chamber—the final burial chamber. He did not claim to understand the purpose of the relieving chambers.

Concerning the sarcophagus in the King's Chamber, Borchardt is of the opinion that its cavity is large enough to hold the royal mummy and its wooden coffin; he finds its closing mechanism to be identical with those of other sarcophagi.

According to him, the value of the cubit used in constructing the Great Pyramid was very close to 0.525 meter.

He then takes up the study of the pyramids' slopes, which the Egyptians expressed in fractional form, using only the numerator (the nonexpressed denominator is invariably 7); this fraction expresses the trigonometric cotangent. This being the case, the Great Pyramid's slope was expressed as 5.5; thus, $\frac{5.5}{7} = 0.7857143$, corresponding to an angle of 51° 51′ 34″.

Concerning the Great Pyramid's base and height, Borchardt, like Petrie, assigns them lengths of 440 and 280 cubits, respectively.[1]

Treating the theories concerning the slope π and the golden section, Borchardt concludes that it is *purely by accident* that these slopes are very close to the actual slope.[2]

According to Borchardt, the only possible explanation for the variation of slope among the pyramids is *whim*—the different tastes of the royal architects and master builders. There are no specific ratios involved in the pyramids' dimensions, any more than there are specific ratios between the various proportions of columns. He assures partisans of the slope π that if they look carefully, they will discover the incommensurable value of the number e.

Taking the opposite tack from the biblical fantasists and certain theoreticians who consider the Great Pyramid to be the "Great All," Borchardt (like Lauer, more recently) considers it to be—mathematically, astronomically, and historically—the "Great Nothing."

Here, I must contradict Borchardt and Lauer. Whereas I am in complete agreement with them in their efforts to combat the biblical fantasists, I cannot agree with them about the ancient Egyptians' mathematical and astronomical knowledge. (Borchardt is amazed at the precision of the orientation of the Great Pyramid's bases, in view of the primitive instruments used.) I will return to this subject later. For now I want to point out one important error: for the Egyptians *of the Old Kingdom,* the cardinal point was not north, but south.

Unlike Borchardt, I share Petrie's opinion that the plan of the Great Pyramid was *absolutely fixed* from the start of construction work. Because—and this, I think, is an incontrovertible argument—why would the ancient Egyptians have *pointlessly* extended the two so-called ventilation ducts of the Queen's Chamber all the way out to the casing if this chamber was to be abandoned? I do not think the architect of the Great Pyramid was *that* crazy!

Actually, as Petrie was the first to suggest, the chamber known as the "Queen's Chamber" was the *serdab* of the Pyramid—that is, the chamber of the "royal double." He found a great quantity of fragments of black rock in this chamber and thought it probable that the statue constituting the "double" was made of basalt and was placed in the four-corbeled niche, which is located *precisely* along the Pyramid's axis. Traces of a stairway and a table for offerings are still clearly visible on the floor in front of the niche. The *serdab* of Kagemni of Mereruka at Saqqara seems to be a copy of this chamber. The two puzzling "ventilation" ducts, *hermetically sealed* with plaques, were not discovered until 1872. Clearly, these are *psychic* ducts, permitting the soul (*ba*) to visit and animate the imputrescible "double" of the royal *tchet.*

Besides Borchardt's work, two other studies concerning the Great Pyramid are particularly serious and interesting. The first was written by Lauer, an architect with the Egyptian Department of Antiquities; the other is the work of Bruchet, who is with the Ancient Architecture Department of the Centre National de la Recherche Scientifique.

A critique of these two works—the best-documented studies available at the present time (1970)—will give me an opportunity to settle the question of the Great Pyramid's destination. A comparison of the views of these two authors, both eminent specialists in the field, should be particularly instructive, as their viewpoints are diametrically opposed. I shall trace these two authors page by page, and my criticism, though occasionally severe, should in no way be construed as tarnishing their reputations, which are fully merited.

Lauer

Lauer's book includes a preface by Father Etienne Drioton, former director of the Egyptian Department of Antiquities, who writes:

> Here is a much-needed, as well as excellent book. If, in Egyptian archaeology (a subject that has the distinction of inflaming even the most phlegmatic of natures), there is an area in which the least reasonable fancies are immediately embraced with enthusiasm, it is, at the moment, that of the pyramids.
>
> Ever since Smyth launched his famous theories during the last century, the error he sowed has proliferated. The subject now abounds in astronomical, mathematical, biblical—indeed, even mystical—theories, each improving on the others and *all* burying this branch of science in a heap of chaff. It has become impossible for the layman to discern the wheat; and if perchance it is presented to him harvested and *painstakingly sorted,* he does not recognize in it the fruit of innumerable lofty ponderings, countless sublime raptures over the unfathomable resources of the mysterious science of the pharaohs. The Egyptologists, with their cautious assertions, seem to him to be blind, naive, or behind the times, or simply as petty scientists disrupted in their routines. Led astray by the many best-sellers on the subject, public opinion is in the process of losing its faith *in true science. . . .*

"True science"! Father Moreux, from the height of his municipal chair in astronomy at Bourges, also speaks of "essential truths"! But how is it possible not to doubt the infallibility of the Egyptological Establishment when its official "chronological canon," backed by Drioton himself, places Menes in the year 3300 B.C., thus committing an error of 2,319 years?

Although I agree with Drioton and Lauer on the necessity of struggling against the infantile mysticism that has infected Egyptology, I have distinct reservations about their views concerning the scientific data contained in the Great Pyramid, as well as its destination. A great many things, it seems, have eluded their comprehension.

Although Lauer's attempt to reconstruct Zoser's Complex at Saqqara is truly praiseworthy, this reconstruction through "anastylosis" required a good deal of creative imagination. But anastylosis can easily lead to "anamorphosis"—that is, to a distorted reconstruction of reality—for anastylosis strongly resembles the paleontologists' comparative anatomy. But while Cuvier succeeded in approximately reconstructing the Palaeotherium from a jawbone fragment, what brilliant engineer would presume to reconstruct a temple from a pile of blocks?

One fact will illustrate my point: I cannot agree with Lauer's reconstruction of the chapels of the "Jubilee courtyard" at Saqqara, where he completes with ten steps a coronation stairway that originally could have comprised no more than seven, in accordance with the "staircase-platforms" placed alongside the solar barques in the *Book of the Dead* (*cf.* Budge, *The Papyrus of Ani,* vol. 1, chap. 110, illus. 35). Moreover, the "step pyramid" of Zoser ought to have seven steps; the uppermost step has disappeared.

Returning from this digression, let us begin to examine Lauer's work. I have no intention of submitting his assertions and viewpoints to a systematic critique, for, like him, I am convinced that the original reason for building the pyramids and their monumental complexes was "to assure the deified pharaoh of the inviolability of his eternal abode, as well as of the persistence of his funerary cult." This fact having been established, however, it is my opinion that the Great Pyramid holds a special place among the royal tombs and merits detailed research more extensive than that devoted to it by Lauer, for I pride myself on my familiarity with the Pyramid, having spent seven years investigating it.

Obviously, I reject all the biblical theories; I also reject the greater part of the pseudoscientific theories—though not all, as certain ones may be true and accurate.

While certain mystics perceive the "Great All" in the Great Pyramid, many Egyptologists (Lauer among them) see it as the "Great Nothing"—that is, they regard the monument only as a royal tomb that is slightly more important than the others. I hold with Jomard (whom Lauer severely, and often wrongly, criticizes) that though the Great Pyramid was obviously erected as a royal tomb, its dimensions were related to precise scientific data.

Many Egyptologists are greatly mistaken in attributing only the most rudimentary scientific knowledge to the ancient Egyptians. I'd like to remind, if not inform, them that the three calendars used in ancient Egypt were as precise as—but much more intelligently designed than—our current Gregorian calendar, whose barbarous structure is worthy of the cavemen. With these three calendars I have been able to reestablish, *to the day,* the Egyptian chronology from the time of Athothis, son of Menes—that is, since 5557 B.C.

Thus we need to adjust the date of the construction of the Great Pyramid, which Lauer sets at around 2700 B.C., by 2,100 years, Cheops having reigned from 4829 to 4766 B.C. Lauer is therefore particularly off in writing (p. 47): "Jomard, moreover, plainly did not know—though this cannot be held against him—the relative time of the construction of the great pyramids in the history of Egyptian architecture."

Lauer claims (p. 87) that "the pyramid is a specifically Egyptian monument." This is a totally unfounded assertion, for the Chaldean ziggurats strangely resemble the Egyptian step pyramids—not to mention the numerous pyramids of Central and South America, the dating of which is still problematical. It is possible that certain recent American discoveries may revive the enigma of Atlantis.

Lauer writes (p. 92):

In an unfinished brick pyramid located at Dashur, the quartzite cask, even after being emptied, still weighs nearly 145 metric tons; as for the sealing slab, which weighs 83 metric tons, it is still in its preliminary position, raised on four temporary posts, as the cask seems never to have been used. These attempts to use the pyramid to ensure the royal mummies' security undoubtedly proved to be insufficiently effective, for eventually, after the second intermediary period, which ended in the formation of the New Kingdom, the pharaohs categorically renounced the practice in favor of the hypogea of the Valley of the Kings carved in the flank of the mountain of Thebes, the highest peak of which exactly formed a *natural pyramid* whose altitude no human construction could match.

"Natural pyramid"? But it is very possible, if not certain, that, like the Sphinx, the mountain was hand-carved well before the Eighteenth Dynasty; digs made around the base of this pyramid might uncover quite a few surprises! In placing Menes' reign around 3300 B.C.—in its view nearly the end of the Neolithic Age!—official Egyptology, imbued with musty biblical notions, seems determined to withhold the Truth. Consequently, in order to explain Imhotep's creations at Saqqara, it has to call upon miraculous intervention by the god Thoth, like the sainted Father Moreux, who does not hesitate to proclaim that "essential truth"—to wit, God alone, through his occult power, directed the construction of the Great Pyramid, the architects and laborers having worked only *unconsciously!* Such nonsense could only hold sway, and for a limited amount of time, among Central African tribes; henceforth, we must take into serious consideration Plato's writings on the subject, as well as the data provided by Berossus and Manetho.

Concerning Davidson's mysterious "displacement factor," which consists of the shifting of the Great Pyramid's entrance 7.29 meters eastward in relation to the Pyramid's meridian, Lauer writes (p. 117, footnote):

Actually, the architects of the Pyramid seem to have been intent on situating the place reserved for the sarcophagus of the sepulchral chamber within the Pyramid's meridian plane. Since the access passage opens on this chamber near the corner opposite the one in which the sarcophagus lies, its axis is necessarily displaced in relation to the meridian plane.

Lauer's argument begs the question by inverting cause and effect; since the access passages were built *before* the chamber, the shifting of the axis could not have been a *consequence* of the position of the sarcophagus.

The reason for the shifting of the Pyramid's passages in relation to its meridian plane is simple. Because of the hollowing of the north face—a feature Lauer seems to be unaware of—the apothem had become a gutter for rainwater. If the Descending Passage had been placed along the apothem, during rainstorms it would have been transformed into a veritable whirlpool.

In the third part of his book Lauer treats the various theories put forth concerning the Great Pyramid; he writes (p. 110):

I wouldn't know how to begin to study—let alone cite here—the countless theories borne of minds having fertile imaginations but lacking any understanding of the requirements that must be taken into account in formulating a hypothesis in archeology, as in any other science. And strange as this may seem, I have known reputable scholars (particularly astronomers and mathematicians), who have always demonstrated the greatest precision and the utmost scientific probity in their own fields, to accept the most astonishing assertions where the pyramids are concerned and construct entire theories upon unverified—and occasionally unverifiable—measurements or data.

I shall therefore merely discuss the principal theories, which I shall group into two broad categories: mystical and scientific. Egyptologists have always dealt with these theories most harshly, and all[3] agree that the great pyramids were royal tombs, including—indisputably—the Great Pyramid of Giza, the most famous of all the pyramids.

Father Drioton, former director of the Egyptian Department of Antiquities, writes:

"The lucubrations recently published (but taken from Smyth's musings regarding the Great Pyramid), which reveal mysterious knowledge on the part of the ancient Egyptians, are beneath notice. Jéquier dismissed these erroneous assumptions once and for all in his article 'Le prétendu sécret de la Grande Pyramide' ['The alleged secret of the Great Pyramid'] published in the *Journal de Lausanne* (January 27, 1947), which ended: '. . . Mind games, harmless fantasies, these lucubrations do not merit the furor they've aroused, but the public cannot be sufficiently warned against a system of prophecy supported by arguments of a scientific cast, when the very bases of these arguments—cleverly disguised—are but inexact data or pure hypotheses and the entire line of reasoning is clearly tendentious.' "

Lauer writes (p. 112):

> While the Egyptologists are thus *unanimous* in rejecting these theories, *they reject the whole lot without allowing for any debate;* they are content merely to ridicule the most absurd, improbable points.

In particular, Lauer cannot accept William Kingsland's assertion that the theory explaining the Great Pyramid's sole purpose as Cheops' tomb is merely a hypothesis, and not a certainty. Egyptology is a complex science requiring interdisciplinary collaboration; while a knowledge of Egyptian linguistics is essential, a knowledge of other, no less important areas is necessary for the comprehension of the Egyptian monuments, and in this field, irony will not suffice. Volney wrote: "If someday a talented man were to add to astronomical knowledge the erudition of Antiquity . . . this man could teach his age a great many things which the *vanity* of ours does not even suspect."

I have already treated the mystical biblical theories put forth by Smyth, Edgar, Davidson, Moreux, Barbarin, Lagrange, John Taylor, and many others. While the majority of the ideas expressed are preposterous, certain of them should not be dismissed out of hand. On the contrary, they deserve our full attention. While the notion of the Great Pyramid as a "Bible in stone" and that of the pyramidal cubit may be absurd, the idea that the monument may have served as the setting for isiac initiations is not. The theosophist H. P. Blavatsky was a great scholar; Schuré and Jomard were certainly Masonic initiates, and it makes sense that certain peculiarities in the Great Pyramid's interior should have made an impression on them.

Moreover, Lauer, who often contradicts himself, admits an esoteric possibility, for he writes (p. 133):

> . . . It is not my intention, certainly, to succeed these authors on a similar ground, but I must simply acknowledge, in defense of some of them, that it is not inadmissible, at first, to suppose—as did Jomard—that an

attempt was made to materialize in the Pyramid the principal data of the science of the time. The architect-priests responsible for building the pyramids must in fact have relied upon the body of their scientific knowledge in order to realize these colossal projects; and since here it was most likely a question of knowledge of an esoteric nature, they may have transposed this knowledge into stone so that it would be revealed to initiates and not to the profane world. I refer the reader to the fourth part of this volume, to the chapter on the scientific knowledge revealed by the pyramids, in which I deal with the question of deciding whether one can accept the reality of such a materialization.

On page 127 Lauer criticizes Adams, who considers the Great Pyramid a material translation, not of the Bible, but of the *Book of the Dead*. According to him, the start of the Descending Passage (located at the Pyramid's seventeenth course) corresponds to the seventeenth chapter of this book. Lauer responds:

Adams claims, for example, that the seventeenth chapter corresponded to Course 17, which rules the Descending Passage's present beginning on the Pyramid's north face. But as the casing has been torn down—and this did not occur until Arab rule—the passage originally must have begun two courses higher up. All the deductions derived from this erroneous correspondence collapse accordingly, and it seems pointless to pursue the discussion.

This harsh and unjustified criticism can be turned against its own author, for when the casing was still intact, the start of the Descending Passage did indeed correspond to the seventeenth course and not to the nineteenth. The start of the Descending Passage is currently located between the fifteenth and the sixteenth course. Lauer's mistake is excusable because he was going by Petrie's figures, but before pronouncing final judgment, it was his duty to verify the facts personally. As the Great Pyramid does not lie within Lauer's operational territory, however, we cannot hold him at fault for his imperfect knowledge of the monument.

Continuing his critique of Adams's views, he writes (p. 127):

Adams mentions the "door of the Horizon," with its two-block arch, under which is found the sign of the horizon sculpted in the stone. But aside from the fact that the shape of this symbol is only very crudely and imperfectly traced, one questions the usefulness of placing this sign at a point which, before the monument was mutilated, was buried 7 meters beneath the layer of masonry that is now gone. What Adams takes to be a figuration of the sign of the horizon or of the rising sun is only a groove cut in the surface of the block, probably during the pillage of the casing or in the course of subsequent investigations. Moreover, the two-block arch over this so-called door is merely an element of the relieving system extending above the entrance passage for at least a few meters, starting from the Pyramid's casing.

Here Lauer's criticism is relevant, even convincing. However, since it is probable that a sort of antechamber was set up behind the Pyramid's swivel door (which Lauer never mentions), it is not unlikely that the name "Luminous Horizon," which is the Pyramid's true name, should have been sculpted so as to be visible only to initiated visitors. For how else are we to interpret the unusual, incomprehensible tetragram (reproduced earlier in this book) carved in the middle of the sign of the horizon?

I agree with Lauer's critique of Edgar's views, but it must be acknowledged that Edgar is one of the authors most familiar with the Pyramid in all its details and that his measurements are, for the most part, accurate.

We cannot linger over the predictions drawn from the "Bible in stone" by the pyramidal visionaries; their case belongs in the province of psychiatry. Only the critique of the scientific theories holds any interest.

THE SCIENTIFIC THEORIES

Jomard was the first to suspect that the Great Pyramid's dimensions might be related to those of the terrestrial globe.

Given the state of the Pyramid in 1800, it is obvious that his measurements could not have been as precise as those of Howard-Vyse, Petrie, and especially the Survey of Egypt. Nevertheless, his measurement of the base, which he sets at 230.902 meters, is a truly admirable result for the time, for it is quite close to the measurement of the edge of the socle (231.093 meters) and that of the real base upon the socle (230.253 meters).

Clearly, the angle he assigned the slope, 51° 10′ (instead of 51° 50′), gave him a height less than that currently accepted. But we must keep in mind that even the Survey's measurements are only accurate to within 0.10 meter for the base and 0.50 meter for the height, because the Survey did not take into account the hollowing of the faces and the angle determining the height was known only to the nearest 30 seconds.

Lauer (p. 135) returns to the subject of Jomard's value for the cubit, 0.462 meter, "which seems as hypothetical as that of Smyth's pyramidal cubit. . . ." Again I must take issue with Lauer's gratuitous assertion. Jomard's cubit is not at all hypothetical; it has the *exact* value of the Egyptian cubit used under the Lagid Dynasty (as well as that of the Greek cubit)—i.e., exactly $1/500$th the base of the Great Pyramid's socle. Obviously, this was not the cubit used under the Fourth Dynasty, but it does in fact represent six-sevenths of the Philaeterian cubit found at the nilometer of Elephantine.

Lauer then mentions a paper I read to the Institut d'Egypte in which I assigned the Philaeterian cubit the value of $1/300$th of a stadium, a unit equivalent to $1/252,000$th of the terrestrial meridian. He does not agree with this; I will come back to this question later.

Lauer then approaches the question of the Great Pyramid's orientation. It is possible to question the Survey's tachymetric results in view of the uncertainty of the position of the Pyramid's corners, since the angle 3′ 6″ corresponds to a distance of 0.20 meter. Nevertheless, so precise an orientation for such a gigantic mass is absolutely remarkable, and it would be hard to obtain even today with modern instruments.

Lauer reviews the possible methods of orientation that the ancient Egyptians might have used. He writes, rather naively:

Thus if we are not dealing here with *simple coincidence* [!], and if such precision was indeed sought, the question is how this precision could have been obtained!

. . . Certain scholars maintain that the preliminary orientation of the Descending Passage (the entrance passage), which was carved in the bedrock even before the bulk of the Pyramid was constructed, would have facilitated the operation. In fact, the passage could have been centered on the polar star of that time, with the passage itself serving as a sighting telescope. Smyth claimed, following the suggestion of another astrologer, Sir John Herschel, that this was a star belonging to the constellation of Draco, whose lower passage would have been 3° 42′ from the pole around 2100 B.C., the date he assigned to the construction of the Pyramid, as well as around 3440 B.C. Unfortunately, Egyptologists are currently agreed that Cheops' reign should be set between 2700 and 2800 B.C.—that is, obviously, midway between these two dates. . . .

It is disconcerting that Smyth and Herschel should have been able to conceive a process of orientation that is, in practical terms, absolutely unrealizable. The idea of attempting to have stonecutters carve—into the bedrock, at night—a descending passage in the direction of a star of the fourth magnitude, scarcely visible to the naked eye, is preposterous.

However, this question does not arise, for two main reasons. First, if the Descending Passage had been oriented according to the polestar of that time, its slope would be 29° 59′, whereas it is 26° 34′, corresponding to cotangent 2. Second, in 4800 B.C., the date of the erection of the monument (*not* 2700–2800, as Lauer informs us), *no visible star corresponded to the North Pole*. I shall return to this question later.

Continuing on the subject of the orientation, Lauer writes:

Somers Clarke and R. Englebach, on the other hand, point out that it was not necessary to bring the polar star into the matter. The orientation could just as well have been obtained—and, in their opinion, must have been obtained—through sightings of a star that rose for a few hours, by taking the bisector of the angle formed by the two positions of its rising and setting.

However, while it might be conceded that this remarkable result attests to a certain astronomical knowledge which provided a practical method of extremely precise orientation, it in no way follows that the edifice itself was intended to be used for astronomical observations.

Clarke and Englebach are absolutely correct; it is Lauer who is wrong. The Great Pyramid was indeed intended to be used for astronomical observations, for at the tomb of Pen-Meruw at Giza, the name of the Great Pyramid *is followed by the determinative reserved for solar temples:*

I will deal with this important question later.

Here is Lauer, word for word, on the most important point concerning the Pyramid's destination (p. 149):

> Another author, Cotsworth (*The Rational Almanac,* 1902), still unscrupulously dismissing every element of the Pyramid that does not fit his theory, sees it as an edifice built solely to serve as a calendar or sundial. This suggestion had already been made, two and a half centuries ago, by Chazelles, a member of the French Academy of Sciences who went to Egypt to study the pyramids; but he did not question the funerary destination of these edifices. Indeed, the traveler Paul Lucas writes . . . that this scholar thought that the kings of Egypt must have intended, in constructing the pyramids for their tombs, "to use them as gnomons or sundials, marking with their shadows the sun's conversions during the solstices."
>
> Cotsworth claims that the Great Pyramid indicated, by the shadows it cast, the various seasons of the year—in particular, the winter solstice, spring equinox, summer solstice, and autumn equinox. The astronomical solar year was thus precisely defined. During the winter half of the year, the Pyramid's north face lay in

shadow, and during the other half, that same face was illumined all day, from the moment the sun rose in the northeast until it set in the northwest. He admits, however, that the transitions between these two different exposures did not occur at the precise moment of the two equinoxes, but rather, because of the special position of the Pyramid, fourteen days before the spring equinox and fourteen days after the autumn equinox.

Cotsworth thinks, moreover, that the pavement located to the north of the Pyramid was laid out solely for the observation of noonday shadows; he provides a sketch of this pavement, laid out—for this reason—in regular squares. Cotsworth adds that this area of the rocky plateau was therefore leveled to a distance of 268 feet (about 90 meters) north of the Pyramid's base, a distance that must have corresponded to the greatest range of the noonday shadow. But this is—alas!— clearly invalidated by the existence of vestiges of the surrounding wall, which limits the paving to less than 11 meters from the Pyramid's base.

Alas, indeed! The plateau to the north of the Pyramid was in fact leveled and paved for over 90 meters, and the presence of a surrounding wall less than 10 meters high could not have blocked the shadow cast by the Pyramid's gnomon at the winter solstice, for this shadow passed over the wall by more than 46 meters. Moreover, Petrie discovered, 90 meters north of the Pyramid's base and parallel to it, a ditch 1.90 meters deep; I will come back to this subject later.

And to close the debate, Lauer writes (p. 151):

While the pyramids were thus able, through the differences in the lighting of their faces, to assume, to a certain extent, the role—moreover, the completely superfluous role—of indicators of the hours and seasons, I have, however, noted that the coincidence, at the Great Pyramid, of the peculiarities described above with the date of the equinoxes is far from manifest. In short, even if this were indeed the case, we are dealing here with nothing more than a mathematical consequence of the monument's extremely precise orientation and the value of the slope of its faces. Could this result have been sought by the builders? I can only perceive it as a whim on their part, indicating, it is true, real geometric and astronomical knowledge, but in no way invalidating the only thesis now unanimously accepted by Egyptologists: to wit, that the Great Pyramid was constructed by Cheops to serve as his tomb.

"A whim of the builders"! What a pleasant jest on the part of one architect vis-à-vis his ancient colleagues! With all due deference to Lauer, his Egyptian predecessors, who antedated him by 6,700 years, were not—as well he knows— "whimsical," and a comparison of the extent of their knowledge with that of certain of our modern architects might not, on certain points, turn out to the latter's advantage.

THE MEASUREMENT OF ANGLES
IN ANCIENT EGYPT

Before tackling the crucial problem of the Great Pyramid's slope, it will be useful to provide a few preliminary explanations concerning the measurement of angles in ancient Egypt. I shall therefore interrupt my critique of Lauer's work momentarily, only to return to it soon, particularly on this point.

The Rhind Papyrus in the London Museum, discovered at Luxor in 1858, contains various accounts of problems and their solutions. Exercises 56, 57, 58, 59, 59A, and 60 relate to the pyramids. The theme of these six exercises consists in determining either the slope given the base and height, or, inversely, the height given the base and slope, or the base given the height and slope. These exercises are assembled in Table II.

In the first five exercises the angle of the slope is expressed, in palms, by the trigonometric cotangent. This cotangent is expressed by the fraction's numerator alone (in palms), the denominator (understood) always being 1 cubit of 7 palms. Thus in order to obtain the true value of the cotangent, one need only divide the slopes mentioned in the papyrus by 7.

In Exercise 60, however, the slope 4 expresses the *true* value of the trigonometric *tangent*. Of the six slopes mentioned, four correspond to the angle 53° 7′ 48″, which is one of the acute angles of the Egyptian Sothic triangle, whose sides are proportional to the numbers 3, 4, and 5.

It should be noted that none of these slopes corresponds to the slope of the Great Pyramid; that is, 5½ according to the Egyptian notation, a slope whose cotangent equals 5½/7, or $^{11}/_{14}$.[4]

$$\text{ctn } \alpha = \frac{OH}{OS} = \frac{b}{h} = \frac{FH}{EF} = \frac{FH}{l}.$$

Rhind Mathematical Papyrus

Exercise No.	Height in cubits	Base in cubits	Slope	ctn α	α°
56	250	360	5$^1/_{25}$	0.720	54° 14′ 45″
57	93⅓	140	5¼	0.750	53° 7′ 48″
58	93⅓	140	5¼	0.750	53° 7′ 48″
59	8	12	5¼	0.750	53° 7′ 48″
59a	8	12	5¼	0.750	53° 7′ 48″
60	30	15	4	0.250	75° 57′ 42″

The numbers in italics are the given data for the problems posed.

Two mathematical ratios are needed in order to define a pyramid:

1. The ratio $\frac{b}{h} = \text{ctn } \alpha$, which defines the slope, thus the general shape.

2. The ratio $\frac{2b}{L}$ or $\frac{h}{L}$, which defines the actual dimensions, L being the unit of length used.

The slope of the Great Pyramid, determined from the facing blocks still in place on the north face, is 51° 51′ (±1′). This angle gives the following values as trigonometric lines.

α =	51° 50′	51° 51′	51° 52′
Sine	0.7862165	0.7863963	0.7865759
Cosine	0.6179511	0.6177224	0.6174936
Tangent	1.2722957	1.2730578	1.2738204
Cotangent	0.7858908	0.7855103	0.7850400

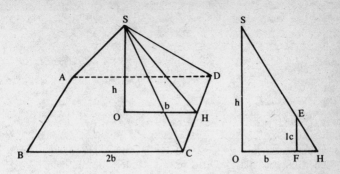

Two remarks can be made concerning these values:

1. The respective values of the trigonometric sine and cotangent are *very* close. By making them equal, the following equation is obtained:

$$\sin \alpha = \frac{\cos \alpha}{\sin \alpha}$$

whence

$$\sin^2\alpha = \cos \alpha \text{ and } \cos^2\alpha - 1 = 0$$

whence

$$\cos \alpha = \frac{1 + \sqrt{5}}{2} = 0.6183981...,$$ which is the value of the golden section (φ).

2. The value of the cotangent is close to $\frac{\pi}{4} = 0.7853981...$ (using the true value of π), or $\frac{22}{7} \times \frac{1}{4} = 0.7857143...$

Each of these two remarks constitutes the basis of a theory, to wit: the theory of the golden slope; the theory of the slope π.

We are now able, according to these two theories, to determine the values of the Great Pyramid's slope and height from the only value that is explicit, the value of the base

	Theory of the golden section	Theory of the slope π (cotg $\alpha = \frac{\pi}{4}$)	
	$\cos \alpha = \varphi$	$\pi = 3.14159$	$\pi = \frac{22}{7}$
$\alpha =$	54° 49′ 38″	51° 51′ 14″	51° 50′ 34″
ctn $\alpha =$	0.7861163	0.7853981	0.7857143
Height:			
from the socle	146.490 m.	146.583 m.	146.525 m.
from the bedrock (+ 0.525 m.)	147.015 m.	147.108 m.	147.050 m.

upon the socle—that is, 230.253 meters. This fact having been established, we can now consider the mathematical theories relating to the pyramids.

THE MATHEMATICAL THEORIES

With his preconceived ideas concerning the scientific naiveté of the ancient Egyptians, Lauer tends to view all the precise data, all the intricate relationships involved in the Great Pyramid, its disconcerting orientation, its angle of slope, the measurement of its base, even its geographical position, as mere coincidence. This attitude is reminiscent of the learned scholars of the sixteenth century, who regarded the fossils they discovered as "nature's little jokes."

The question of the mathematical theories, which proves to be most important, was the subject of a paper read to the French Academy of Sciences on June 23, 1947, by the mathematician Paul Montel.

In this paper Montel lends support to Lauer's thesis, and his conclusions are the following:

1. The shape of the pyramids depends solely upon the ratio

$\frac{b}{h}$ (b = half of the base, h = height).

. . . Thus, if one wished to preserve in the edifice a number whose mystical virtue or scientific value seemed worthy of defying the centuries, the ratio b/h would be fixed and the external shape entirely determined. Consequently, if other significant numbers are discovered in the ratios of the monument's dimensions, it should be inferred that the relationship defining them is a consequence of the imposed initial relationship, and not that a new intention has been added to the first.

2. After having studied the slopes ϕ and π mathematically, Montel, apparently preferring the former as the most likely in the doubtful case of an imposed initial condition, adopts Lauer's conclusions and concedes that

> . . . only considerations of a technical nature guided the builders in the choice of dimensions. It was essential that they be able to verify easily, on the site, the slope of the casings and, above all, the slope of the ridges, which governs the layout of the pattern of the cornerstones, which were set in place prior to the lateral facings. In the case of the pyramid of Cheops, they chose the slope $^9/_{10}$ for the ridges and, consequently, $^{11}/_{14}$ for the faces. Thus, a single technical requirement determined the Pyramid's shape, and this shape entailed the presence of numbers close to notable constants.

These conclusions, despite the seemingly logical reasoning behind them, invite the following major objections:

While the ratio b/h, which is a dimensionless number, is *in itself* sufficient for determining the *general shape* of a regular pyramid, *it is not sufficient for the actual realization of a particular pyramid*, for an infinite number of mathematically similar pyramids would fit the description.

The question of orientation aside, in order to effect a concrete realization, one of the two parameters, b or h, must be set arbitrarily.

Therefore, there is nothing to prevent the size of the chosen parameter from corresponding to a preconceived idea—astronomical, geodesic, or other. Moreover, the size of this parameter may or may not depend on the value of the unit of measurement being used.

In sum, a regular, concrete pyramid is totally defined by *only two* ratios (and not by *only one*, as Montel would have it), to wit: (1). the ratio $\frac{b}{h}$ defining the slope, thus the general shape; (2). either the ratio $\frac{b}{L}$ or the ratio $\frac{h}{L}$, L being any length chosen *arbitrarily* as a unit of measurement—cubit, stade, terrestrial radius or meridian, even the ineffable divine pyramidal cubit.

On the Slope ϕ, or the Golden Section

It might be helpful to review what the golden section is, mathematically: it is the number which, increased or diminished by 1, is equal to its inverse; whence the equation:

$$x \pm 1 = \frac{1}{x} \text{ or } x^2 \pm x - 1 = 0.$$

There are thus two golden sections that are the positive roots of the preceding equation. These two roots have a value of $\frac{\pm 1 + \sqrt{5}}{2}$:

$$\phi = 1.61803398\ldots \text{ and } \varphi = 0.61803398$$

Without going into a study of the special mathematical properties of these two golden sections, let us recall that they respectively measure out the two segments obtained by dividing a given length (a) into mean and extreme ratio. This is the "golden section" of the ancient Greeks, in which the whole (a) is to one of the parts (x) as x is to the second part (a − x).

Whence the proportion: $\frac{a}{x} = \frac{x}{a - x}$

Moreover, the numbers ϕ and φ respectively measure out the sides of regular star-shaped convex decagons inscribed in a circle whose radius equals the unit used.

The number ϕ also equals the ratio of the sides of regular star-shaped convex pentagrams inscribed in the same circle. Let us not overlook yet another singular and important property, to wit: $\phi^{n+1} = \phi^n + \phi^{(n-1)}$.

We have seen that the slope of the Great Pyramid, determined from the facing blocks still in place along the north face, is $\alpha = 51° 51' (\pm 1')$. Now, it is a strange and remarkable fact that:

$\varphi = 0.61803398 = \cos 51° 49' 38''$ The angle so
and $\phi = 1.61803398 = \sec 51° 49' 38''$ defined is thus, to the nearest minute, that of the Pyramid.

Going along with Lauer (p. 190) in this matter, Montel writes:

> In the Great Pyramid of Cheops, among the Giza group, the oldest ratio known goes back to Herodotus, who described it in the fifth century B.C., 2,500 years[5] after [the Pyramid's] construction. According to his account, the Egyptian priests assured him that the area of each equilateral triangle is equivalent to the square having as its sides the Pyramid's height, which gives the relationship $b^2 = ab$, with a designating the apothem and b half of the base.

This is *entirely wrong,* and it is curious that Montel's Hellenist colleagues should have let such errors pass! First of all, there is nothing in Herodotus' text to suggest that this account was provided by Egyptian priests. Moreover, Herodotus' text is completely different:

> Each front thereof is eight plethra long, (for it is square), and the height is the same. . . .[6]
> It is square, eight hundred feet each way, and the height the same. . . .[7]

Nowhere does Herodotus say that the faces are equilateral triangles, and at no point does he make any mention of the surfaces. The side of 8 plethra gives, for the base, a value of 246.26 meters instead of 231.40 meters, the true value of the length of the base upon the bedrock. This error is understandable in the case of a traveler who had little regard for mathematical accuracy and was content to report the common opinion, according to which the Pyramid was as high as it was wide, an assertion one frequently finds among the Arab authors.[8]

In conclusion, the theory of the slope ϕ, or the golden section, the premises of which rely upon a false interpretation of Herodotus' text, must be classified as *improbable.*

Still, if the golden slope had been real, the relationship $h^2 = ab$ would have led to an angle of slope α satisfying the following trigonometric relationships:

$$\cos \alpha = \sin^2 \alpha = \operatorname{ctn}^2 \alpha = \varphi$$
$$\text{and} \quad \sec \alpha = \operatorname{cosec}^2 \alpha = \operatorname{tg}^2 \alpha = \phi$$

leading to the equations:

$$\sin \alpha \; \text{tg} \; \alpha = 1 \quad \text{and} \quad \cos^2 \alpha + \cos \alpha - 1 = 0$$
$$\text{whence} \quad \cos \alpha = \frac{-1 + \sqrt{5}}{2} = \varphi.$$

This being the case, Lauer has no right to claim that the ancient Egyptians' mathematical knowledge was slight, since they would have been capable of solving a quadratic equation. It is true that while Montel is inclined to acknowledge the golden slope, Lauer does not agree with this opinion; according to him, it is the $^9/_{10}$ slope of the ridge that played the primordial role—a plausible hypothesis, perhaps, but not at all certain.

It is very possible that the stereotomic outline of the angle blocks was obtained by projecting a length AN equal to $^{10}/_9$ the height AB, and drawing parallels from this point to the ridges NP and NP'. (See Fig. 1.) However, the outline can be obtained just as easily by projecting the lengths AD and AC (readily obtained with a gauge), equal to $^{11}/_{14}$ the height AB, along the upper ridges and tracing parallels to the ridges. (See Fig. 2.)

Since the number of angle blocks is *infinitesimal* compared to the number of lateral blocks, it is *certain* that the stereotomic outline was executed according to the slope $^{11}/_{14}$, and not according to the $^9/_{10}$ slope of the ridge, as Lauer would have it.

The Slope π

If the slope of the Great Pyramid does indeed correspond to the relationship $\text{ctn} \; \alpha = \dfrac{\pi}{4}$, there follows an important consequence.

We have, in effect:

$$\text{ctn} \; \alpha = \frac{\dfrac{b}{2}}{h} = \frac{\pi}{4} , \quad \text{whence} \quad 4b = 2\pi h.$$

In other words, *the perimeter of the Great Pyramid's base is equal to the circumference having as its radius the Pyramid's height.*

STEREOTOMIC OUTLINES OF THE CUTTING SCHEMES
USED FOR THE GREAT PYRAMID'S BLOCKS

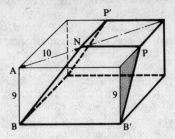

Fig. 1. The cut of an angle block, according to Lauer

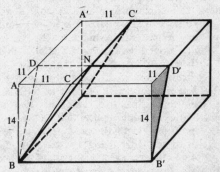

Fig. 2. My version of the cut of an angle block

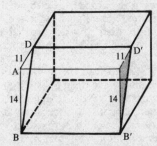

Fig. 3. My version of the cut of a lateral block

This important relationship—which to Lauer is "mere coincidence"—brings us back to the inscription found in the mastaba of Pen-Meruw, in which the Great Pyramid bears the determinative reserved for *solar temples*.

Thus it is not unlikely that the Great Pyramid's dimensions should be related to geodesic measurements, as Jomard claimed, and this despite the assurance of Lauer, who writes (p. 194): "But even if such statements could have been made, they would have been only appendant ideal qualities that were added to the determining reasons of a practical nature, which I intend to explain." For Lauer, these "determining reasons of a practical nature" are limited exclusively to the cutting of the ridge blocks according to the most easily realized outline.

The Great Pyramid *must* have been a solar temple, for why would it have had a platform if not to hold a gnomon? Moreover, how are we to explain (barring suppositions about the "whims" or "jokes" of the builders) the existence of *four solar barques* around the Pyramid? The obvious answer is that two of them were intended for the sun god Khnum, the two others being reserved for King Cheops.

Most of the Egyptian pyramids, having as their slope 5¼ (tg α = ¾), have an outline that represents two adjacent isiac triangles. Now, Plutarch reports that the sacred Egyptian triangle represented both the cosmos[9] and the divine Osiris-Isis-Horus triad. This being the case, if the isiac pyramid represented the terrestrial globe and if the perimeter of its base was considered to be equal to the circumference having as its radius the Pyramid's height, the value of π would have been equal to 3, the same value assigned by the Bible with respect to the bronze sea of Solomon's temple (1 Kings 7:23): "And he [Hiram] made a molten sea, ten cubits from the one brim to other: it was round all about, and his height was five cubits: and a line of thirty cubits did compass it round about."

This value of 3, ascribed to the ratio of a circumference with its diameter, must have been a distant memory carried down from predynastic times. In assigning the value 5½ to his pyramid's slope, Cheops must certainly have wished to fix in his funerary monument a more exact value for π, to wit, $^{22}/_7$. That is all it took for him to be considered an iconoclast, an atheist, and to be dishonored by the sacerdotal college of his time.

There is nothing, moreover, to controvert the possibility that the length of the base might have been related to the value of an arc of the terrestrial meridian. That is what remains to be proved; I will return to this subject later.

The Isiac Slope

The Rhind Papyrus includes no problem related to the Great Pyramid's 5½ slope. Moreover, no other Egyptian pyramid, to my knowledge, has this slope.

However, the Great Pyramid, wonder of the ancient world, must have been the subject of special studies, and problems dealing with this 5½ slope would have been no more difficult to solve than those concerning the slope 5¼, with which four out of the six problems related to the pyramids deal. And this lack in the papyrus poses another problem. Could it be that the Great Pyramid's slope was not exactly 5½, as Petrie and Borchardt insist, and that the problem posed would therefore have greatly surpassed the average student's capacity? For, in my opinion, the Rhind Papyrus was simply a student's notebook.

The fact is, the pyramid of Cheops is not, like the others, a regular pyramid: its faces are curiously hollowed and its top is truncated. Moreover, it is very possible that its base *did not have as its value an exact number of cubits* measuring 0.524 meter (440 of these, according to Petrie and Borchardt). Alas, unless a papyrus dealing with the problem is unearthed, this question will never be settled.

This isiac slope of 53° 7' 48", corresponding to ctn α = 5¼ = 0.750, is simply the value of the largest acute angle of the sacred Egyptian triangle. The meridian section of most of the Egyptian pyramids (that of Kephren in particular) thus appears as an isosceles triangle, with a base of 6 and a height of 4, comprising two adjacent isiac triangles. This fact is *formal proof* that the Pyramid's shape could have been dictated, not by a simple concern for ease of execution, but by a *guiding symbolic idea*—a possibility that Lauer and Montel stubbornly refuse to admit.

The symbolism was expressed not only *in the Pyramid's shape,* but also *in its color,* for the Great Pyramid—as well as the pyramid of Kephren—*was painted red,* like the Sphinx's face. The Great Pyramid was the solar temple of the ram-headed god Khnum, whose son Cheops was thought to be; it was "Khufu's Horizon," and naturally its color was that of the sun setting in the western horizon.

I will return later to this question of the painting of the pyramids, a possibility that Lauer will not admit, despite tangible, irrefutable proof.

THE MEASUREMENT OF THE EARTH BY THE ANCIENT EGYPTIANS

The authors concerned with ancient geodesy report that the first real attempt to measure an arc of the meridian was made by Eratosthenes, between Syene and Alexandria, under Ptolemy Euergetes I, *c.* 230 B.C. For this information, they rely on texts by Pliny and Strabo.

> Similarly it is reported that at the town of Syene, 5000 stades South of Alexandria, at noon in midsummer no shadow is cast, and that in a well made for the sake of testing this the light reaches to the bottom, clearly showing that the sun is vertically above that place at the time. . . .[10]

> But as to the question whether the earth is as large as he has said, later writers do not agree with him; neither do they approve his measurement of the earth. Still, when Hipparchus plots the celestial phenomena for the several inhabited places, he uses, in addition, those intervals measured by Eratosthenes on the meridian through Meroë and Alexandria and the Borysthenes, after saying that they deviate but slightly from the truth.[11]

> Beyond there are forests, in which is Ptolemais, built by Ptolemy Philadelphus for the purpose of elephant-hunting and consequently called Ptolemy's Hunting Lodge; it is close to Lake Monoleus. This is the district referred to by us in Book II, in which during the 45 days before midsummer and the same number of days after midsummer shadows contract to nothing an hour before noon, and during the rest of the day fall to the south,

while all the other days of the year they fall to the north; on the other hand at the first Berenice mentioned above, on the actual day of the summer solstice the shadow disappears altogether an hour before noon, but nothing else unusual is observed—this place is 602½ miles from Ptolemais. The phenomenon is extremely remarkable, and the topic is one involving infinitely profound research, it being here that the structure of the world was discovered, because Eratosthenes derived from it the idea of working out the earth's dimensions by the certain method of noting the shadows.[12]

It is also stated that in the Cave-dwellers' city of Berenice, and 4820 stades away at the town of Ptolemais in the same tribe, which was founded on the shore of the Red Sea for the earliest elephant hunts, the same thing occurs 45 days before and 45 days after midsummer, and during that period of 90 days the shadows are thrown southward.[13]

In the regions of Meroë, and of the Ptolemaïs in the country of the Troglodytes, the longest day has thirteen equinoctial hours; and this inhabited country is approximately midway between the equator and the parallel that runs through Alexandria (the stretch to the equator being eighteen hundred stadia more).[14]

At present, on the island of Elephantine, there still exists a well, which I myself have seen, about 5 meters in diameter and 8 meters deep, which could have been Pliny's historical well. But in examining it one perceives that the precision regarding the lack of shadow at the bottom of the well is questionable, given its diameter, which is too great for its slight depth (perhaps it is partly filled in at the present time). During Eratosthenes' time the island of Elephantine (latitude 24° 5′ 23″) no longer marked the position of the tropic, which was then located at latitude 23° 44′ 8″ 3. The tropic coincided with the position of the well around 3200 B.C.—that is, during the Twelfth Dynasty. Pliny's statement thus represents only a distant recollection.

The latitude of Alexandria, derived by measuring 21,440 stadia[15] from the equator, is 30° 55′ 10″, instead of 31° 10′—an admissible error, in view of the difficulty of defining the equator at that time. The measurement of 5,000 stadia from Alexandria to Syene is much more significant, because it is not subject to the displacement of the tropic; it corresponds to a difference in latitude of 7° 8' 34". This being the case, the latitude of Syene would have been 24° 1' 26", instead of 24° 5' 25".

Such an error on the part of Eratosthenes, entailing 4 arc minutes, is inconceivable. There is only one plausible explanation, and that is that the southern extremity of the arc of the meridian measured by Eratosthenes was not the well on the island of Elephantine (which would have had to have been, by the strangest coincidence, *exactly* 5,000 stadia from Alexandria), but a well on the island of Philae, whose latitude is precisely 24° 1' 23". The two obelisks there, still standing today, must have been erected for the purpose of marking the southern end of the measurement. Moreover, the very name of the cubit derived from Eratosthenes' measurement—the "Philaeterian" cubit, or the "wonder of Philae"—seems to prove it ($\phi\iota\lambda\alpha\iota\tau\epsilon\rho\alpha\sigma$).

Eratosthenes' second measurement, from Berenice to Ptolemais, extending 4,820 stadia, corresponds to a difference in latitude of 6° 53' 8". It is certain that the northern end of this arc of the meridian must have been exactly determined at the same latitude as the southern end of the Alexandria-Philae arc. This being the case, the Alexandria-Ptolemais arc of the meridian had a value of 9,820 stadia, or 14° 1' 42".

We now know the precise value of the various degrees of the terrestrial meridian as they relate to latitude. Between the latitude 17° (very close to that of Ptolemais, the exact location of which is still unknown) and the latitude of Alexandria, 31° 10', the average value of the degree is 110,771 meters (1 minute = 1,846.19 meters; ½ minute = 923.095 meters). Consequently, the length of the Alexandria-Ptolemais arc of the meridian is 1,553,932.51 meters, which gives Eratosthenes' stadium a value of *158.242* meters.

Since Eratosthenes' stadium equaled 300 cubits, it follows that the value of the cubit was 0.5275 meter. That is *exactly* the value of the cubit marked on the nilometer of Elephantine studied by P.-S. Girard.[16]

One important fact should be noted: the line occupied by each cubit on the nilometer is indicated *in Greek symbols*. It is therefore certain that the construction of this nilometer dates from the Lagid Dynasty and that its scale conforms to the results of the measurement of the earth made by Eratosthenes.

In sum, we should pay heartfelt tribute to Eratosthenes and his royal bematists for the truly prodigious exactitude of their cubit, the "wonder of Philae."

This digression concerning Eratosthenes' measurement of the earth leads us directly back to the Great Pyramid of Giza. The cubit of 0.52367 meter used by the builders of the Pyramid is very close to the Ptolemaic Philaeterian cubit of 0.5275 meter. Since the value of the latter is connected to the measurement of the terrestrial meridian, it is probable that the cubit of the Fourth Dynasty was as well. Obviously, this suggests a knowledge of the roundness of the earth dating from the early dynasties; that is, from 4800 B.C. and perhaps even earlier.

The Great Pyramid was not only the tomb of Cheops, but also—and *above all*—the temple of the sun god Khnum. The hieroglyphic determinative found in the tomb of Pen-Meruw at Giza leaves no doubt in this respect. One could cite as complementary proofs the red coating with which the Pyramid was covered; the existence of *four* solar barques; the regard in which it was held by the Sabean sun worshippers; and, above all, the hollowing of its faces, designed to allow the equinoxes to be determined precisely—not to mention its slope, unique in Egypt, giving the value of π.

Is it therefore so unlikely that the value of the base should be related to the value of an arc of the meridian? For it is not without reason that:

1. The value of the Greek cubit corresponds exactly to $1/500$th of the base (0.462 meter); this cubit is described by the ancient Arab authors as being "the cubit of the just hand."

2. Al Mamun, who had most of the Giza pyramids opened *c.* 820 A.D., set the value of the Arabian cubit at $1/400$th of the Pyramid's base (0.5775 meter).[17] It is also curious that, upon his return to Baghdad, Al Mamun had a measurement of the meridian carried out in the desert plain of Sinjar.

3. The value of the "quarriers'" cubit (*diraa mimari*) has a value of 0.77 meter; that is, $1/300$th of the Great Pyramid's base.

Lauer can call upon "chance" all he likes, but no one with

any sense would go along with him. For from these facts it becomes obvious that the length of the Great Pyramid's base was of the utmost significance and was certainly in accord with the dimensions of the terrestrial globe. Many Egyptologists will protest that it is utter madness to claim that a measurement of the terrestrial meridian could have been made in 4800 B.C. (yes, 4800 B.C.); I am certain that the madness is not mine.

While to Lauer the slope is a "whim" on the part of the builders, to me the slope assumes a special significance—it proves that the Great Pyramid's dimensions are directly related to the result of the measurement of an arc of the meridian, and the value of the base should be able to show us the precision attained by the Egyptians under or before the Fourth Dynasty.

The *average* value of the Egyptian degree depends on the arc being measured. This value is:

110,771 m. from Meroe to Alexandria:
    ½ sexagesimal minute = 923.092 meters.[18]
110,817.5 m. from Philae to Alexandria:
    ½ sexagesimal minute = 923.52 meters.
110,865 m. from Memphis to Alexandria:
    ½ sexagesimal minute = 923.92 meters.

The values of the monument's bases are the following:
  Length of the base upon the socle: 230.253 m.
  Perimeter: 921.012 m.
  Length of the edge of the socle: 231.093 m.
  Perimeter: 924.372 m.
  Length of the base of the socle upon the bedrock:
    231.393 m.
  Perimeter: 925.572 m.

In my opinion, two referential lines alone could have served as a standard of measurement: (1) the Pyramid's real base upon its socle; (2) the edge of the socle, which could be measured precisely. In the first instance, the precision obtained by the bematists would have been within 0.20, 0.27, or 0.31 percent, depending on the arc of the meridian measured. In the second instance, this precision would have been within 0.14, 0.09, or 0.05 percent—remarkable results for the time.

All this sheds new light on the astronomical and geodesic knowledge of the Egyptians of the Fourth Dynasty in 4800

B.C. In having Eratosthenes undertake a new measurement of the terrestrial meridian, Philadelphus and Euergetes, who were open-minded about scientific research, wished to verify the ancestral value embodied and found in the Great Pyramid. The value of the ancient cubit (0.524 meter) was corrected, and the new cubit (0.527 meter), dedicated to Isis, goddess of Philae, was called the "Philaeterian" cubit, or the "wonder of Philae," for the city that was located midway on the Meroe-Alexandria arc of the meridian. Eleven centuries later, Al Mamun attempted the same verification in the plain of Sinjar.

Lauer categorically states that the measurement of the earth could not have been carried out under the early dynasties. However, he knows better than anyone the extent of the scientific and technological knowledge required to build a complex such as that of the pyramid of Zoser and its temples; what can be said, then, of the Giza complexes?

The construction of a complex such as that of Cheops involved difficulties beyond accurate surveying. The ancient Egyptians lacked precision instruments analogous to our stadias and theodolites, which permit correct triangulations—but even this is not entirely true, for they were already using trigonometry and understood the tangent and cotangent. The point is the ancient Egyptians did not need triangulations in order to measure their meridian. They knew how to determine a north-south bearing at night as precisely as we can, by proceeding to the two transections made by a star along a knotted cord stretched approximately east-west. Concretized by aligned benchmarks, this north-south bearing was "surveyed" by a group of about a hundred bematists, and the average of the number of paces they took was the equivalent, in terms of precision, of the triangulation of a base (which is sometimes uncertain). Apropos of this, let me mention that I have discovered a number of cairns in the desert, along the Alexandria meridian, west of Wadi Natrun. These cairns do not follow any particular course but are aligned exactly north-south. Are they vestiges of the measurement made by Eratosthenes, or of an earlier measurement?

I am thoroughly convinced that the ancient Egyptians carried out a measurement of the earth during or before the Fourth Dynasty and that the results of this measurement were embodied in the perimeter of the Great Pyramid, whose sides are perfectly oriented and whose slope gives the value of π.

There is no doubt that the pyramids are the tombs of kings, but, as Jomard pointed out, they *also* "preserved for us a reliable model of the size of the terrestrial globe and the invaluable concept of the invariability of the pole." I would simply correct Jomard's passage by rephrasing it in the singular, for only the Great Pyramid served this function; the others retained the classical isiac pattern with its cross-sectional dimensions proportional to 3, 4, and 5.

Lauer writes (p. 200):

In sum, at the time that the great pyramids were being built, geometry does not seem to have progressed beyond an *intuitive,* utilitarian empiricism. The architect-priests, when confronted with difficult technical problems, sought the best practical solutions; a mind totally given over to material exigencies cannot also be devoted to pure, disinterested speculation.

However, he then contradicts himself, agreeing with Abel Rey that it is possible the Egyptian priests

might have possessed important knowledge—carefully amassed and preserved in the secrecy of the temples—resulting from patient observations made in the course of the long centuries separating the construction of the first pyramids around 2900 B.C.[19] from the dawn of Greek mathematical thought, starting in the sixth century B.C.

As far as geometry, in particular, is concerned, the analysis of such famous edifices as the Great Pyramid must have figured prominently in the speculations of these priests, and it is perfectly conceivable that they should have succeeded in discovering—undoubtedly, quite a long time after [the edifices] were erected—coincidental properties never dreamed of by the builders.

"Coincidental properties never dreamed of by the builders"—there's a dialectical explanation worthy of

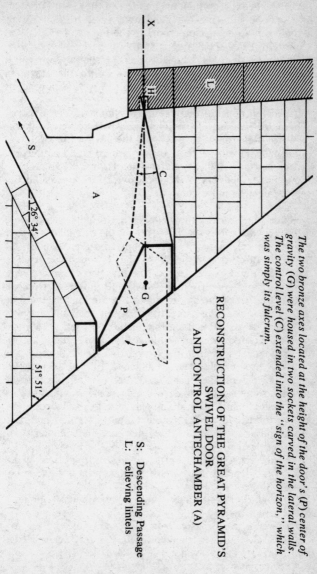

The two bronze axes located at the height of the door's (P) center of gravity (G) were housed in two sockets carved in the lateral walls. The control level (C) extended into the "sign of the horizon," which was simply its fulcrum.

RECONSTRUCTION OF THE GREAT PYRAMID'S
SWIVEL DOOR
AND CONTROL ANTECHAMBER (A)

S: Descending Passage
L: relieving lintels

181

Father Moreux, for whom the builders of the Great Pyramid, mere puppets having the illusion of total freedom, were actually only unconscious tools in the hands of God, Who secretly directed their actions and thoughts!

Before finishing with Lauer's book, I should point out a significant error he makes in reference to the Egyptian calendar. Concerning the latter, he writes (p. 188, footnote):

> . . . It is generally agreed that one must go all the way back to the third of the 1,460-year Sothic cycles—that is, to the year 4211 B.C.—for the institution of this calendar. However, there is no reason it could not have been started 1,460 years later—that is, in 2781 B.C.—by one of the builders of the great pyramids, a possibility that might be more plausible.

Lauer's calendrical knowledge is out of date. There were *three* calendars in Egypt, not just one: the calendar of Upper Egypt, the calendar of Lower Egypt, and the calendar "of the ancestors," or "of the Two Lands," which was used in both Upper and Lower Egypt. The first two calendars were "mobile" and comprised 365 days; the third was tropical. The institution of the first calendar was well before the time of Menes; the second dates from the year 5557 B.C. and was instituted by Athothis upon the death of his father, Menes. As for the third, it was in use under Kaiechos, second king of the Second Dynasty, in 5329 B.C., and its institution was probably predynastic, whence its name, "of the ancestors."

In conclusion: The upshot of Lauer's opinion is that the architects and master builders of the Great Pyramid had only very limited mathematical knowledge; all their works show an overriding concern for simplicity, particularly in regard to the angular coefficients; there are no mathematical, astronomical, or mystical relationships in the Pyramid, and if perchance such relationships seem apparent, either they are mere coincidence or they are the mistaken interpretations of visionary theorists.

If I have subjected Lauer's book to a stringent critique, it is because it seemed absolutely necessary to do so since it is considered "authoritative" in Egyptological circles. My criticisms are not meant unkindly, for I readily acknowledge that there are many memorable passages in his work.

Bruchet

This author provides a very objective study of the monument, along with artistically executed sketches. Taking the opposite stance from Lauer's in regard to the ancient Egyptians' scientific knowledge, he concludes—with good reason—that the architects of that time were easily the equals of their modern counterparts.

I find Bruchet's ideas interesting, even though I disagree with him on many points. He, too, is intrigued by the Pyramid's interior layout, which cannot be compared to that of an ordinary tomb. According to him, the Great Pyramid must be a *simulacrum* of a tomb because the Ascending Passage was blocked off *even as construction was underway,* before the Grand Gallery and the King's Chamber had been laid out. I cannot agree with him on this matter, and I will take the liberty of criticizing him with respect to certain parts of the Pyramid he was unable to visit or observe closely.

Like Lauer, Bruchet reproduces (on p. 27) Petrie's sketch of the Pyramid's northeast ridge, but with a slight variation: he shows the casing block imbedded *directly* in the bedrock. As I said earlier, this, in my opinion, is *impossible* because the entire Pyramid rests on a socle 0.524 meter thick, which projects 0.42 meter beyond the base of the casing. This socle was used in the Pyramid's orientation, which would have been impossible but for it, given the hollowing of the faces, which no author other than Petrie mentions. It is the cornerstones *of the socle,* 0.69 meter thick, that are imbedded 0.27 meter in the bedrock.

Bruchet makes the same mistake (p. 33) as Lauer and Montel in regard to an alleged text by Herodotus referring to the slope ϕ.

Bruchet thinks there may have been some kind of antechamber at the entrance to the Descending Passage. This is not impossible; I would even say that it is probable, for a certain amount of space was necessary in which to swing the mobile door mentioned by Strabo, which was clearly analogous to the one found in the bent pyramid at Dashur. Nonetheless, aside from Petrie (*The Pyramids and Temples of Gizeh,* illus. 11), who provides a simplistic sketch (with the height of the Descending Passage's entrance reduced by half: 0.65 meter), no author has attempted a plausible reconstruction of the swivel door pointed out by Strabo.

My reconstruction, based on meticulous observations, has the advantage of providing a correct explanation of the mysterious "sign of the horizon," which is simply the fulcrum of the swivel door's control bar (see p. 181). It should be noted, in this regard, that the horizontal plane transecting the center of gravity of Strabo's door in fact transected the "sign of the horizon" and coincided with the plane of the floor of the "Queen's Chamber," the Pyramid's *serdab*.

In discussing the eastward displacement of the Descending Passage in relation to the Pyramid's meridian plane, Bruchet deduces that the structure's final dimensions were fixed well before construction was begun; this is absolutely certain (and contrary to Borchardt's views).

Concerning the Descending Passage (p. 50), Bruchet criticizes Moret in regard to an alleged landing located directly beneath the opening of the Ascending Passage; according to him, "there was nothing in the floor of the lower passage to suggest that one had reached a junction."

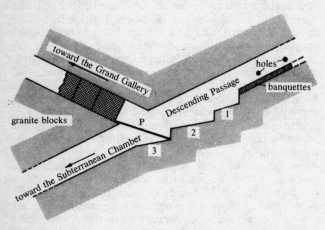

This is an error on Bruchet's part: he did not observe the Descending Passage very closely, since he does not mention the two lateral banquettes, which are 18 centimeters deep and 30 centimeters high and extend down to three steps located near the opening of the Ascending Passage. The top step (1) is 0.70 meter long (height: 25 centimeters); the second (2), 2.25 meters, forms a veritable platform (height: 35 centimeters); the third (3) is 1.57 meter long (height: 50 centimeters). Moreover, Bruchet does not note the ten holes (5 centimeters in diameter) dug in the east wall, which were probably designed to hold crampons supporting a handrail.

One important fact should be pointed out here: the extension of the floor of the Ascending Passage ends exactly in the hollow of the third step. Therefore we can assume that it was equipped with a wooden ramp in order to permit ascent to the Grand Gallery and the central chamber (the King's Chamber) during the entombment—or, as I believe, during the isiac ceremony of the transferral of the divine *ka*. Moreover, we find the same setup at the Grand Gallery's entrance, enabling one to climb up over the Horizontal Passage of the *serdab* (Queen's Chamber).

Bruchet (p. 35) adopts Smyth's musings concerning Polaris, which presumably allowed the bearing of the Great Pyramid's Descending Passage to be determined. He writes: "In this period, nearly five thousand years ago, this star [Sirius], the brightest in the constellation Canis Major, had a rival, 'Alpha Draconis.' " A rather pitiful rival, for Alpha Draconis is only a star of the third magnitude, scarcely visible to the naked eye! Besides, in 4800 B.C., when the Pyramid was built, *no* visible star represented the north pole.

I do not agree with Bruchet (p. 37) that Al Mamun "was forced to begin his search blindly." In my opinion, the location of the entrance to the Descending Passage was common knowledge. Al Mamun merely repierced a four-thousand-year-old tunnel, as his august personage could not be permitted to climb under the granite blocks in the narrow passage leading to the Descending Passage.

More reasonable is Bruchet's remark (pp. 40–41) concerning the location of the entrance to the Descending Passage at the seventeenth course, which created the problem of having to raise the royal coffin up a slide nearly 20 meters long at an angle of 52 degrees. His argument has a certain value in that it supports the theory that the King's Chamber was never Cheops' tomb. However, it is possible that a stairway cut right into the casing existed at the time.

The reasoning that follows (pp. 43–46) concerning a possible antechamber located behind the swivel door is quite valid. As for the portal's symbolic significance, the question remains unresolved for the time being. (See my explanation in the preceding pages.)

Bruchet then proceeds (pp. 50–51) to a dissertation on the limestone plug that, according to him, must have concealed the granite blocks obstructing the Ascending Passage. In my opinion, this limestone plug never existed, for the three steps in the Descending Passage would have revealed the presence of any anomaly in the construction. He then takes up the question of the origin of the piece of granite obstructing the Descending Passage; in my opinion, it simply came from the third plug block, which, having been broken during the first attempt to unblock the passage, was thrown into the Descending Passage by the despoilers.

The rest of the chapter, concerning the total impossibility of two successive changes of plan in the course of the Pyramid's construction, is clear, realistic, and irrefutable.

It is a pity that Bruchet was unable to reach the interior of the Subterranean Chamber and had to be content with the findings of Howard-Vyse, Perring, Petrie, and Jacques Vandier. He states (p. 58, art. 48) that the Subterranean Chamber is still cluttered with debris from the well and that, since 1838, no one has thought to clear it out. This is an erroneous statement, for Baraize had the Subterranean Chamber completely cleaned; the photographs I provide of the chamber should serve as formal proof of this fact. I myself have recorded all the dimensions of this strange chamber, which, destined to play a major role in the isiac initiation ceremonies, was never an "abandoned chamber." (This is one area in which I agree, at least partially, with Bruchet. I will come back to this important question later.) The two sketches he provides are obviously defective, since he was unable to penetrate the interior. Still, using logic, he was able to derive the better part of the incomplete data in his possession. He is correct in affirming that it was not an abandoned chamber. I know the chamber well, having visited it many times, and to me this is an *indisputable* fact, despite the rash judgments formed by certain well-known Egyptologists.

According to Bruchet (p. 79), the Ascending Passage *was blocked from the time of its construction,* because it was totally impossible to make the three plug blocks slide into it from the Grand Gallery. The Great Pyramid was thus but a simulacrum of a tomb, and no one was ever entombed there.

Although I strongly support Bruchet's esoteric viewpoints in certain respects, I cannot accept this statement. In my opinion, the three plug blocks were stored in a lateral recess connected to the Descending Passage by a narrow shaft. After the portcullises of the King's Chamber were closed and the three plug blocks set in place, this narrow pit was obstructed, at the point where it opened on the Descending Passage, with cemented blocks that were later removed by the first despoilers. This shaft under the granite blocks still exists, but the lateral recess[20] is now unrecognizable; enlarged, it is now part of "Al Mamun's" hole.

Bruchet treats the difficult subject of the Pyramid's "well" (pp. 76–84). He admits that he was unable to reach it—which is obvious, given the sketch he provides of it.

The "grotto," situated at the level of the bedrock and slightly above it, is less than 2 meters high, not 9 meters. The well is *tangent* to the grotto and does not transect it (see the cross section and description provided earlier). It is a pity that Bruchet was unable to climb down the well; in the dust and darkness this is a rather impressive feat.

With reason, Bruchet is of the opinion that the well was dug for the evacuation of the workers charged with closing the portcullises of the King's Chamber and placing the plugs at the bottom of the Ascending Passage. But he maintains that the well, or the part of it included in the masonry, is as old as the Pyramid itself (which is *inconceivable*); for, like the "psychic" ducts, it was correctly laid out and not crudely bored *through* the existing masonry.

In order to make the Grand Gallery's north landing meet the descending shaft formerly used by the workers, the stonemasons must have known where the shaft came out at the level of the floor—which was a simple matter, since the shaft was accessible where it opened onto the Descending Passage near the Subterranean Chamber. This connection was made, in my opinion, under Ramesses II, 3,550 years after the monument was erected, when it was decided to use the lower chamber once again for the minor isiac initiation and the central chamber for the major initiation.

Concerning the so-called Queen's Chamber, Bruchet (pp. 85–97) shows clearly that it could not have been, as Borchardt and Lauer claim, the sepulchral chamber of a second plan, which was itself later abandoned.

Concerning the apertureless (!) "ventilation ducts," the author puts forth a particularly unusual and, in my view, worthless hypothesis. He writes:

> Since they weren't designed either for ventilation or as a connection to the outside, why do we not find actual acoustic ducts ending in sound boxes? This assumption implies the existence, in the Pyramid's bulk, of other compartments unknown at present. It also presupposes that we are dealing here with a room whose function was in no way funerary, but whose layout was required to fill an important role in a very regulated ritual. . . .

He then reviews the various purposes to which the four-corbeled niche located in the chamber's east wall could have been set, and he is inclined to see it as a site reserved for the statue of a god.

To my mind, there is no doubt that the "Queen's Chamber" was simply the Pyramid's *serdab,* containing the statue of Cheops' "double," the two dead-end ducts being but "psychic" ducts intended for the visits of the deceased pharaoh's *ba,* or soul.

THE GRAND GALLERY (pp. 98–110)

In regard to this gallery, Bruchet asserts first of all that one thing is certain: no one prior to Al Mamun was able to penetrate this far. In my opinion, this is a rather flimsy assertion.

In the technical supplement relating to the gallery (art. 128), Bruchet counts the same number of holes in both banquettes—twenty-eight times two (fifty-six for both sides)—and notes: "It is proper to add to these those located in the southeast and southwest angles of the upper horizontal landing, which brings their number to fifty-eight."

The count is inexact; there are twenty-eight slots in the east banquette and twenty-seven in the west banquette, including the two slots in the square of the upper landing. The twenty-eighth, lowermost slot in the west banquette is now occupied by the opening of the well, the banquette having been cut into at this point.

I have already shown that the Grand Gallery was the "gallery of the ancestors," containing twenty-seven facing pairs of statues of Cheops' predecessors, his two statues being located, appropriately, on the upper landing, on either side of the entrance to the chamber of the portcullises. As I pointed out earlier, Cheops was the twenty-eighth king of Egypt starting with Menes.

Bruchet criticizes and disproves the hypothesis that these slots were used for erecting a scaffolding with a floor designed to hold the blocks to be used in closing the Pyramid's passages. He notes that the slots do not all have the same dimensions or depth and that their restraining beds are set at an angle.

In the conclusion of his book (p. 163), Bruchet states that for an indeterminate length of time these slots must have served as housings for pieces of wood supporting emblems or something else entirely.

THE ANTECHAMBER (pp. 111–19)

For Bruchet, the 0.90-meter-high step (the "Great Step") has an esoteric significance: ". . . It announced the appearance of an essential element in the interior layout."

He describes the chamber and calls attention to the granite lintel, a false valve composed of two superincumbent elements, the upper one showing a horseshoe-shaped projection that he considers to be the letter *tau*.

According to Bruchet, the three granite portcullises, whose bearings are visible, *were never set in place*. In a footnote he mentions Vandier's opinion:

It is curious that no trace of these enormous monoliths has been found: every preparation had been made to receive them (the platform in the Grand Gallery, the slots in the Antechamber), but it is possible that they were never brought into the Pyramid. Indeed, it seems improbable that the violators, having succeeded in breaking the portcullises, should have gone to the trouble of clearing away the fragments while following a particularly difficult course.

Bruchet demonstrates the inanity of Borchardt's attempt to reconstruct the manner of closing the portcullises *using three poles as pulleys.* Thus far Bruchet is perfectly correct, but he is wrong in claiming that the portcullises were not lowered. They were indeed lowered, with the help of three large poles, which, being *wedged,* could not function as pulleys—indeed, the east side was arranged so as to prevent *any rotation.* I have dealt with this question elsewhere, by showing the role of the double lintel in the closing process, a role that no one else has yet suspected.

THE KING'S CHAMBER (pp. 120–28)

After having provided the dimensions of the room, the sarcophagus, and the ventilation ducts, Bruchet writes:

> Even the greatest skeptics must yield to the evidence! The cask probably never held a body; indeed, after studying the blocks in the Ascending Passage, I am certain that this must have been the case. Moreover, the presence of the two ducts connecting the King's Chamber with the air outside made this room unfit for the preservation of a mummy. There is absolutely no explanation for these ventilation ducts if one accepts the sole hypothesis of the tomb. . . . Moreover, if the desired outcome had been to permit the deceased king's soul to exit toward the light, a single shaft would have sufficed. . . . In the construction plan, it would have been easier to have [these shafts] proceed horizontally rather than build them through regular courses at a rather steep angle. Such a solution would have avoided the problem of having to see that they were sealed from the outside, and also the problem of their filling up with rainwater and dust raised by sandstorms. If this is the direction they were given, it was only, it seems, out of a concern for better ventilation, in order to allow a freer and, above all, more rapid change of air. . . .

However, he adds:

> The only fact I can deduce is that these ducts were not created solely for utilitarian reasons; they served a more ritual function as well, concerning which there is not much I can say.

As I see it, the two "ventilation" ducts of the King's Chamber, like those of the *serdab,* were sealed at both ends with plaques; thus they could not become plugged up with desert sand. They were psychic ducts which were opened under Ramesses II in order that the "central chamber" might be used in the second degree of the isiac initiation.

One error of Bruchet's should be pointed out; he writes (p. 126), "I must add that the height corresponding to the level of this chamber is itself equal to the radius of a circumference equal in length to the perimeter of the base." This statement is false; the radius of the circumference equal in length to the perimeter is the Pyramid's actual height up to its graphic summit.

Bruchet notes that the east-west axis of the King's Chamber coincides with the Pyramid's axis, and he adopts Petrie's figures for the room's dimensions. He thinks it is possible to deduce from these data the fact that the chamber is located at the Pyramid's center of gravity. This is incorrect: a pyramid's center of gravity is located three-quarters of the way down from its summit—that is, at one-quarter its height starting from the base, and not at two-sevenths, as Bruchet maintains.[21]

THE RELIEVING CHAMBERS (pp. 129–34)

Concerning the quarriers' graffiti discovered in the relieving chambers, among which is found a cartouche with the name "Khnum-Khufu,"[22] Bruchet queries whether Khufu represents a pharaoh who ruled conjointly with Cheops; he believes that it was indeed Cheops who built the Great Pyramid, but that he dedicated it to the god Khnum. I have already discussed this matter.

THE SPHINX

First let me point out an error on Bruchet's part: he ascribes to the Sphinx a length of 57 meters, instead of 71.80 meters including the paws.

Is the Sphinx a mysterious symbol, effigy of a king or a god?

Concerning its age, Maspero believes that its *predynastic* construction is forever lost in the mists of time and that it represents the god Horakhty, "Horus of the two places of light."

Bruchet is inclined to believe that the Great Pyramid and the Sphinx belong to the same complex, and that the Sphinx, beneath Cheops' features, represents the god Khnum.

WHAT IS THE GREAT PYRAMID? (pp. 159–66)

As this chapter concludes Bruchet's interesting study, I feel I should provide extracts of the main passages, since the author's ideas agree, *in part,* with my own. He writes:

> . . . But let us review briefly the main aspects of its layout. The most likely course would be to continue believing that the Subterranean Chamber was indeed meant to house a corpse—that of Cheops, as it happened. It is nonetheless true that this chamber was *deliberately left unfinished*; access to it must have remained open, or very nearly so.
>
> These reservations induce me to amend the customary rationale. I would say, rather, that the chamber was thought to be meant to house a corpse. While it was indeed hollowed out so as to represent what must have been a funerary cave, its abandoned appearance exudes an aura of uselessness. . . . [23]
>
> If the conclusions that end this book are correct, we have here proof that the material, physical plane represented by the lower part, though containing pitfalls and dangers, is, on the whole, merely an expression of the finite and of vanity. It is fitting, therefore, that we should seek the solution elsewhere, higher up.
>
> Once its relieving system had been set up, the upper chamber, as well as the chamber directly beneath it, was no longer accessible except by way of the "well." This is the final conclusion arrived at in the course of my description and in the accompanying discussion. [24]
>
> If Cheops was not entombed in the lower cave of the Pyramid, where, then, is his tomb?

Bruchet then takes up Herodotus' account and questions why it should not be taken as accurate. And concerning the high temple located to the east of the Pyramid, he writes:

> Why couldn't this temple be simply a jubilean monument? And perhaps also the monument in which the

transmission of the *neter* between the deceased king and his heir apparent took place. Why could it not have been there that the latter came to receive the two crowns?[25]

Concerning the Antechamber, Bruchet writes:

As with a real tomb, it is indeed a question of a recess for the portcullises; but here this recess was only conceived as a simulacrum.

As for the horseshoe-shaped projection of the "false door" lintel, still in place, Bruchet sees in it the hieroglyph of the letter *T,* having great symbolic significance; according to him, it represents the principle of universal equilibrium! I have provided another, completely unsymbolic and highly practical explanation.

In regard to the sarcophagus, Bruchet states that it never contained Cheops' remains. He recalls that, in the pyramid of Sekhem-Khet, which Zakariah Goneim discovered in 1953, the hermetically sealed alabaster sarcophagus was *empty!*

. . . However, the presence of a mortuary sheaf placed not far from it proves that funerary rites were indeed performed. This sheaf was composed of Ferula, an aromatic plant from Libya, which archaeological texts associate with the jubilean feasts of the *sed.*[26]

Bruchet's conclusion agrees with my own on many points, though not all. He writes:

If the Pyramid is not a tomb, it is either a cenotaph, or the hiding place of a secret closely linked with the funerary rites, or, finally, a place where death and resurrection meet—all in all, a place of "initiation."

This does not preclude its having other missions, more or less discernible in its external and internal symbolism . . . and nothing prevents the Pyramid from aspiring, at the same time, to a more positive destination. Moreover, if the master builder intentionally set certain secrets—cosmogonical, mathematical, astronomical, etc.—in the Pyramid's dimension, volumes, and shapes, I do not think he would have done so . . . unless the various chambers had been assigned a more specific function.

In order to become a *son of Horus* and incarnate the *neter* of the race, the future king, it seems, had to submit to a veritable training. . . .

Is it feasible to suggest—without running the risk of grossly misinterpreting the Egyptian soul—that in order to achieve this state of omnipotence, the king did *not* have to go through all the magical and other kinds of rites? Before he possessed this knowledge, the king was assuredly prepared. . . . It seems logical to concede that during his life on earth, he had to undergo the indispensable initiations.

Let us recall, in this respect, that the majority of the sovereigns of this era seem to have been very knowledgeable. To some, the ancient Egyptians ascribed treatises on astronomy, medicine, or magic; to others, books on alchemy or hermetism. Cheops is among the latter group.

In order to treat all the gods as equals, it was essential that the king ascend all the degrees that would bring him up to their level.

It is absolutely necessary that we forget what we are—that is, twentieth-century Westerners—if we wish to understand what a *son of Horus,* possessor of the royal magic power, was.

The initiation is a death followed by a resurrection into a new life. Osiris himself is but an initiate, and all that separates the old king who dies and the young prince who will incarnate the *neter* is a long funereal vigil. . . .

Thus ends the book.

If I have insisted on submitting Lauer's and Bruchet's work to a thorough and occasionally harsh critique, it is because the comparison of their ideas—these two authors, both specialists in architecture, are at opposite poles—permits a closer grasp of the Great Pyramid's true destination. It is now up to me to express my own views on a subject that I know well (having verified all of the Great Pyramid's dimensions, external as well as internal) and to present my views for criticism, which I hope will be as constructive and harsh as my own.

First, however, I must point out that if I have not cited Maspero, it is because he never made any specific, firsthand study of the Pyramid. This is also true of Jacques Pirenne, from whose work I will, however, extract two interesting passages that agree in part with my own thought.

Pirenne

This author writes (*Histoire de la civilisation de l'Egypte ancienne* [Paris: A. Michel, 1961], vol. 1, p. 211):

In the Great Pyramid of Cheops, the chamber of the sarcophagus, where the royal mummy was kept, is connected with the outside by means of two passages that emerge midway up the Pyramid so as to allow the royal soul to leave and reenter its mausoleum at will.

Topped by its golden point, which sparkles under the rays of the sun, it is, like the sun itself, the tabernacle in which the supreme god, in the form of the royal soul, joins the earth. It is the sacred place where, in the mortal remains of a king, immortalized as a mummy, the spirit of the world contrives to take on concrete form. Thus, without leaving the earth, the pyramids touch heaven. And the bodies of kings, living gods, carefully enshrined in [the pyramid's] immense womb, are like the souls of the world, both present on this earth and raised to heaven with the pyramid's help.

Pirenne clearly understood the role of the two so-called ventilation ducts in the King's Chamber. Like the ducts in the Queen's Chamber (*serdab*), they must have originally been hermetically sealed by plaques. If one subscribes to the belief that they were open ever since the Pyramid was erected, then it is impossible to claim, as many Egyptologists do, that the "central chamber" was ever Cheops' burial chamber. I will come back to this subject later.

As for the "golden point," I do not know upon which data or text the author relies. I believe the presence of a gnomon is undeniable, since the Great Pyramid was the solar temple of the god Khnum; his hieroglyphic determinative, distinguished by Reisner in a Giza mastaba, leaves no doubt in this regard and explains the necessary presence of a platform.

Pirenne poses the question of whether the pyramids were painted (p. 236, fn. 204), a possibility Lauer denies. This fact is certain, and I will take up this matter in a special section.

THE EGYPTIAN MYSTIQUE

Our mentality, that of twentieth-century Westerners, makes it difficult for us to understand the mentality of Egyptians of the fifth millenium B.C.[27]

Throughout history, Egypt was a melting pot in which various ethnic mixtures continually took place, so it is logical to find there multiple religious concepts, with each nome having its own particular gods. A synthesis of beliefs, attempted by Akhnaton, proved impossible. Two religious cults prevailed, however: the Thinic or Hermopolitan, which worshipped Osiris; and the Heliopolitan, which worshipped the sun god Ra.

A curious Ra-Osiris amalgam was to develop after the early dynasties. Though immortal, as the son of Ra, the pharaoh had, like Osiris, to be assassinated upon the death of his predecessor, in order to be reborn through the magic of the isiac rites. Moreover, he had to die and be reborn symbolically every twenty-eight years (*sed*[28]), as Osiris was assassinated during the twenty-eighth year of his reign.

The Egyptian of the pharaonic Old Kingdom was deeply religious and totally convinced of the mysterious, occult powers of magic. He believed implicitly in the reality of the gods and was certain that representations of them, magically alive, could force them to remain in contact with the earth and with man. In his mind there was no doubt that the pharaoh, the possessor of the divine *mana,* was the son of Ra and could communicate directly with the god. He was certain that magical practices could "animate" statues and confer on them strange faculties. For example, the Sphinx (Harmachis, Horus on the horizon) was thought to have the power, in the steadiness and force of his gaze, to compel the sun god himself to rise each morning in the eastern horizon. Magically, the gigantic statue *enchained* the sun god along his orbit and forced him to return daily.

Just as the Demiurge, through its *Word,* created the world, the words pronounced by the king were supposed to materialize immediately. The texts of offerings engraved on the walls of tombs were magic, and thought to materialize "at the sound" (*perit kheru*). A visitor reading a text aloud would be enough to make the "responding" servants (*ushebtiu*) come to life and serve food to the deceased.

The entire mentality of the Old Kingdom was marked by *imitative magic,* which is also found in the ceremonies of the "mysteries" of the Middle Ages and even now in the celebration of the Christian mass and in the Masonic rites.

The Hermopolitan Mystique

The legend of Osiris is well known. Enclosed in a coffin through trickery, Osiris was thrown into the Nile by his brother Set and Set's fellow conspirators. His body, which Isis sought and found at Byblos on the Syrian coast, hidden under a tamarisk and brought back to Egypt, was again dismembered by Set. Nevertheless, Isis, with the help of her son Horus as well as the jackal god Anubis and the ibis god Thoth, reassembled the scattered remains. Osiris' reconstituted body was brought back to life through Isis' magic.

According to Plutarch, the assassination of Osiris took place on the 17th day of the month Athyr in the twenty-eighth year of his reign. In the tropical calendar of the "Two Lands," this date corresponds to the winter solstice (December 21 in the Gregorian calendar).

Starting with the Old Kingdom, the raising of the *dad* pillar, a magical representation of Osiris' resurrection, took place each year on the 19th day of Athyr. This pillar, generally thought of as an acacia stripped of its branches, was actually, in my opinion, the representation of the four obelisk pillars (seen in a row) used at Heliopolis, Tanis, Mendes, etc., in determining the solstices and equinoxes. Since they were used to check the *stability* of the seasons, they became the symbol of it.

However, since the winter solstice was in Egypt the time of renewal and germination, and thus of the resurrection of nature, the 19th day of Athyr, the date of Osiris' resurrection, was also considered to be the date of Ra's resurrection. Therefore the two gods Ra and Osiris became identified with each other.

At Dendera, in order to symbolize this resurrection for all to see, grains of wheat were incorporated, forty-five days in advance, in an effigy of Osiris made of Nile mud. On the 19th day of Athyr, when the wheat had sprouted, Osiris was declared risen.

Osiris had thus become both a sun god and an agrarian god; but, in that he incarnated resurrection, he was also the god of the dead. As such, he presided over the judgment of souls. The soul of the deceased, having surmounted pitfalls and trials and passed through the seven infernal portals guarded by terrifying spirits, arrived in the last room, and there, in Osiris' presence, the weighing of the soul took place. If its weight did not exceed that of the feather of Maat, goddess of justice and truth, the soul was proclaimed "just of voice" (maa-kheru) and admitted to eternal life in the underworld of Amenti, the western empire of the blessed. In the event of an unfavorable weighing-in, the soul of the deceased was swallowed on the spot by the devouring monster Amemet.

There was nothing particularly attractive about this underworld life of the soul in Amenti. Up to the time of the Sixth Dynasty, only the king could lay claim to a luminous afterlife in the company of his father, Ra, by means of the Heliopolitan ritual ceremonies.

It is certain that this royal prerogative was the cause of the period of civil disorder in Egypt, a religious as well as social revolution that took place between the Seventh and Tenth Dynasties. Funeral temples were sacked, tombs violated, the isiac mysteries exposed. From that time on, the "plebian" had as much claim to celestial light as the pharaoh himself.

During the first six dynasties, however, the pharaoh was *sole* master of not only the earthly fate of his people, but also their fate in the beyond. For the pharaoh alone possessed a portion of the divine *ka,* and he alone was in constant contact with the deity. As the son of Ra through theogamy, he was the *mediator* between heaven and earth. It was thus essential that his portion of the divine *ka* remain on earth forever and pass, after the king's death, into the body of his successor.

This *ka,* a part of the cosmic generative force, should be compared to the *mana* of African and Polynesian clans, which is thought to be preserved through the *ritual manducation* of ancestors. And does not the Christian priest magically eat Christ's *mana* in the form of bread and wine to this day? It is not impossible that in Egypt, in prehistoric times, the new king should have been compelled to consume his predecessor's brain and heart ritually. It is even conceivable that since Osiris reigned only twenty-eight years, his successors were permitted to reign for only the same period, at the end of which they were put to death. This would explain the ceremony of the *sed,* a ceremony of imitative magic permitting the suppression of the criminal ancestral ritual custom.

The Heliopolitan Mystique

As opposed to Osiris, god of Hermopolis, god of the dead in the underworld, the Heliopolitan god Khepri-Ra-Atum is the god of light and life. Only the king's soul, after its periplus through Amenti and its vindication before the tribunal of Osiris, had the prerogative of ascending to heaven in order to join the solar barque of his father, Ra.

Up to the end of the Sixth Dynasty the Egyptian mentality was satisfied with the Hermopolitan concept and its shadowy afterlife. It was enough for the Egyptian of the Old Kingdom to be convinced that his fate on earth as well as in the beyond was forever presided over by his dead king.

How could this be?

According to the primitive Egyptian mystique, the king's person was composed of two elements: the *body* (*tchet*) and the *spirit,* the latter being composed of three distinct principles: the *ka,* the *ba,* and the *akh.*[29] The *ka,* as I said earlier, is a portion of the divine *ka,* of divine omniscience, of the universal *mana* (the *ka* was the royal perquisite); the *ba* is the theoretically immortal soul, the being's personification; and the *akh* is the power that generates and receives waves, the *aura* of spirits, connected to the life of the perishable body (*khet*).

Upon the king's death, therefore, it was essential: (1) to keep his body latently alive, in order that his *akh* might allow him to remain in contact with his soul (*ba*), which had joined the solar barque; and (2) to keep the divine *ka* connected to the earth by forcing it to pass magically into the body of the king's successor. Such were the goals of the royal isiac funerary rites.

1. We are ill informed concerning the tapping of the

deceased king's *ka* and its transferral into the body of his successor. It is probable that, after the king's death, his successor had to die by symbolic assassination in order to attain the supreme initiation; the priests' magic could then effect the transferral.

2. The magical operation of the transferral of the *ka* was followed by the mummification of the royal body. Since the preservation of the mummy could not be ensured eternally, a statue (the "double"), usually made of diorite or basalt and placed in a special chamber (the *serdab*), had, like the mummy itself, to undergo the rites of the opening of the mouth and eyes. Then it could act for the mummy, having become—like the latter—magically alive.

A second statue of the king, draped in the osirian shroud and having itself undergone the rites of animation, was placed in the *naos* of the cella of the funerary temple adjoining the pyramid. The king or high priest came there each morning to repeat the rites of the opening of the mouth and eyes, and to pronounce *the name of Ra,* the seventy-third secret divine name, which Isis extorted by means of a serpent's bite.

Alive once more, the royal mummy and its doubles would become the receptacles of the deceased king's *akh,* the power that generates and receives waves, permitting communication with the soul (*ba*) sailing in the solar barque.

3. The *ka* and the *akh* being, in this manner, sustained on earth, the ascension of the soul, or *ba,* to heaven became the ultimate phase of the royal deification. But first the soul had to descend into Hades and appear before the tribunal of Osiris. In this regard, it conformed to the lot of all souls, according to the Hermopolitan concept.

Once declared *maa-kheru* ("justified"), the soul could then attempt the ultimate test: ascension into heaven in order to join the solar barque. It is uncertain, however, whether the pharaoh's heart had to be weighed, for the king, son of the sun god, was considered to be moral perfection incarnate.

4. The sky, whence the rain falls, could only be an immense basin full of water, the universal ocean, the celestial *nut* upon which the solar barque sails; the provision of the morning and evening barques placed near the pyramids was thus indispensable.

The priests certainly did not subscribe to this childish concept of the firmament, but it was a carry-over from ancestral beliefs that had to be respected. This was also true of those ingenuous ladders found in the *Book of the Dead* which were raised to the sky in order to permit the soul to ascend. These were later replaced by the steps of the pyramid, whether obvious or disguised under facing.

How was it possible to effect this prodigious ascent into space while shielding the soul from the relentless terrestrial attraction? Even if its weight did not exceed that of the "feather of Truth," the soul, like light, was thought to possess a materiality that, however faint, constituted an insurmountable obstacle to its ascension. Just as protons must be projected into space by centrifugal force, so it was necessary to provide the soul with sufficient energy to overcome both the solar blast (centripetal force) and the earth's gravity.

From where was this energy derived?

First of all, from the deity, by giving the tomb a pyramidal shape whose section magically represented the divine triad. According to Plutarch, the sacred Egyptian triangle, with sides proportional to the numbers 3, 4, and 5, represented, respectively, Osiris, Isis, and Horus. Starting with the Fourth Dynasty, all the Egyptian pyramids followed this pattern. Only the Great Pyramid at Giza strays from this rule, and the fact that the slope of the pyramid of Cheops was not isiac is perhaps one of the reasons he was dishonored by the priests of the time.

Because of this divine pyramidal pattern, the Hermopolitan triad was directly linked to the success of the extraordinary miracle of the *ba*'s ascension into heaven.

Did the ancient Egyptians believe, as some people now think, that the pyramid's four faces enabled them to tap cosmic energy, particularly the rays of the blazing star Sirius (Isis to the Egyptians)? Although extremely doubtful, this theory of the tapping of energies is not impossible. In 1969 a team of American scholars, supplied with ultramodern equipment and an IBM computer, attempted to locate the "spaces" in the pyramid of Kephren by counting the cosmic particles (mesons and muons) that traverse the pyramid under all its azimuths.

But even if this theory is incorrect, the construction of the grandiose pyramidal complex was not "an idle and foolish ostentation of royal wealth," as Pliny calls it, but a *grandiose act of faith,* materializing the mysticism of a people convinced that their future destiny was linked to the success of the royal soul's miraculous ascension into heaven. To be sure, this opinion was not held by all—particularly not by those pariahs of various nationalities, the slaves or prisoners who, like beasts of burden under a rain of blows, hauled the monstrous blocks used in building the sepulcher of the all-powerful monarch claiming supreme divinity.

With the help of the *Book of the Dead* and the frescoes found in the tombs, we can attempt, without running the risk of committing flagrant errors, to reconstruct the funerary ceremonies that took place during the burial of a king under the Old Kingdom.

For the Egyptian people, thoroughly religious and mystical, this day was crucial; it passed in an atmosphere of exacerbated anxiety, close to a collective insanity. This collective insanity is not peculiar to ancient Egypt: throughout the world, up to the present day, there have been incredible scenes attributable to the political or religious fanaticism of crowds.

The king's body (*tchet*), having undergone the mummification processes in the valley temple for seventy days and having been subjected to the last rites of the opening of the mouth and eyes, was finally placed in its three coffins, one inside the other, then escorted in a cortege up to the pyramid's entrance by way of the covered passage.

While the professional female mourners raised strident cries and laments to heaven and clawed their cheeks till the blood ran, the coffin slid down the descending passage to the subterranean chamber, whose granite walls defied eternity. It was then placed inside the sarcophagus, which had awaited the royal mummy since the pyramid was built.

The royal furniture had been placed in the adjoining chambers several days earlier. Thus the "respondants" were able to continue to ensure service to His Divine Majesty.

Once the final ritual lustrations and fumigations were completed, the heavy lid was slid over the royal remains as the college of priests, slowly and arduously climbing back up the descending passage while chanting liturgical prayers, left the pyramid's interior. A terrible roar, which caused the entire pyramid to tremble for minutes on end and reverberated to the very center of the earth, announced the fall of the heavy granite portcullises and the final isolation of the deceased king from the outside world. In the heavy silence that followed, the laid-out mummy was alone in the presence of its soul, which, hovering about the sarcophagus, had to attempt the supreme test and take flight toward heaven.

The sacerdotal college returned to the great funerary temple to the east of the pyramid. The mourners' laments ceased. The ancient *Maneros* resounded, amplified boundlessly by the multitude crowding the square—a haunting sight in which was revealed all the psychic force of an aroused people, bordering on insanity.

Appearing at last atop the peristyle, the high priest announced the good news: the "double" in the *naos* had shown itself and the royal soul had happily boarded Ra's divine barque! And while the sun at its zenith darted forth its scorching rays, a frenetic joy exploded: The king is god! Ra's barque is forever stable!

As if in affirmation, way up in the sky the millennary circle of sacred hawks silently wheeled, without a single wing-stroke, in the orb of the radiant sun.

Alas, the stability announced by the high priest was far from eternal; this sacred despotism was not to outlast the Sixth Dynasty. Fifteen hundred years after Menes there occurred a revolution that was at once social and religious, plunging Egypt into misfortune and desolation. The royal pyramidal tombs were defiled and sacked, the isiac rites exposed, the statues of kings smashed to bits and consigned to the trash heap. For the people had suddenly tired of being mere outcasts, eligible only for a miserable afterlife in the shadowy Amenti, to be spent contemplating the greenish flesh of the god of the dead, while the royal soul lived on in the light! The people wanted to be able, like the pharaoh, to attain to heavenly life in the azure firmament, to aspire to the "journey of Millions of Years" through the stars. So the Heliopolitan rites were democratized, and every Egyptian was able to build himself a pyramidal tomb, however modest—his own "pointed cubic stone."

Let us heed "The Admonitions of an Old Sage":[30]

> In the sublime Hall of Justice, the writings are taken away, and the secret places are thrown open. The magical formulas are disclosed and become inefficacious (?), because men have them in their memory. The poor man attains to the condition of the divine Ennead. This rule of the Hall of the Thirty Judges is disclosed. The secrets of the land, whose bounds are unknown, are disclosed . . . The Serpent (the protector of the Palace) is taken from his hiding-place. The secrets of the Kings of Upper and Lower Egypt are disclosed . . .
>
> There is no more sailing to Byblos to-day . . .

Once the revolutionary fever had been assuaged, the kings of the Eleventh and Twelfth Dynasties resumed the construction of sumptuous pyramidal tombs, which, although equipped with secret chambers disguised with incredible ingenuity, were no less immune to vandalism than those built by their predecessors.

Under the Eighteenth Dynasty a new trend developed. At Thebes, on the west bank of the Nile, an entire mountain, carved into a pyramid,[31] was used by kings and their families collectively. Interminable descending passages plunge deep into the bedrock, toward the center of the sacred pyramidal mountain dominating the Valley of the Kings. Out of over five hundred tombs discovered up to the present (including sixty-two magically inviolable royal tombs), only one has come down to us nearly intact, that of Tutankhamen, Neb Kheperu Ra!

Had the magic isiac rites and formulas by this time lost their power? *Sic transit gloria mundi!*

THE IMPORTANCE OF THE NAME

In so-called primitive societies it is believed that, through magic, "the sign creates the thing, and the word the event." Thus it is only necessary to express a thing *ritually* for it to materialize magically. That is the Egyptian theory of "the voice that emerges" (*per kheru*), which is simply the dogma of the "Word."

Nothing exists before it has been named; to call a creature by its name is to create, to give birth to its personality, in order then to dominate it. This is why in the book of Genesis, chapter 2, God allowed Adam to name every living creature.

The name is one of the aspects of the *ka;* it animates the body it penetrates. That which no longer has a name no longer exists. To *mutilate* a being's image while simultaneously making *its name disappear* is to annihilate it forever by destroying both its earthly and its divine life. This is why the Christian bishops ordered that the Egyptian "living statues," which had undergone the rites of the opening of the mouth and eyes, be methodically mutilated and their names effaced.

If in the course of the performance of a "mystery" a living creature (or its figuration) plays the historical role of a god or a hero, *it is identified cabalistically* with the latter, on the express condition that it bear the latter's secret name. This secret name would be that which a mother mysteriously confers upon her child at the moment of birth, and it is generally unknown to the being who unconsciously bears it. The primary goal of the isiac initiation is the Socratic "Know thyself"; for whoever does not know his secret name, the name of his *ka,* cannot claim to be his own master.

Knowing the *ka* name of a god allows one to become the god's master. In this respect, the legent of Isis' cobra is much more interesting than that of the serpent in Genesis.

Isis, desiring to dominate Ra and become immortal, wishes to succeed in learning the god's secret name. She models a serpent out of clay, which comes to life through the action of the sun's rays and magical incantations. Upon Isis' order, the cobra bites the god Ra during his daily round. Since the bite causes him terrible suffering, Ra convokes the council of the gods and begs Isis, the great magician, to ease his pain.

"O, tell me thy name, holy father," Isis answers him, "for he shall live whose name shall be revealed." Ra, aware of the danger, tries to elude the question. Finally, overcome by pain, Ra pronounces his name, after having provided successively the seventy-two names by which he is known to man. "I consent that Isis shall search into me, and that my name shall pass from me into her." (In the hieroglyphic text this name is represented by a heart: *ib.*)

And when the time arrives "for the heart . . . to come forth," Isis tells her son Horus to state the god's name. Thus Ra had delivered up, with his heart, his true name, his cabalistic name, the secret of his power. According to the cabala, in fact, God has seventy-two known names and one ineffable name, unknown to man, which only the seven archangels might pronounce.

The supreme isiac initiation (the second and last stage of the initiation) had as its sole purpose the transmission of this name, which constituted *the Word*. For in order that the god's cabalistic name should remain among men forever, Isis established the initiation and the isiac mysteries, the rites of which were, according to Diodorus Siculus, the means of achieving immortality.

Unfortunately, very little is known about these initiatory rites, which must have borne some analogy to the Eleusinian mysteries. There are only a few representations on the walls of the temple at Dendera to tell us anything at all, and they lead us to believe that the laying on of hands and magical magnetic passes were essential; but the incantatory words that accompanied these rites have not come down to us.

However, it is possible that these rites were partially transmitted—in distorted and defiled form—by certain initiatory sects. The collations of the major orders of the Catholic Church, for instance, are clearly marked by isiac memories. Other esoteric sects (Sabean, Druse, Essenian, etc.) have preserved part of the Egyptian magical rites.

Freemasonry, in its first three degrees, is certainly very close to the isiac rites. But since the Masonic rites have come down to us in the West by way of Judaism, they bear the indelible stamp of the Jewish saga. They are, moreover, not very old; they certainly postdate the Christian chronology. They lack any initiatory value from the fourth to the thirty-third degree.[32] Few Masons are aware that their work within the temple is carried out under the aegis of the Egyptian trinity.

The radiating delta is simply the representation, in cross section, of the isiac pyramid; it is the double triangle representing the divine triad Osiris (3), Isis (4), Horus (5). The eye at the center of the delta is simply Osiris' hieroglyphic name:

Usir

In most of the temples of the Grand Orient and in all those of the Grand Lodge, one will note the addition of the Hebraic tetragram I E Vo E. This addition is a *veritable spoliation*.

The flaming five-pointed star is simply Sirius = Sothis = Isis. The addition of a *G* (God) inside the star of Isis can be attributed to the Scottish masons.

The interlacing cord encircling the temple is simply a series of *sau* amulets, magic Egyptian fetishes of divine protection. Moreover, in heraldry, the knotted cord is the protective symbol of the Widow and decorates the exterior of her coat of arms. In the masters' distress signal to the "Widow's children," the lodges' ritual indicates that "Free Masons are the sons of a widow and that this widow is Isis."[33]

THE EMBLEMS OF A MASONIC LODGE

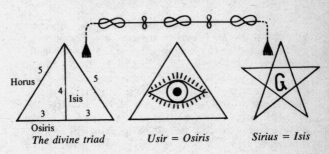

Horus 5 — 5
4 Isis
3 — 3
Osiris
The divine triad   *Usir = Osiris*   *Sirius = Isis*

In Freemasonry, during the initiation to the degree of master, the companion no longer plays the role of Osiris; the latter has been replaced by Hiram, the architect of Solomon's temple. As Hiram, the companion is supposed to be assassinated, then brought back to life through the joint efforts of the Master of the lodge and the two guardians playing the respective roles of Horus and Anubis. The scenario is thus identical to that of the resurrection of Osiris. It is both curious and amusing to note that in this exclusively male sect the Master ritually plays the part of a woman, the goddess Isis. Whereas the Greek Eleusinian initiatory rites are essentially feminine, women are totally excluded from the Judeo-Masonic ritual ceremony . . . and yet the initiation comprises two successive rebirths, thus two deliveries. How, then, can the elimination of women be justified? The Grand College of rites ought seriously to reconsider this matter.

In Egypt, the ceremony of Osiris' resurrection in the new king must have taken place in a nearly identical manner. Ritually dead (perhaps drugged), the king's successor was placed in a sarcophagus which, according to the rather inexplicit ritual represented at Dendera, must have been located in an upper chamber, whereas the deceased king's (Osiris') remains were taken down to a lower chamber.

The cabalistic name that the high priest murmured during the animation has not come down to us. Could this be the "Lost Word" the Rosicrucian knights seek in vain?

In Yaschar's curious book,[34] we find the following text concerning Joseph's vizierate:

> . . . According to another custom, any man who knew how to speak the seventy tongues could mount all seventy steps up to the king's throne, but whoever did not know all seventy tongues could only climb as many steps as he knew tongues. A special law of the Egyptians, in force at that time and strictly observed, stated that no one was fit to rule and govern his country if he did not know how to speak the seventy tongues . . . and an angel gave Joseph the gift of speaking the seventy tongues.

This odd text is *certainly* directly related to the isiac initiation, and the term that Migne translates as *langue* ("tongue") must have actually been the *word* characterizing the initiatory degree attained; these "passwords" must have been the seventy-two different names of the deity: Khepri, Ra, Atum, Horus, Harsiesis, Harmachis . . .[35]

The "legend of Ra," which I outlined earlier, may help us to understand. Ra, bitten by Isis' magic serpent, gave his seventy-two divine names successively before divulging his *real name,* the secret of his power. And Isis established the initiations in order that the name of the sun god should remain in the memory of men eternally. It is probable that *only* the pharaoh and the high priests possessed this name, which magically enabled them to subdue the deity.

It is obvious that in order to become a possessor of the name, the pharaoh had first to attain the seventy-two initiatory degrees. The sublime name was imparted to him only upon the death of his predecessor; he then had to die a second time, before his third birth. For, according to Hermes Trismegistus, the initiate is he who has twice died and thrice been born.

During the first degree of the initiation, after a preparatory period, the neophyte, placed in the depths of a subterranean pit symbolizing the female reproductive tract, is supposed to die there and come back to life. In texts found in the pyramids this resurrection is conceived of as the goddess Nut actually giving birth. After having crawled along the uterine passage, the neophyte emerges into a chaotic subterranean chamber, its floor uneven and strewn with hemispheric monticles well known to Freemasons. This is the domain of the "rough stone," symbolizing the spiritual and moral state of the profane world against which the neophyte himself will have to struggle. His task will be to carve his "pointed cubic stone," symbol of the moral perfection necessary in order to become an *epopt* (seer).

After a harsh interrogation concerning the esoteric knowledge he has already acquired, the neophyte undergoes purification by three elements: water, air, and fire. He has now become a *myst*.

At the highest degree of the initiation, only attained under the Old Kingdom by the pharaoh and the grand hierophant, the *epopt* had to personify Osiris, be assassinated like him, and have his body laid out in the central chamber, where mysterious rites put him into contact with the divine *ka*. He was then, like Osiris, called back to life, through the joint efforts of the high priestess, playing the role of Isis, and two hierophants playing the roles of Horus and Anubis.

The layout of the Great Pyramid's chambers and passages is comparable—though not identical—to that of the crypts of the temple at Dendera. This temple contains no less than

DENDERA

Map of Crypt No. 7, used in the major isiac initiation, and of the central chamber, or "chamber of the resurrection" (G).

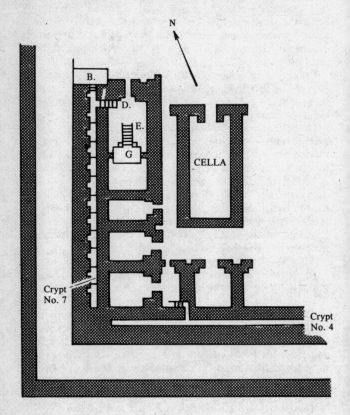

twenty crypts built into its thick walls and superimposed at various levels accessible via narrow stairways or secret entrances sealed by mobile stones.

It is not impossible that the periplus reserved for the highest degree of the isiac initiation under the Lagid Dynasty should have been that of Crypt No. 7, made up of a long subterranean pit 25 meters (40 cubits) long, 1 meter wide, and 1.80 meters high, transected along its entire length by 20-centimeter-high projections. This pit ends in a stairway with *three* steps, by means of which one reaches a small chamber (B). On the west side of the pit are located niches housing sculptures of deities.

Toward its north end, on the right, is found a stairway (D) with *four* steps, leading to an inner courtyard.

In the *center* of this courtyard is located a small temple (G), called, for some unknown reason, the "chapel of the new year." It would have been more logical to name it the "chapel of the resurrection." It is reached by a stairway having *seven* steps, framed by two Hathoric columns. On the ceiling is depicted Nut as she daily gives birth to the sun. The rays of the renascent sun fall upon a sarcophagus from which the head of the goddess Hathor is emerging, and causes two plants to sprout.[36]

It is curious to find the representation of the goddess Hathor, Isis' double, in Osiris' place, framed by two stalks of what looks like sprouting wheat. Had the isiac mysteries evolved under the Lagid Dynasty to the point of approaching the Eleusinian mysteries, so that Hathor was identical with Demeter?

It is certain that a sarcophagus, which has since disappeared, was located directly beneath the representation on the ceiling.

Obviously, we are dealing here with an initiatory temple. We find in the Masonic catechism:

Q. How did you reach the Central Chamber?
A. By a stairway that I climbed by three, five, and seven steps.

The importance of the name is shown particularly in the *Book of the Dead*. Entrance into Amenti, the divine domain, is contingent upon knowing all the names of the gods, the

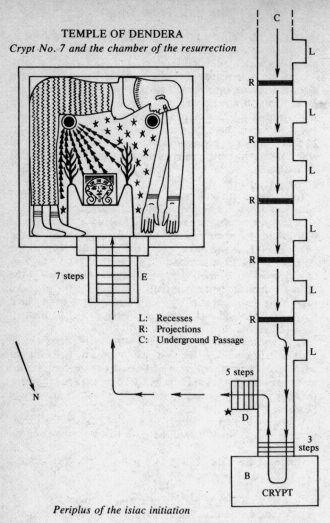

TEMPLE OF DENDERA
Crypt No. 7 and the chamber of the resurrection

7 steps   E

L: Recesses
R: Projections
C: Underground Passage

N

C

L

R

L

R

L

R

L

R

L

R

L

5 steps

D

3 steps

B

CRYPT

Periplus of the isiac initiation

The "chamber of the resurrection," located in the center of the courtyard, shows on its ceiling a representation of the goddess Nuit, symbol of nature, giving birth to the sun, Ra, at each winter solstice. The latter's rays cause Osiris' wheat to sprout, a symbol of resurrection.

goddesses, the forty-two "followers of Horus," as well as the names of the guardians of the seven doors and the ten portals. These doors themselves, thought to be alive, would not open unless the soul of the deceased pronounced their names correctly! More important, the very ground of Amenti would allow no access until its secret name had been uttered.

The knowledge of all the names constituting the "passwords" (about seventy in all) was indispensable to the soul of the deceased wishing to reach Osiris' throne in Amenti. To protect against a failure of memory, it was necessary to mention these names in a ritual placed on the mummy's body. In the ritual of Ani one can read:

> Nothing evil can befall me in this sanctuary of Maat for I know the names of the gods and of "those who follow Horus"! . . .
> Hail to you, Great God, master of the Truth! . . . I know you, I know your name; I know the name of the forty-two gods who live here, in the chamber of Maat . . .

Alas, the ineffable name handed down to us by Isis, which allowed humanity to be freed from the ascendancy of the gods, seems to be permanently lost. Tragic historical events have amply demonstrated the inefficacy of the isiac rites. The lost word seems destined to remain forever lost, despite claims to the contrary made by the Rosicrucian knights who have set off in search of it. Today the isiac survivance is but partially transmitted by the Masonic lodges, as well as by certain mysterious, very exclusive sects spread throughout the world.

But despite the symbolic rebirth of Hiram in each new master, the isiac rites seem to have vanished forever. "That which is scattered" seems destined to remain so eternally. Osiris, Aton, Adonai, Adonis, Hiram—all are dead, and over the vestiges of their obliterated tombs let us repeat this poignant, prophetic lament that Hermes Trismegistus, as quoted by Lactantius, addressed to Asclepius:

> . . . There will come a day when it will seem that it was in vain that the Egyptians guarded the cult of the gods with a pious spirit and a conscientious religion; and all their holy veneration, having served no purpose, will

be defeated. Divinity will leave the earth and return to heaven; it will abandon Egypt, and the land which was once the seat of the sacred doctrines will be empty and deprived of the presence of the gods.

For strangers will fill this region and the earth; not only will the doctrines be neglected, but—a fate even harsher—it will be, so to speak, in the name of the law that religion, piety, and the divine cult will be prohibited and persecuted. Then this very holy land, the site of sanctuaries and temples, will be full of corpses and tombs.

Why weep, Asclepius? What is even more painful, more lamentable, Egypt herself will submit to this influence; the worst evils will intoxicate her. This very holy land, lover of divinity, mistress of saintliness and piety, will set the example for the worst acts of cruelty. Men will inspire such repugnance that the world will cease to be admired . . . darkness will be preferred to light, death will seem more useful than life.

People will no longer raise their eyes toward heaven; the religious person will be thought crazy, the irreligious person will pass for a sage, madmen will be regarded as powerful, scoundrels will be taken as men of good faith . . . Yes, believe me: whoever devotes himself to the cult of the soul will do so at the risk of his life. A new law will be instituted: it will have nothing to do with what is holy, or with anything religious that is worthy of heaven and its celestial inhabitants; no one will believe in all that. There will be a painful divorce between the gods and men. Only the destroying angels will remain, intermingling with humanity; they will lead the wretched into all the sins of pride, into wars, depredation, fraud, into everything contrary to the true nature of souls . . .

O Egypt! Egypt! Of all thy doctrines, only the fables will survive, and thy posterity will no longer believe in them; there will subsist only words, engraved on stones, to attest to thy piety . . .

NOTES

1. Since the Great Pyramid's actual north base above the socle—the only datum that is certain—measures 230.253 meters, the value of the cubit used is 0.523 meter, and the height of the

214

Pyramid, up to its imaginary summit, is 0.5233 x 280 = 146.524 meters.

2. The figures 440 and 280 cubits proposed by Petrie, then Borchardt, are only hypothetical; but it is odd that Borchardt does not mention that, according to this hypothesis, the Great Pyramid's slope is actually related to the value of $\pi - {}^{22}/_7$ brought back from Egypt by Pythagoras.

   We have, in fact, 4 cotg. $\alpha - {}^{22}/_7 = \pi$.

3. All, with a few noteworthy exceptions, such as Alexandre Varille and Isha Schwaller de Lubicz.

4. It has been shown that in the majority of the pyramids the isiac slope corresponded to tg $\alpha = {}^{4}/_3$. Moreover, the Rhind Papyrus gives a very interesting value for π: $\pi = tg^4 \alpha = {}^{4}/_3{}^{4} = 3.1605$ . . . , a value useful for certain approximations. The ancient Egyptians were, therefore, not that ignorant from the mathematical standpoint.

5. Actually 4,400 years.

6. Herodotus, II, 124, tr. Powell.

7. Herodotus, II, 124, tr. Rawlinson.

8. It should be noted, in Lauer's defense, that in a paper read to the Société Française d'Egyptologie on June 29, 1949, he acknowledged his error regarding the interpretation of Herodotus' text, an error he ascribes to Moreux and not Montel (out of deference to the Institut de France?).

9. Since the Greek term signifies both "world" and "universe," it is possible to infer that the Great Pyramid's dimensions related to those of the *earth-sun* system. Certain authors have acknowlededge this as a possibility, but I believe that this hypothesis clearly belongs in the improbable sector.

10. Pliny, Book II, LXXV (tr. Rockham).

11. Strabo, Book I, 4:2 (tr. H. L. Jones).

12. Pliny, Book VI, XXXIV (tr. Rockham).

13. Pliny, Book II, LXXV (tr. Rockham).

14. Strabo, Book II, 5:36. (tr. H. L. Jones).

15. Eratosthenes divided the terrestrial circumference into 252,000 stadia, the stadium being essentially a unit of the arc such that 70 stadia equal 6 arc minutes. This division of the circumference into 252,000 stadia is specifically Egyptian. We know that the Egyptians, in expressing their fractions, never used numerators greater than 1, except for the fractions ⅔ and ¾. They would write, for example: "Divide 8 by 9; results = ⅔ plus ¹/₆ plus ¹/₃₀ plus ¹/₄₅." In astronomy, as in geodesy, they had to adopt a system of dividing the circle into fractions that would give numerous aliquot parts. Now, it should be noted that the number 2520 is the *smallest common multiple* of the first ten integers, and that the number 252,000 will admit 144 divisors.

16. *Description de l'Egypte*, vol. 6.

17. The value of this cubit (*diraa baladi*) was set, by khedivial decree in 1891, at 0.58 meter, in order to ensure a simpler relationship with the decimal metric system.

18. It could be posited that the Egyptians of the Fourth Dynasty were ignorant of the sexagesimal division of the circle. This is an *a priori* objection, not based on any proof. I myself am certain that more than military confrontation existed between Egypt and Chaldea and that there were cultural ties as well.

19. With a very minor error of 2,000 years! (4900 *B.C.*)

20. This recess is analogous to the one located in the west wall of the passage leading to the Subterranean Chamber, but larger.

21. Another comment that could be made in this regard, using the Subterranean Chamber's floor as the plane of reference, the heights of the Pyramid's base, the Queen's Chamber (serdab), and the King's Chamber are very close to 60, 100, and 140 cubits—that is, to heights proportional to the numbers 3, 5, and 7.

22. This cartouche is found not only in the relieving chambers, but also on one of the rocks at Wadi Magharah.

23. I do not agree with this viewpoint at all, and if Bruchet had been able to visit the Subterranean Chamber, he would be convinced, as I am, that it played a major role during the initiation of Cheops' successor.

24. This is a mistake. During the supreme initiation of Cheops' successor, the Ascending Passage was not blocked, whereas it was, on the contrary, the "well" that was sealed by the masonry core. The section was not joined with the Grand Gallery until the reign of Ramesses II, 2,550 years after Cheops' death.

25. In my opinion, this "transferral of the divine *ka*" must have taken place in the Pyramid's "central chamber." The corpse of the deceased king was laid out beside the sarcophagus, in which lay the royal heir, plunged deep in a drug-induced sleep. It was then that the magic isiac rites took place, followed by the resurrection—after which, in the *serdab* (middle chamber), the rite of the opening the mouth of the "double" was performed. These isiac rites were performed *upon the king's death*, before mummification. The enthronement and coronation of the new king took place right after the entombment of the royal mummy, in the temple of Ptah in Memphis or the temple of Ra in Heliopolis.

26. Concerning this matter, Laurer writes (*Les Pyramides de Sakkarah*, published in Cairo by L'Institut Graphique Egyptien, 1961): "The constructional incline arrives, at 28 metres below the level of the basis of the enclosure, in a vast underground room, where we can still see a beautiful sarcophagus made of alabaster, shut not by a cover but a vertical sliding panel on one

of the smaller sides toward the north. This trap being down gave the hope at a certain moment that the sarcophagus might be untouched, but it was completely empty. In the inclined passage at the place where it is cut out by the pit, lay a large heap of alabaster and hard stone vessels and also some big jars made of baked clay with plugs bearing the seal of Horus Sekhem-Khet, to whom without doubt this pyramid was dedicated. At some distance from there a small deposit of gold jewelry was collected from the soil of the gallery itself. Among the objects found were some gold objects and bracelets together with a small box having the form of Saint James cockleshell and pearls.

"Why were these jewels here, if as Zakaria Goneim assumed, the king was never buried in his sarcophagus? The enigma continues, and could be explained only by a systematic clearing of the whole funerary site of Sekhem-Khet."

It is quite probable, if not certain, that there existed at least two superimposed chambers in each pyramid; the lower chamber was reserved for the royal mummy's sepulcher, whereas the upper chamber was the site of the transferral of the *ka* once the isiac rites had been completed. The upper chamber's empty sarcophagus—having become sacred and untouchable—was hermetically sealed.

The ritual of the feasts of Osiris at Dendera fully confirm this hypothesis; the Osiris of the preceding year, symbolized by a clay statuette sprinkled with grains of wheat, was brought down from the upper tomb to the lower tomb, while Socharis, Osiris' successor for a year, occupied the upper tomb.

27. Many authors have dealt with this question. To my mind, the authoritative source is Alexandre Moret; no other author has investigated the Egyptian mystique as extensively as he.

28. This festival of the *sed*, analogous to the "mysteries" of the Middle Ages, was performed by the pharoah himself, assisted by the queen playing the role of Isis, two high priests playing Anubis and Thoth, and the eldest prince acting as Horus. The king, with the help of the other participants, raised a pillar (*dad* or *djet*, symbolizing Osiris) lying on the ground. Once the pillar had been raised, the revived Osiris again became the emblem of survival, stability, and virility.

The feast of the *sed*, or royal jubilee, signified the feast of the end (the tail) of a twenty-eight-year period and its renewal. A representation of the erection of the *dad* pillar by Amenophis III has been preserved for us in an Eighteenth Dynasty tomb.

But the ceremony of the erection of the *dad* did not take place only at the royal *sed*; since Osiris had become an agrarian god, the ceremony was repeated each winter solstice at Busiris (now Abusir) on the Nile branch Damietta. Herodotus describes the feast in these terms: "I have already told how they keep the feast of Isis in the city of Busiris. After the sacrifice all the men and all the women, many tens of thousands of persons together, tear their breasts; but for whom they tear their breasts, it was not piety in me to say. (Book II, 161, tr. Powell). This last phrase of Herodotus' represents a vow; he had received the first degree of the initiation.

29. It is probably that the word *cabala* (*cabbalah*), which designates the science of communion with spirits, is derived from the synthesis of these three principles: *ka–ba–akh*.

30. "The Admonitions of an Old Sage," Leyde manuscript. See Alexandre Moret, *The Nile and Egyptian Civilization* (New York: A. A. Knopf, 1927).

31. As in the case of the Sphinx of Giza, it is possible that this pyramidal mountain, unquestionably carved by hand, antedates the historic dynasties. There is a lot that remains to be explained in the Nile Valley, and it would not surprise me if the unexpected discovery of tombs at a level 150 meters higher than the Valley of the Kings were to take us back to the phantasmagorical divine dynasties.

32. It could be that Moses' schism (1462 *B.C.*) was related to the new Atonian ideas that were dawning from the time of Amenophis III (1432 *B.C.*) and were concretized seventy years later, under Amenophis IV (Akhnaton—1395 *B.C.*)

   In view of the close assonance of *Adonai* (the Hebraic God), *Adon* (the Phoenician sun god), and *Aton* (the Egyptian sun god), this hypothesis is not unreasonable.

33. It should be noted that in the rite of Mizraim, in which the proliferation of degrees passes understanding, the passwords at the ninetieth and final degree are "Isis" and "Osiris."

34. Yaschar, *Le Livre du juste: dictionnaire des apocryphes* (*Migne*), vol. 24, p. 1206.

35. Yaschar mentions the number *70*; this is probably a copyist's error.

36. In Isha Schwaller de Lubicz's work *Her-Bak, Egyptian Initials* (tr. Ronald Fraser [London: Hodder and Stoughton, 1967], (Vol. I, p. 249), we find a very lovely reproduction of the ceiling of the chapel of the resurrection at Dendera. Above one of the two plants we find the hieroglyphic word *isd*, which would be the name for Balanites, one of the sacred trees of Egypt.

   I have not been able to locate this hieroglyph in any of my photographs. Moreover, the habit of the plant depicted is very unlike that of Balanites, which is a thorny-branched *tree*; the plant seems to correspond to sorghum, corn, or a variety of giant wheat.

CHAPTER 5

THE GREAT ENIGMAS

THE GREAT PYRAMIDS WERE PAINTED

The question of the painting of the pyramids was the subject of two papers I read to the Institut d'Egypte on May 7, 1934, and March 2, 1953; I provide here the essential passages.[1]

. . . As I proceeded to measure the casing stones of the Great Pyramid, a peculiar fact attracted my attention. Some detached blocks lined up a few meters from the Pyramid, which apparently had once been part of the facing, showed a curious red-brown tint on their flat, sloping side.

To what phenomenon could this tint—which the blocks' other surfaces did not have—be attributed? To time? Light? To the sand—as unferruginous as it was—that had covered the blocks for so long? It is hardly likely, for the other surfaces would have shown the beginnings of a similar transformation. Moreover, a knife blade penetrates the colored surface with difficulty and cuts through the other surfaces easily.

Chemical tests gave me an immediate result: the facing blocks were coated with a paint having a ferrous oxide base (red ochre). Powder obtained by scraping the surface of a block was treated with hot diluted hydrochloric acid; the filtrate showed the intense red and blue colorations characteristic of ferrocyanide and potassium sulphocyanide. Tests carried out onother parts of the sample were negative.

It remained to determine the kind of adhesive used. Cold diluted hydrochloric acid does not affect the colored coating, whereas it sets off a lively effervescence in other parts of the sample.

Moreover, it is clear that, for a width of approximately one-half millimeter, the superficial coating is of a different nature than the subjacent limestone rock.

The question of the adhesive materials used by the ancient Egyptians lends itself to controversy; no hypothesis concerning these substances (oils, gums, blood, etc.) could be proved satisfactorily.

Abulfeda's statement[2] is sufficiently curious to be worth noting: "At Memphis are found the ruins of ancient monuments, consisting of polished blocks covered with figures. The stone is coated with a green oil or oil of another color; and this oil has remained intact to this day, without having been altered, over so long a period of time, by the sun or the inclemencies of the atmosphere."

The chemical analyses prove the undeniable presence of calcium and silica. The presence of an organic also seems likely, for when placed over a flame, the colored portion takes on a tint that is plainly blacker than the subjacent calcium.

However, it was necessary to verify this fact. The second pyramid still retains part of its casing, which definitely seems to be colored red; this red tint was attributed at first to granite, then to the pyramid's great age, and finally to lichens. It should be pointed out that there are large pink trails clearly visible on the pyramid's lower blocks; descending from the pyramid's summit, these trails undoubtedly stem from the dissolution of the facing blocks that are still in place. Fragments taken from the pyramid's casing, when subjected to chemical tests, showed the same reaction as those taken from the facing blocks of the Great Pyramid. We must also keep in mind that the Sphinx's face is also painted red; Pliny informs us that it was painted because of a cult.

Why should this not have been the case with the Great Pyramid as well?

However, formal proof of the fact that the Great Pyramid was painted came to me in the course of a separate examination of the rather deteriorated casing stones found on the Pyramid's south face. E. Baraize and I ascertained that some of these blocks showed, on their uppermost horizontal surfaces, traces of red paint corresponding to the breaks between the rocks that had been placed directly above them; the coating was clearly thicker and showed *fins*. There could no longer be any doubt: *The Pyramid's facing had been painted*.

The second paper I read to the Institut de l'Egypte concerns spectral analyses carried out in the laboratories of the Sorbonne. These analyses were essential, for Lauer, in his book on the pyramids, had cast doubt upon my conclusions. Having still had in my possession four fragments from the Great Pyramid's facing, I entrusted them to Professor Boulanger, head of general chemical research at the Sorbonne.

Mr. Boulanger submitted three of the fragments to chemical analysis, not wishing to damage the fourth (now at the Louvre), which showed in places smudges of a red coating 2 millimeters thick, the sight of which alone would dismiss any possible doubt.

The chemical analysis corroborated the analyses made previously in Cairo. Unfortunately, Mr. Boulanger's death cut short his research, which was completed by his daughter, Françoise Boulanger, assistant professor at the Faculté des Sciences. The Sorbonne's great spectrograph was used for this purpose.

Françoise Boulanger reported the following:

Mr. Pochan entrusted us with limestone fragments taken from the Great Pyramid's external facing, which showed, on their flat surface, a reddish coloration.

We have demonstrated that this flat, colored surface

contained elements chemically different from those making up the stone itself.

Our technique consisted, first of all, in registering, for each of the three fragments, the comparative spectrum emission of the innermost part of the stone (that is, the part farthest from the reddish part) and the outermost part (that is, the part corresponding to the coloration). This comparative analysis was rendered necessary by the fact that the colored part apparently cannot be obtained apart from the stone.

As one can see in the attached spectra,[3] the elements found in the superficial reddish coating *and not in the stone* are: *iron, manganese, phosphorus*, and *sodium*.

In addition, as phosphorus is among the rare metalloids that reveal themselves spectrographically, we tried an alkaline treatment with a view toward investigating the other possible anions, and we found—again, by comparison—that the colored coating contained *chlorine* and traces of sulphate; we can assume that the sulphate is in the form of calcium sulphate.

The fact that we found phosphorus and sodium leads us to posit the existence of an organic element accompanied by these two elements.

The presence of iron and manganese fully explains the reddish coloration observed.

We consider these facts to verify Mr. Pochan's hypothesis, to wit, that the Pyramid was indeed painted.

Paris, May 5, 1950

As the study of the spectra will confirm, the results obtained by Françoise Boulanger corroborated those found through ordinary qualitative chemical analyses, while adding some new elements. In addition to showing *the lack of iron* in the bulk of the limestone rock and its presence in the superficial coating, these spectral analyses demonstrate this to be true of *manganese* as well.

Iron and manganese are thus *superficial, external additions*; these elements could not have come from the rock itself, since it does not contain them. Now, it should be noted that manganese salts have long been used in painting as *siccatives*. It is thus natural to conclude that the organic matter revealed by the presence of phosphorus and sodium was simply *oil*.

The following passage from Pliny, (book 36:58) is pertinent:

> Maltha is prepared from freshly calcined lime, a lump of which is slaked in wine and then pounded together with pork fat and figs, both of which are softening agents. Maltha is the most adhesive of substances and grows harder than stone. Anything that is treated with it is first thoroughly rubbed with olive oil.

The only possible conclusion is Professor Boulanger's *express* conclusion, to wit, that it is indisputable that the Great Pyramid (as well as the pyramid of Kephren) was indeed covered with a plaster paint having a base of red ochre or hematite. Moreover, I should mention that Caviglia had also discovered traces of a red coating or paint in various places along the base of the second pyramid, as well as on blocks from the east and west sides of the Great Pyramid's facing; and that Howard-Vyse discovered, near the north base, a quantity of red stucco or mortar made of crushed granite and a red stone similar to one still used by stone cutters, called *mokra*. And, in conclusion, let us recall the passage from Maqrizi concerning the pyramids of Giza: "When they were completed, they were covered from top to bottom with *a colored brocade*." The term *brocade* must be a copyist's error or misinterpretation, for this would have been impossible in my opinion, the word *mokra* should be substituted for the word *brocade*.

THE ORIENTATION OF THE GREAT PYRAMID

The average shift in the orientation of the faces is 3′ 6″ according to the Survey of Egypt. Given the present state of the Pyramid's faces, this slight error may be due to the imprecision of the tachymetric survey itself. At any rate, the extraordinary accuracy of the orientation poses a problem. How with the primitive means available to them, were the ancient Egyptians able to orient such an edifice so precisely?

Ingenuously, Lauer writes: "Thus if we are not dealing

here with *simple coincidence*, and if such precision was indeed sought, the question is how this precision could have been obtained." The question remains, as far as he is concerned, answerless. And, pressing on to the subject of the illumination of the faces during the equinoxes, Lauer adds: "Could this result have been sought by the builders? I can only perceive it as a whim on their part." A whimsical remark!

The question of the orientation of the Great Pyramid has preoccupied numerous authors, and many hypotheses have been put forth. It is astonishing that renowned astronomers should have proposed solutions that are, *in terms of practicality*, impossible. This is particularly true with regard to the perforation of the Descending Passage, which was the first task executed after the precise laying out of the Pyramid's four corners.

The claim that the Descending Passage was dug while sighting some star near the North Pole is ridiculous for many reasons—among them two important ones:

1. In the year 4800 B.C., the true date of the erection of the Great Pyramid, *no* visible star represented the North Pole; Herschel's and Smyth's Alpha Draconis is just a myth.

2. The Descending Passage's angle of slope is 26° 34' (corresponding to cotangent 2), *not* 29° 58' 51", which it would have to have been in order for the pole to be discernible from the bottom of the Descending Passage.

The most substantial, best-documented study concerning the orientation of the pyramids has come from Professor Zbynek Zaba, director of the Czechoslovakian Institute of Egyptology at the University of Prague.[4]

The hieroglyphic texts he cites are conclusive; the orientation of the Ptolemaic temples was arrived at astronomically through the points intersected along a line by one of the stars in Ursa Major.

An inscription found in the temple at Edfu relates a royal oration by Euergetes II:

I take the staff and I grasp the handle of the mallet; I grasp the cord with Sechat. I have turned my regard according to the movement of the stars, and I have set my sight on Mshtyw [Ursa Major]. The god who is the indicator of time was standing beside his merkhet. I have established the four corners of thy temple . . . [pp. 58–60].

. . . He [the king] built the great square of Ra-Horakhty to conform with the horizon holding his disc; the cord was stretched there by Her Majesty herself, holding the stake in her hand with Sechat; he wound his cord with He-Who-Is-to-the-South-of-His-*Wall*, in a task perfect for all time, it having been established along its angle by the majesty of Khnum; He-Who-Makes-Existence-Unfold stood up to see his shadow [; it] was perfectly long, excellently long, properly high and wide, the task executed with excellent workmanship, equipped with all his belongings, *sprinkled with gold*, decorated with colors; its appearance was similar to Ra's horizon.

The preceding text is explicit enough for us to understand the ancient Egyptians' methods of operation. During the Lagid Dynasty the star used for determining the meridian belonged to the constellation Ursa Major; this was probably, according to Professor Zaba, the star Eta Ursa Majoris (Alkaïd), whose present declination is 49° 38′ 14″ N.

The sighting operations required a moonless night. All desert dwellers know that the starry Egyptian sky is sufficiently luminous for a cord, especially one covered with gold powder, to be seen at a distance of 50 meters.

The purpose of the ceremony of the "stretching of the cord" by the king himself was to obtain an "artificial horizon," the cord being stretched, in an initial attempt, about 2 cubits approximately east-west, over perfectly level ground.

The sighting apparatus (the *merkhet*), which I will attempt to reconstruct schematically according to its hieroglyphic diagram, was placed in the center of the area, directly beneath the middle of the stretched cord.

Borchardt studied two vestiges of these instruments which were at the Berlin Museum, and compares them, correctly, to graphometers. One of them, made of ivory, bears a partially obscured inscription. On this subject Professor Zaba writes (p. 57):

Borchardt's assumption, according to which the second determinative of the word *itn* is a mistake for the determinative for "moon," is plausible enough. It concerns the dual [determinative] *itnwy* ("the two balls"); that is, those of the sun and the moon, since the word appears to have been used in the sense of "ball" only in regard to the sun and the moon, and not in regard to the stars. It should thus be translated as: "I am familiar with the movement of the ball of the sun and the ball of the moon and the stars, each according to its position."

I will permit myself to suggest a hypothesis, that, in my eyes, is more plausible: The "two balls" were each pierced with a hole and strung on the cord; they were used to mark the guiding star's points of intersection and were placed along the cord according to the indications of the observer equipped with his *merkhet*.

While the problem of the orientation of the Ptolemaic temples seems to have been solved, the question of the orientation of the great pyramids of Giza remains open. The problem is particularly puzzling in the case of the pyramid of Kephren, which is located 15 meters below the level of the carved bedrock north of it; thus its orientation could not have been based on sightings of Ursa Major. In my opinion, during the Old Kingdom the guiding star was not in the Northern Hemisphere but in the Southern Hemisphere, and the cardinal point was south, not north. The hieroglyphic diagrams seem clearly to support this hypothesis.

Assuming that the cardinal point was south, east was to the observer's left, west to his right. Now, the diagrams are explicit:

ibt = east, *left*; *imnt* = west, right.

Moreover, the "priest of the hour," or "watchman," was called *rsy*, from *rswt* (south).

It is probable that the guiding star chosen was of the first magnitude; there are many of these in the Southern Hemisphere. Four stars in particular are capable of serving this function:

Alpha Carinae (Canopus), declination: 52° 40′ S.
Alpha Scorpii (Antares), declination: 26° 18′ S.

Alpha Piscis Austrani (Fomalhaut),
    declination: 29° 58' S.
Alpha Canis Majoris (Sirius), declination: 16° 38' S.

The mode of operation was identical to that used under the Lagid Dynasty. In an initial process the cord was stretched *approximately* east-west. In order to obtain the correct east-west orientation, all that was necessary was to measure two equal lengths along the bearings defined by two intersections of the cord made by the same star.

Once the cord had been restretched in this direction, the same stars' points of intersection were again determined. The midpoint (M) of the points of intersection determined the north-south direction with great precision.

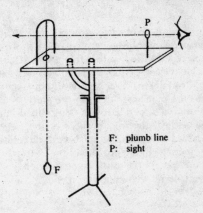

F: plumb line
P: sight

Reconstruction of the merkhet
according to its hieroglyphic diagram

In my opinion, the guiding star chosen must have been either Antares or Fomalhaut, as Canopus' trajectory was not high enough above the horizon.

Since the Great Pyramid was destined to become the temple of the sun god Khnum, it had to be oriented with the greatest precision. The very first condition to be met was that the Giza Plateau be leveled and surveyed. Then excavation of the Descending Passage could begin, followed by the laying out of the Pyramid's socle.

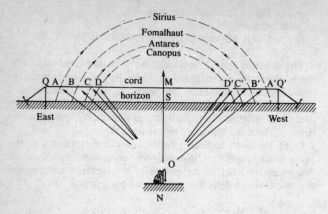

In the course of the work it was *impossible* to make any correction whatsoever; the general plan of the monument was *definitively* established well before the first course was set in place. The Great Pyramid's hollowed faces increased the difficulty of obtaining a precise orientation—more reason to believe that the plan was set from the start.

Once the Pyramid's meridian was determined in the manner described earlier, the four corners of the ridges of the socle could be established, the east-west direction having been defined since the initial process of the "stretching of the cord." The outline of the base, including the 0.92-meter hollowing toward the center of each side, could then be traced on the leveled bedrock.

THE EXCAVATION OF THE GREAT PYRAMID'S DESCENDING PASSAGE AND "WELL"

One critical problem was the excavation of the Descending Passage, which was the first operation to be carried out after the leveling, surveying, and orientation. It was necessary to determine its point of impact in the rock exactly, 48 meters south of the north base and 7.30 meters east of the Pyramid's meridian plane. This eastward displacement, a consequence of the hollowing of the north face, had no other purpose than to avoid flooding in the Subterranean Chamber during storms.

Although constructing a slope gauge for digging the Descending Passage posed no problem (because its angle, 26° 34', corresponds to cotangent 2), the orientation of the perforation of the bedrock did. For the Pyramid's entire interior layout was linked to the *impeccable* placement of the Descending Passage on a plane *strictly* parallel to the Pyramid's meridian plane.

It is absurd to propose that this orientation was made according to some star close to the pole, especially Alpha Draconis, a barely perceptible star of the fourth magnitude—for in 4800 *B.C.*, the date of the erection of the monument, this star was not close to the pole. A process that was at once *simple* and *precise* was required. In my opinion, this process consisted in aligning the two poles AB and CD 7.30 meters east of the Pyramid's north-south meridian. These two poles could have been set 20 cubits apart—with the first pole (B) located 10 cubits from the entrance to the Descending Passage—and have had respective heights of 5 and 15 cubits. Under these conditions, the AC bearing would have shown the stonecutters the *exact* direction in which to drill.

Once the piercing of the Descending Passage had been accomplished, the drilling of the Subterranean Chamber had to be carried out. But before this work could be begun, it was necessary to ensure that descending workers would not

THE EXCAVATION OF THE DESCENDING PASSAGE AND "WELL"

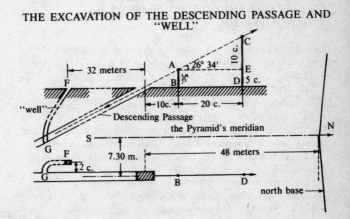

interfere with their fellow workers climbing back up the Descending Passage, bearing stone-cutting debris.

Therefore a shaft (FG) was made parallel to the Descending Passage, 32 meters south of where the bedrock was pierced by the Descending Passage, and 2 cubits west of the latter. This shaft, called the "well" for some unknown reason, was supposed to end at a point (G) about 15 meters from the Subterranean Chamber's entrance.

According to Herodotus, it took ten years to complete the passage and the subterranean *chambers*. In my opinion, it could not have taken more than two years to dig the Descending Passage and the "well," in addition to excavating the Subterranean Chamber and its blind passage. Since Herodotus' uses the plural, "the subterranean *chambers*," it is possible—indeed, probable—that Cheops' sepulchral chamber and the annexes needed for his funerary furniture are still undiscovered at the level of the Nile at the time; that is, 58 meters beneath the Pyramid. The actual erection of the Pyramid could not have been begun until the causeway had been completed, because it was indispensable in transporting the blocks uphill. Thus the erection could not have been begun until the eleventh year; it required another twenty years' effort to complete.

THE GREAT PYRAMID AND THE DETERMINATION OF EQUINOXES AND SOLSTICES

In a paper read to the Institut d'Egypte in September 1935, I pointed out a singular phenomenon relating to the Great Pyramid. I will only reproduce here an extract from an article that appeared in the newspaper *La Bourse egyptienne* [The Egyptian Exchange] at that time:

Mr. Antoniadi, astronomer at the Meudon Observatory, recently revealed in an admirable book on Egyptian astronomy[5] the profound knowledge that presided over the construction of the pyramids.

Yesterday evening Mr. Pochan, to whom we already owe the discovery of the red paint that once covered the pyramids, revealed quite a curious phenomenon to the

Institut d'Egypte. It seems that the Great Pyramid constituted a precision instrument that allowed the date of the equinoxes to be determined exactly.

Mr. Pochan's attention was drawn to the curious irregularity of the south face. It seems at first glance to be, or to have been, absolutely flat. But it is nothing of the kind. The Great Pyramid's south face is composed of two planes that meet each other at an angle measuring approximately 27 minutes. Petrie tried to explain this anomaly by assuming that the casing was thicker toward the center of the face. Mr. Pochan provides another explanation that shows greater respect for the extent of the builders' knowledge.

On the day of the equinox the sun, as it rises and sets, lights this face in such a way that a curious phenomenon, which Mr. Pochan calls the "flash," occurs. Mr. Pochan describes it as follows:

> *A.* At sunrise the shadow cast on the ridge SB sweeps across the left (western) part of the south face from left to right. This is what I would call "the flash phenomenon"; it lasts for about 20 seconds.
>
> *B.* The western part (ASM), which is then illuminated, contrasts with the eastern part (MSB), which

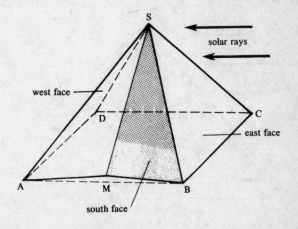

is still in shadow. This phenomenon is clearly visible for four to five minutes.

When the sun sets, the phenomenon is *reversed*:

A. The eastern part (MSB), which is illuminated, contrasts with the western part (ASM), which is already in shadow.

B. The shadow of the ridge AS sweeps rapidly across the eastern part (MSB) from the left to right.

This curious phenomenon is increasingly visible from March 21 to June 21, the summer solstice; at this date, when the sun is high on the horizon, it occurs at around 6:40 A.M. and 5:20 P.M.

It occurs for the last time at the autumn equinox, at which date the phenomenon is seen only in the morning, at six o'clock, whereas at the spring equinox, it is seen only in the evening, at six o'clock.

The equinox can thus be precisely determined to within twelve hours. Infrared photography has allowed us to see this phenomenon clearly; when the casing was still in place, it must have had much greater effect and visibility. . . . In the photographs the shadow cuts the two parts of the south face so

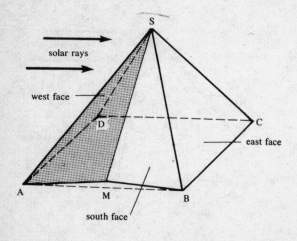

neatly that one would think one were seeing a fifth ridge on the Pyramid.

This phenomenon is not peculiar to the south face; the north face, similarly hollowed, presents the same phenomenon. It can even be assumed that it was the north face that was used for observations, since there extends before it a vast, carefully leveled and paved esplanade over 100 meters long.

One important fact deserving special emphasis proves that the hollowing of the faces was in no way a "whim" on the part of the builders: the angle of hollowing at the level of the bedrock is approximately 27 minutes. Now, the variation of the sun's declination at the equinoxes is 23 minutes per twenty-four hours! We have here obvious proof that the ancient Egyptians were astronomically much more advanced than our modern Egyptologists suspect.

The singular phenomenon of the first "flash" that I described might explain the comments made by Solinus, Ammianus Marcellinus, and Cassiodorus to the effect that the pyramid "*absorbed*" its own shadow. However, this statement could also be interpreted to mean that in Cheops' time, during part of the year (from March 1 to October 14), the obelisk-gnomon atop the Pyramid's platform cast no visible shadow at true solar noon.

But the Great Pyramid, solar temple of the god Khnum, equipped with its obelisk-gnomon, must have also been used in determining the winter solstice and solar noon.

On the subject of obelisks, Pliny writes (Book 36:15):

The one in the Campus was put to use in a remarkable way by Augustus of Revered Memory so as to mark the sun's shadow and thereby the lengths of days and nights. A pavement was laid down for a distance appropriate to the height of the obelisk so that the shadow cast at noon on the shortest day of the year might exactly coincide with it. Bronze rods let into the pavement were meant to measure the shadow day by day as it gradually became shorter and then lengthened again. This device deserves to be carefully studied, and was contrived by the mathematician Novius Facundus. He placed on the pinnacle a gilt ball, at the top of which the shadow would

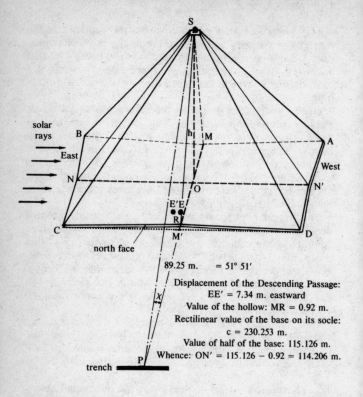

89.25 m. = 51° 51′

Displacement of the Descending Passage:
EE′ = 7.34 m. eastward
Value of the hollow: MR = 0.92 m.
Rectilinear value of the base on its socle:
c = 230.253 m.
Value of half of the base: 115.126 m.
Whence: ON′ = 115.126 − 0.92 = 114.206 m.

The Pyramid's true height above its socle up to the top of its gnomon was:

$$h = ON′ \times tg\ \alpha = 114.206 \times 1.2730578 = 145.39\ m.$$

At the winter solstice, the elongation of the shadow cast by the gnomon (OP) was maximal. During Cheops' time, the height of the sun on the Giza horizon at noon was x° = 90° − 54° 19′ 9″ = 35° 40′ 51″.

As a result, PO = h · cotg · χ = 204.95 m.

The shadow cast was thus located 204.95 − 115.70 = 89.25 m. from the foot of the Pyramid.

be concentrated, for otherwise, the shadow cast by the tip of the obelisk would have lacked definition.

I am inclined to think that the accomplishment was but a miniaturized replica of Cheops' grandiose achievement. Like Rome's Campus Martius, the Great Pyramid's north esplanade was leveled and paved, and I tend to see proof that the determination of the winter solstice was effected on the Giza Plateau in the fact that there exists a trench dug in the bedrock, discovered by Howard-Vyse on March 29, 1837. This incision in the bedrock north of the Great Pyramid lies parallel to the base at a distance of approximately 100 yards (91.40 meters) and is 6 to 7 feet (1.83 to 2.13 meters) deep.

Since the obliquity of the ecliptic was 20° 21′ 17″ in Cheops' time (c. 4800 B.C.), the angle between the Pyramid's axis and the sun's bearing at noon on the day of the winter solstice was 54° 19′ 9″. Consequently, the shadow projected by the gnomon had a length of:

$$147.09 \text{ m.} \times \tan 54° 19′ 9″ = 204.95 \text{ m.}$$

The end of the shadow cast (P) was thus located at:

$$204.95 \text{ m.} - 115.7 \text{ m.} = 89.25 \text{ m.}$$

Now, the trench in the rock is located at a distance of about 90 meters, and its depth is about 2 meters; therefore, it must have been used by observers placed inside it to verify the position of the solar disc in relation to the point of the obelisk-gnomon, whose shadow passed 46 meters above the Pyramid's surrounding wall. Moreover, it can be assumed that a line corresponding to the two hundred days during which the gnomon's shadow was projected beyond the surrounding wall at noon must have been carved in the pavement, perpendicular to the middle of the base.

Was the shape of the gnomon surmounting the Pyramid's platform, like the hieroglyphic determinative of the mastaba of Pen-Meruw, a squat obelisk, similar to the one found at the solar temple of Niuserre at Abu Gurab?

It is not unreasonable to suppose that Marcus Manilius, the poet and mathematician, who certainly traveled in Egypt, should have been interested in the Great Pyramid and have learned from the priests that it had once been surmounted by a sphere. The latter, if it existed, was no longer in place in 440 B.C., for Herodotus would not have omitted to mention it. In order exactly to eclipse the solar disc at the winter solstice, it must have had a diameter of 1.87 meters, and the trench discovered by Howard-Vyse would have been indispensable in detecting the phenomenon accurately.

Why else would this vast esplanade have been laid out before the Pyramid's north face, if not to carve on the pavement the daily graphic curves marked by the gnomon's shadow? Egyptologists who subscribe to the "Great Nothing" school of thought will see this conclusion as morbid imagination, but all the evidence points to it. Knowledge, money, work, human lives . . . Cheops spared nothing to create a unique masterpiece, superhuman, unmatched for knowledge, grandeur, and beauty! Yes, beauty, for despite its imposing mass, the Great Pyramid rose soaringly atop the Giza Plateau, dominating the valley and the desert sands, its scarlet faces flaming in the golden sunset. "Khufu's Horizon" proclaimed the alliance of man and God.

The Great Pyramid's Triple Destination

At the end of this study of the Great Pyramid it seems fitting to take stock and to state its destination definitively and succinctly.

Pliny was wrong to see it as "an idle and foolish ostentation of royal wealth," and Jomard was quite correct in stating that though the Great Pyramid was a tomb, it was the tomb of a king who wished to hand down to posterity the knowledge of scholarly Egypt, a king, moreover, who foresaw that the Pyramid would be used as a place of initiation.

Professor Zaba is entirely of this opinion, for he ends his scholarly work *L'Orientation astronomique dans l'ancienne Egypte,* with the following sentence: "One should not, therefore, consider the pyramids solely as monuments attesting to the megalomaniac arrogance of the theocratic despots who had them built, but rather as monuments to the culture, knowledge, and progressive technology of the age in which they were erected."

To be sure, the Great Pyramid was—and is to this day, in all probability—the tomb of King Cheops, who remains, 58 meters deep in the bedrock, jealously guarded by the waters of the Nile. The three known chambers had a single esoteric destination: the strange, chaotic Subterranean Chamber was the site of the second, symbolic birth of Cheops' successor; the middle chamber, known as the "Queen's Chamber," was simply the *serdab* containing the statue of the royal "double"; and the central chamber, known as the "King's Chamber," was the sanctuary used for the magical transfer of the divine *ka* from the not yet mummified royal cadaver to the body of Kephren, stretched out in the sarcophagus in a drugged sleep. His awakening, after the ritual ceremonies of imitative magic, symbolized his third birth and marked the conclusion of his ultimate initiation, his body having become the receptacle of the godhead.

Once the miracle was effected, the central chamber became a *sacred place*. Access to it was henceforth forbidden to mortals, and the granite portcullises were lowered on *an empty tomb*. The Subterranean Chamber, accessible through the Descending Passage's swivel door, alone continued to serve a function—it was the site of the first stage of the isiac initiation. Such was the Great Pyramid's esoteric and primordial role.

But the Great Pyramid was more than the tomb of Cheops' and the site of his successor's supreme initiation; it was also the temple of the sun god Khnum, and as such, its external shape was related to the shape of the earth. While its pyramidal shape and red color were presumed to play a role in the tapping of solar and sidereal energies, its dimensions embodied those of the terrestrial globe and its roundness; its slope, in fact, gave the value of $\pi = 22/7$, and its perimeter the value of a half-minute of the arc of the meridian. What is more, its curiously hollowed faces allowed the equinoxes to be determined to within twelve hours, while the shadow of its gnomon, shifting along the vast esplanade laid out before the north face, allowed the winter solstice, the hour, and, above all, true solar noon to be determined.

The occurrence of such a masterly achievement (as much in terms of the technology involved in the construction as in terms of the mathematical and astronomical knowledge it embodies) in 4800 B.C. revolutionizes our opinion of the scientific knowledge possessed by the ancient Egyptians. It is unlikely that we have yet reached the bounds of our

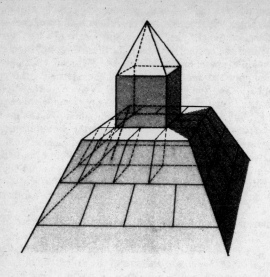

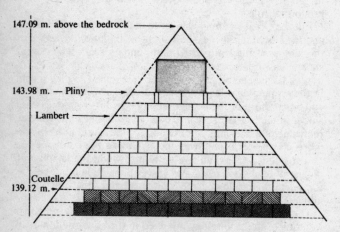

147.09 m. above the bedrock

143.98 m. — Pliny

Lambert

Coutelle
139.12 m.

**AN ATTEMPT TO RECONSTRUCT THE SUMMIT
OF THE GREAT
PYRAMID OF GIZA**

astonishment, for new archaeological discoveries, opening up as yet unsuspected horizons, are still possible—indeed, probable.

THE CALENDARS OF ANCIENT EGYPT

How can one doubt that the Great Pyramid was arranged thus astronomically when one finds in Maqrizi the following passage concerning the two obelisks of Heliopolis only one of which is still standing, the other having toppled on September 4, 1258:

> This town was formerly called Ramsas, and Ain Shams ("The Source of the Sun") was a temple to which pilgrimages were made from every point along the horizon; it was one of those ancient temples to which pilgrims flocked . . .
>
> Ain Shams is the *temple of the sun* at which there stand two columns so wondrous that nothing more beautiful has ever been seen, nor anything even approaching their beauty. They are about 50 cubits high and are set on the surface of the ground. Between the two of them stands the statue of a man mounted on a charger. They are capped by two copper points . . . When the sun enters the first minute of Capricorn—that is, on the shortest day of the year—the sun reaches the southernmost of the two obelisks and culminates at its

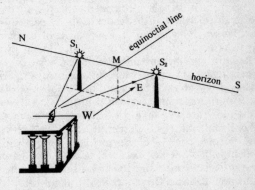

summit; when the sun reaches the first minute of Cancer—that is, on the longest day of the year—it reaches the northernmost obelisk and culminates at its summit. These two obelisks thus form the two extremities of the solar swing, and the equinoctial line passes exactly midway between the two. The advent and passage of the year is thus contained between these two obelisks; at least this is what the competent scholars say.

In Egyptian *peh* means "to attain to, reach forward, arrive at." Thus passover is the day on which the rising or setting sun has reached the equinoctial median.

I believe there must have been two observation posts, both located along the equinoctial line, one to the west, the other to the east of a line between the two obelisks, which allowed the equinoxes and solstices to be determined to within twelve hours.

If the ancient Egyptians set up such solar observatories not only at Heliopolis (northern ON) but also at Tanis in the delta, Hermonthis (southern ON), Esneh, and Edfu in Thebaide, it was surely according to a precise plan.

In a paper I read to the Société Française d'Egyptologie on February 10, 1954, concerning the calendars of the ancient Egyptians, I pointed out that three different calendars had been used simultaneously in the Nile Valley for thousands of years, whereas Egyptologists had recognized only one, known as the "*mobile*, or *vague* calendar." I said if anything was "vague," it was their competence in the astronomical and calendrical field. (As the reader might suspect, this paper was a bit acrimonious.) The Egyptian civil calendar certainly was not "vague," for it constituted an invariable standard for the measurement of time. What *is* vague—comical, really—is to presume to measure a given size precisely, using an elastic standard of variable size. And this is what our Gregorian calendar, with its stupidly unequal months and years without a constant value, presumes to do. Thus one smiles at the condescension of Eduard Meyer, one of the famous pundits of Egyptology, who ridicules the Egyptian mobile calendar because, he says, it is based on a totally artificial concept: "Its months aren't months, its seasons aren't seasons, even its year it not a year!"

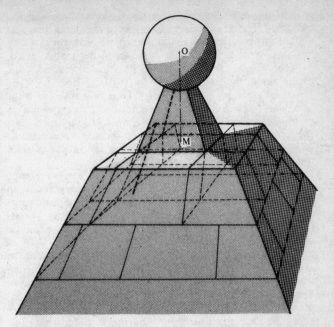

Despite our vanity we must recognize our clear inferiority to the ancient Egyptians in this because the Egyptians knew more than 7,500 years ago that there are two distinct problems in regard to the duration of time: its intrinsic, formal measurement, and its concordance with the seasons. That is why they devised two distinct calendars: the *chronological calendar*, in which the value of the year is immutable (365 days = 12 equal months + 5 epagomenal days); and the *tropical* (or seasonal) *calendar*, in which the value of the year is variable, its duration being incommensurable with that of the solar day.

Before discussing these any further, it is necessary to recall that: (1) Egypt was, before Menes, composed of two distinct states, Lower Egypt and Upper Egypt, each having its own chronological calendar in which the first day of the year was called, respectively, the 1st of Thoth and the 1st of Mesori; and (2) their historical archives, which unfortunately are now lost, were based on these distinct calendars.

Why the label "*mobile*" for the Egyptian chronological calendar? The answer is simple: The first day of the year shifted through the seasons in the course of the ages.

The original starting point common to the mobile calendars of Upper and Lower Egypt was connected to a phenomenon that was *peculiar in its fixity*, since it is still produced at the present time, after thousands of years, at the same date in the Sothic or Julian calendar. This astronomical phenomenon consists of *the heliacal rising of the star Sirius*, the star of Isis (Sothis). When this occurs, one sees, at daybreak, the star of Isis also rising up in the eastern horizon, and, to its right, the first ray of the sun.

The date of the simultaneous rising of the sun and Sirius, which is invariable for a given place, does vary according to the latitude of the observation point. More specifically, this date corresponds to July 20 in the Julian calendar for Thebes (the 1st of Thoth) and to July 25 in the Julian calendar (the 1st of Mesori) for Tanis.

Now, while this rising took place on the 1st of Thoth or the 1st of Mesori for four years, in the fifth year the phenomenon was observed a day late; that is, it occurred on the 2nd of Thoth and the 2nd of Mesori for Upper and Lower Egypt, respectively. There was thus a calendrical shift of one day every four years, which explains the qualifier "mobile" given the two chronological calendars. Thus, for the heliacal rising of Sirius to occur exactly on the respective first days of the year (the 1st of Thoth and the 1st of Mesori), a time lapse of $4 \times 365 = 1,460$ years was necessary. This is what is called the "Sothic cycle"—a concept that is essential in reconstructing the Egyptian chronology. (Please see Table VII.)

Thus, it was enough to know the date, *in the mobile calendar*, of Sirius' heliacal rising during the year of a historical event to place that event in the Sothic cycle in progress. The Greeks, for their Olympics, simply copied the Egyptians; the games were to begin at the heliacal rising of Sirus at Olympia on July 29th in the Julian calendar.

Since there were distinct mobile calendars for Upper and Lower Egypt, obviously there were two parallel branches of Sothic cycles whose starting points were staggered by 145 years.

Upper Egypt's last Sothic cycle ended in 139 A.D. (year 2

of the reign of Antoninus), and that of Lower Egypt in 284 A.D. (year 1 of the reign of Diocletian).

Conjointly with the two chronological calendars peculiar to Upper and Lower Egypt, a *common seasonal tropical calendar* known as the "calendar of the ancestors" or the "calendar of the Two Lands" was also in general use. Its additional days were determined according to the full moons falling on the epagomenal days and were supplemented by one day for each cycle of Apis (25 years) and of the Phoenix (509 years). Thus conceived, the tropical calendar "of the Two Lands" was as precise as the Gregorian calendar we use today.

As for the introduction of the Egyptian calendar, most Egyptologists are of the opinion that this could not have occurred before 2780 B.C.; some, however, concede the date of 4242 B.C. I do not hesitate to assert that the three aforementioned calendars are predynastic and that it is necessary to go back many thousands of years—indeed, even as far back as the demigod-king Thoth, who gave his name to the first month of the Theban calendar; that is, according to Eusebius, to 15588 B.C.

Imaginary hypothesis? Fabrication? Not at all! I am convinced that future discoveries will prove me absolutely right!

NOTES

1. *Bulletin de l'Institut d'Egypte,* vols. 16 and 35.
2. Albufeda, *Geography.*
3. *Cf. Bulletin de l'Institut d'Egypte,* vol. 35 (1952-53), spectral plates 1, 2 and 3.

    The principal characteristic rays of the elements revealed exclusively in the colored coatings are the following (wave lengths expressed in angstroms):

Phosphorus:	rays 2,534 and 2,535.7
Manganese:	rays 2,576.2 and 2,596.7
Iron:	rays 2,706—2,712—2,718—2,721
Sodium:	rays 3,302.5 and 3,303.1

4. *L'Orientation astronomique dans l'ancienne Egypte et la procession de l'axe du monde* [Astronomical orientation in ancient Egypt and the procession of the Earth's axis] (Prague: Edition de l'Academie Tcheslovaque des Sciences, 1953).
5. Eugene Michael Antoniali, *L'astronomie égyptienne depuis les temps les plus réculés* (Paris: Gauthier-Villars, 1934).

CHAPTER 6

THE VICISSITUDES
OF THE GREAT PYRAMID

THE STATE OF THE GREAT PYRAMID
THROUGH THE AGES

Before attempting a historical account of the Great Pyramid,
it will be useful to gather, in chronological order, the various
elements of information that have come down to us.

Herodotus (c. 430 B.C.)

According to his description, the Pyramid was intact, at
least externally. He mentions that the causeway and the
subterranean chambers took ten years' work. He reports
that these subterranean chambers were built to serve as
Cheops' tomb, on a spot transformed into an island by means
of an underground canal diverting the flood waters of the
Nile.

He provides no description of the chambers known at
present. We cannot conclude from his silence that he did not
know about them, for, considering his reticence concerning
the isiac religion, it is probable, if not certain, that he had
been initiated and was thus sworn to absolute secrecy.

Diodorus Siculus (*c.* 56 B.C.)

According to him, the Pyramid was intact; he writes: "The stones remain to this day still preserving their original position and the entire structure undecayed," and he indicates that it ends in a platform 6 cubits long. However, like Herodotus, he is silent concerning the interior layout.

He is the only author to mention a step carved in *one* face of the second pyramid, and it seems, in fact, that this must have been so, at two-thirds the height, but on all four faces.

Strabo (*c.* 24 B.C.)

He is the only author to mention the mobile stone that closes off the Great Pyramid's entrance and "which, once raised, reveals the entrance of a tortuous gallery, or Descending Passage, leading to the tomb."

Like Herodotus and Diodorus Siculus, he offers no information concerning the interior layout.

Pliny (*c.* 20 A.D.)

He is the only ancient author to give the exact measurements (in Roman feet) of the three pyramids and the Sphinx.

It is curious that he was able to give a rather accurate vertical height for the Pyramid's "well" (in Egyptian cubits). How was he able to obtain this datum? It is certain that he did not descend into the "well," for he stated *it was thought* to catch flood water.

It is likely that these four authors had all been initiated and were thus bound to respect the law of silence. Religion, in my opinion, is the reason for their silence concerning the Pyramid's interior layout.

Solinus (*c.* 250)

He points out the phenomenon of the consumption of the shadow.

de Telmahre (*c.* 830)

He visited Egypt during the reign of Al Mamun. He gives 500 cubits as the value of the Great Pyramid's base and 50 cubits as the length of the Descending Passage. The latter datum is important; for it means that during Al Mamun's time the Descending Passage was already blocked at exactly the same spot where Greaves, Norden, and the members of the French Expedition to Egypt were halted.

Masudi (*c.* 940) and Abd-al-Latif (*c.* 1200)

Both these authors, and many other Arab authors, report that the two great pyramids were covered with hieroglyphic inscriptions.

d'Anglure (1395)

He witnessed the demolition of the casing of one of the pyramids, probably the pyramid of Kephren.

Maqrizi (*c.* 1400)

He reports that according to Ibrahim Wassif Shah:

> Calif Abdallah-Ali-Mamun-ben-Harun el-Rashid (813–33) ordered that the Great Pyramid be opened. And it was for him that the hole was made that is still gaping today: fire, vinegar, and levers were used for this; blacksmiths worked at it; and considerable amounts of money were spent on it. The thickness of the wall was about 20 cubits [9.20 m.] . . .

The latter datum has its importance, for the entire tunnel, leading to the granite blocks in the Ascending Passage, has a length of 38 meters. This excavation was thus made *prior* to the time of Al Mamun, who merely had the passage *reopened* by perforating the facing and six or seven courses behind it, which had been put back in place during a restoration of the Pyramid, probably under Ramesses II.

Ibrahim Ben Ebn Wassif Shah adds that the Great Pyramid was covered from top to bottom with a "brocade" of color.

Pierre Belon (1540)

Belon states that the third pyramid was, during his time, in a perfect state of conservation.

Lambert (1630)

He reports that there were twelve blocks forming the summit of the core, that the platform measured 20 spans (4.84 meters) in length, and that at the center of the twelve stones there was one that in length and width surpassed human belief.

Edward Melton (1661)

Melton states that the Great Pyramid did not end in a point, but included a platform topped by a statue.

John Greaves (1638)

Greaves points out that the Queen's Chamber, which was pervaded by a bad odor, was coated with stucco, and was full of piled-up debris, and that the well, extremely congested toward the bottom, had notches in which to place one's hands and feet. He notes the two ducts in the King's Chamber. He is silent concerning "Al Mamun's" hole.

Norden (1737)

He correctly describes the Great Pyramid's interior; the level of the Ascending Passage could not be reached except by way of the opening in the Descending Passage, which had been obstructed earlier. He does not mention "Al Mamun's" hole at all but reports that the Queen's Chamber was littered with stones and the well was plugged up.

The French Expedition to Egypt (1799)

"Al Mamun's" hole was unknown, for it was obstructed by debris. The members of the Expedition had to use the despoilers' opening, as the Descending Passage was still blocked.

The well was plugged up; Colonel Coutelle tried to clear it (without success, for lack of time). The first relieving chamber was accessible.

Gerard de Nerval (1842)

He also had to make use of the despoilers' opening in order to succeed in penetrating the Pyramid. He mentions numerous graffiti made by Napoleon's Old Guard and the inscription freshly engraved by Lepsius on the Pyramid's fronton.

Perring and Caviglia (1835)

They cleared the Descending Passage, the Subterranean Chamber, and the well.

Howard-Vyse (1837)
He found the Descending Passage cleared down to the Subterranean Chamber and the latter cluttered with stones and debris; the blind passage was open.

Baraize and Barsanti (1917–32)
They subjected the entire Pyramid to a methodical cleaning.

At present (1970) access to the Queen's Chamber and the "well" is forbidden; moreover, the Descending Passage is again obstructed by debris and desert sand carried in by rainwater, making the entrance to the Subterranean Chamber impassable.

THE CONSTRUCTION

According to Borchardt, whose views seem to be widely accepted in Egyptological circles, the plans of the Great Pyramid were modified *twice* during the course of its construction. In his opinion, the Subterranean Chamber (initial plan) is an *abandoned* chamber, as is the middle chamber, known as the "Queen's Chamber" (second plan). The upper chamber, known as the "King's Chamber," containing the sarcophagus, was the realization of the third plan.

For many reasons it seemed to me *impossible* that this should have been the case; I go along with Petrie in asserting that the plan of the Great Pyramid was established *once and for all, before work began.* Indeed, the pyramidal complex of Cheops forms *a coherent whole;* it would have been impossible to alter it even slightly after the completion of the primordial geodesic operations determining the orientation, and the laying out of the border of the sides of the base, the value of which was connected to that of a minute of an arc of the meridian.

One fact whose importance has eluded all those who have attempted studies of the Great Pyramid is the *hollowing of the faces* in an astronomical design, which required that the Descending Passage's entrance be displaced 7.34 meters (14 cubits) east of the meridian plane. This displacement of the Descending Passage was an absolute necessity, for the north face constituted an immense gutter for rainwater, the flow of which might have been considerable during a storm. Placing the Descending Passage's *mobile door* in the center of this gutter would inevitably have meant the total inundation of the Subterranean Chamber. This, quite simply, is the reason for Davidson's "displacement factor."

This eastward displacement of the Descending Passage must have posed a delicate problem for the architect in charge of construction in determining the passage's point of impact in the bedrock precisely; for its placement was connected to that of the Descending Passage's future mobile door in the Pyramid's facing, which could not be put in place until construction work had been completed. Once the Descending Passage had been started, *nothing* could be changed.

The various stages of construction can be established as follows:

FIRST STAGE

The primordial, most important stage consisted of the topographical work: the strict leveling of the plateau, particularly along the sides and the northern esplanade; the laying out of the base, following the precise orientation of the sides and taking into account the hollowing of the faces; and the absolutely precise determination of the Descending Passage's point of impact (A) in the bedrock, 14 cubits east of the Pyramid's meridian and 100 cubits (52.40 meters) from the middle of the north face.

I discussed earlier the method the Egyptian topographers used to determine north-south bearings; they employed the intersections made by stars of the Southern Hemisphere along an artificial horizon composed of a cord stretched east-west. This method required that the ground be perfectly leveled.

SECOND STAGE

The second phase consisted of constructing the causeway to be used in transporting the blocks brought in the Turah quarriers' feluccas. According to Herodotus, this causeway measured 5 stades (920 meters) long and 10 fathoms (18.50 meters) wide.

During this time the excavation of the Descending Passage

(AF) was carried out, backed up by a shaft (CF) (incorrectly called the "well") contrived about 4 meters west of the axis of the Descending Passage and along a plane parallel to that of the latter, its entrance being 160 cubits (83.80 meters) from the center of the Pyramid's north socle. This shaft allowed laborers to *descend,* as the Descending Passage was reserved for their *ascending* co-workers bearing baskets loaded with stone-cutting debris.

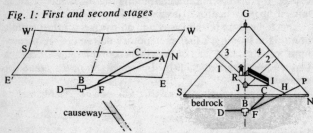

Fig. 1: First and second stages

Fig. 2: Completion of the Pyramid

The perforation of the Descending Passage was followed by the excavation of the Subterranean Chamber (B) and its blind passage (D).

According to Herodotus, it took *ten years* to lay out the causeway and construct the subterranean *chambers.* He mentions that Cheops' sepulchral chamber was arranged in such a way that the sarcophagus was located on an island surrounded by water brought in from the Nile by an underground canal. He says the same was true of the pyramid of Kephren, except that the latter lacked the underground canal supplying Nile water.

Herodotus' account should not be rejected *a priori* because we now know the arrangement of the Subterranean Chamber could not have required more than two years' work. The strange resonance in this room suggests the probable existence of an immense lower chamber as yet undiscovered. I discussed this possibility earlier.

THIRD STAGE

The completion of the causeway made it possible to haul the blocks to be used for the Pyramid's socle.

Obviously, the most critical task was the necessarily impeccable alignment of the blocks constituting the socle of the Pyramid, with its four hollowed faces. Upon this socle, and it alone, depended the chances for building the entire edifice perfectly, since the future positioning of the casing blocks would be obtained by arranging the blocks 1 pygon (0.43 meter) parallel to the edge of the socle.

Once this was done it was possible to begin constructing the core, by superimposing successive courses and laying out the upper part of the Descending Passage (HP) and the Ascending Passage (HI), including, on the west side of the latter, a lateral recess for the temporary storage of the three granite plugblocks. This recess was connected vertically with the Descending Passage by means of a narrow shaft that allowed the laborers assigned to block the passage to withdraw afterwards.

The opening of this narrow shaft must have been carefully sealed with cemented blocks. It was by reopening this hole, that the first despoilers were able to penetrate the Pyramid's interior. It still exists and was in use up until the time "Al Mamun's" hole was unplugged.

The interior layout continued with the construction of the Horizontal Passage (IJ), the *serdab* (J), and its two psychic ducts (1 and 2).

It should be noted that once the first course was set in place, the shaft (CF) reserved for the descending laborers was sealed. The connection of the shaft with the Grand Gallery (IC) was made through the masonry, probably under Ramesses II, over 2,000 years later.

FOURTH STAGE

This stage consisted of laying out the Grand Gallery and placing, along each of the two lateral banquettes, the twenty-eight facing pairs of statues of the rulers of Egypt starting with Menes; then laying out the chamber of portcullises, the King's Chamber, the two psychic ducts (3 and 4), and setting the sarcophagus in place.

FIFTH STAGE

Construction of the relieving chambers and completion, by tiers, of the core. Then, arrangement of the platform and placement of the gnomon. During this work the construction of the "lower temple" and "upper temple" (the latter was adjacent to the Pyramid's east face must have taken place.

SIXTH STAGE

This must have consisted of setting the casing blocks in place, dressing them, and applying a cement-base plaster paint made of crushed granite and red hematite; for, like the Sphinx and the pyramid of Kephren, the Great Pyramid was painted red.

SEVENTH STAGE

This final stage consisted of, first, raising the surrounding wall, which was about 4 cubits (2.10 meters) high, and arranging the four solar barques, two to the east and two to the south, then installing a pavement 1 cubit thick along the entire northern terrace and carving in the bedrock, parallel to and about 90 meters from the north face, a trench 1.90 meters deep to be used in determining the winter solstice.

At that point, the finished Pyramid awaited the mummified royal remains. But was it the privilege of the sarcophagus found in the upper chamber to hold the corpse? I do not think so; in my opinion, this sarcophagus must have been used *solely* for the transferral of the divine *ka* into Kephren's body after his initiation in the Subterranean Chamber.

Once the transferral of the *ka* had been carried out, the central chamber had become a sacred place, forbidden to all, and *the portcullises were lowered on an empty tomb*.

As for the royal mummy of Cheops, it must still lie— protected by the waters of the Nile—58 meters deep in the bedrock, beneath the Pyramid, the solar temple of the god Khnum.

At any rate, whether the upper chamber served as the royal sepulcher or simply as the site of the transferral of the divine *ka*, there is no doubt—despite the denials of Bruchet and the biblical dreamers'—that the three portcullises were lowered and that the passage to the Antechamber was obstructed with a granite block. The deep brutal gashes that the despoilers left in the walls constitute irrefutable evidence.

The inhumation of the royal remains was necessarily followed by the rites of the opening of the mouth of the "double" lodged in the niche in the *serdab* (Queen's Chamber). The Horizontal Passage leading to this chamber was probably then obstructed.

Finally, the three granite blocks provisionally stored in the niche located on the right side of the Ascending Passage were set in place to block the passage. This niche, as I mentioned earlier, was connected to the Descending Passage by means of a narrow shaft whose opening was later sealed with cemented blocks.

At that point, only the Subterranean Chamber, reserved for minor initiations, remained accessible by way of the Descending Passage equipped with its swivel door.

Guarded by the priests of the sacerdotal college of the "upper temple," to whom the cult of the deified deceased king had been entrusted, the Pyramid seemed eternally indestructible and inviolable. Alas, it can be assumed that, as was the case with the royal hypogea of Thebes, the priests-guardians of the Pyramid were its first despoilers.

THE SUCCESSIVE SPOLIATIONS

A detailed analysis of ancient sites and documents has led me to the following historical accounts.

First Spoliation

This was probably the work of the priests of the Pyramid, starting from the beginning of the reign of Menkaura, or Mykerinos (4700–4637 B.C.). Mykerinos had embraced the Heliopolitan god Ra and rejected the god Khnum of Upper Egypt; therefore, his tomb remained inviolate up until the time of Al Mamun (815 A.D.).

The Great Pyramid's Subterranean Chamber, reserved for first-degree isiac initiations, was abandoned, and access to it was forbidden. Then the priests of the Great Pyramid, knowing the location of the egress of the narrow shaft used by the laborers assigned to block up the Ascending Passage to withdraw, forced the cemented blocks that sealed its opening on the Descending Passage, and thus reached the Ascending Passage by circumventing the granite blocks.

But their most difficult task was wresting the granite plug that sealed the entrance corridor of the Antechamber

(chamber of the portcullises); the deep marks they left over the "Great Step" at the top of the Grand Gallery attest to the laboriousness of this task.

Reaching the Antechamber and climbing over the portcullises, which were still in place, the despoilers attacked the south wall, carving a narrow passage in the granite arch of the access corridor of the chamber of the sarcophagus.

SECOND SPOLIATION

The true spoliation of the Great Pyramid probably took place toward the end of the Sixth Dynasty (4123 B.C.). At that time a social revolution was raging, and the tombs were systematically pillaged. It is not inconceivable that the sacking of the Great Pyramid was—at least at the start of the revolutionary turmoil—encouraged by the priests, who had long since stolen the most precious objects. Hadn't Cheops, the schismatic king, imported the usurper god Khnum of Upper Egypt into the fiefs of Ptah and Ra? It was thus fitting that his works be destroyed and his name erased forever from the memory of man.

In a paroxysm of hatred and vengeance, the people erupted in frenzied vandalism (cf. Herodotus and Diodorus Siculus). The tunnel of the Descending Passage, reopened by the priests, was judged to be insufficient for the great sack; so the Pyramid's facing was smashed and a horizontal excavation 35 meters long was made through the masonry core, ending at the three granite blocks that sealed off the Ascending Passage. The fifty-six paired facing statues in the "gallery of the ancestors" (Grand Gallery) were broken to bits; their royal names, sculpted at the level of the third corbel, were chiseled out; and the divine debris of the representatives of absolutism ended up on the trash heap. *Sic transit gloria mundi!*

The statue in the *serdab*, Khufu's basalt "double," was also destroyed, as well as the table of offerings, his funerary furniture, and the *ushebtiu* ("respondants") in charge of seeing to his welfare in the beyond. The destruction of the granite portcullises of the Antechamber cleared the way to the chamber of the sarcophagus, the cover of which was broken; but the desecration of the royal mummy seems most unlikely, as the sarcophagus was probably empty.

Herodotus' and Diodorus Siculus' accounts concerning

this matter seem to be veracious. One eventuality the priests of the Pyramid certainly did not anticipate—the "upper temple" and its annexes were also completely destroyed and burned.

The turmoil, as much social as it was religious, persisted from the Seventh through the Ninth Dynasty (4123–3977 B.C.). The contemporary papyruses that have come down to us describe the lamentable state in which Egypt found itself at the time:

> If thou dost think of burial, it is a grief for the heart, it is what brings tears, troubling a man. Nevermore wilt thou rise towards heaven, to see Ra, the Sun of the Gods. . . . They who have been carved in pink granite, for whom chambers have been made in the pyramid, who have achieved works of beauty, the builders who have become gods—their offering-tables are empty, like those of the neglected dead, who died on the shore, without survivors.
>
> Bodies have gone, and others have remained (in their place), since the time of our Ancestors. The Gods (deceased Kings) who once lived sleep in their pyramids, and the nobles also, the glorious ones, are buried in their tombs. They built houses, of which the place no longer exists. What, then, has become of them. I have heard the words of Imhetep[1] and Hardedef,[2] whose sayings are repeated everywhere. Where are their places now? Their walls are destroyed, their places no longer exist, as if they had never been.[3]

THE RESTORATION OF THE GREAT PYRAMID UNDER RAMESSES II

Over two thousand years passed, and the disemboweled Great Pyramid remained deserted until the accession of Ramesses II (1287 B.C)

An inscription carved in the bedrock opposite the pyramid of Kephren informs us that his minister of labor, Mai, "grandee of the temple of Maat," and Seankh-Pa, superintendent of construction at the temple of Amon in Thebes, worked on restoring the two great pyramids of Giza. Beneath the inscription is found, carved deep in the bedrock, the same mysterious symbol that is sculpted in the ceiling of the Great Pyramid's Subterranean Chamber.

It can be assumed that the purpose of the work undertaken at the Great Pyramid was to put it to rights so that isiac initiations could be resumed.

I have already pointed out that under the Old Kingdom only the pharaoh could attain to the complete initiation. When Cheops died, Kephren had to undergo this initiation. After his first symbolic rebirth upon leaving the Subterranean Chamber's uterine (blind) passage, Kephren, like any newborn baby, was plunged into the purifying lustral water of the square pit placed in the uneven floor of the chamber of Chaos (which should come as no surprise to Masonic initiates).

After the ritual interrogation concerning his esoteric knowledge conducted by the hierophant, the future pharaoh had to climb the Descending Passage, then the Ascending Passage and the gallery of his ancestors, in order to scale the Great Step to the chamber of the portcullises and to penetrate, entering back first, the Pyramid's central chamber, the chamber of the sarcophagus.

There he had to die symbolically a second time, in the course of a magic ceremony, so that his predecessor's divine *ka* could enter his own body. The initiate, according to Hermes Trismegistus, is he who, twice dead, is thrice born.

Once the ceremonies of the transferral of the *ka* had been completed, the central chamber, *having become a sacred place*, had to be permanently closed off: the portcullises were lowered and the Ascending Passage was sealed with three granite blocks.

The revolution that erupted toward the end of the Sixth Dynasty was both social and religious. The day was past when only the pharaoh could aspire to celestial light, while his subjects themselves contented with eternally contemplating the god Osiris' greenish flesh in the shadowy regions of hell. Henceforth, everyone, according to his merit, could aspire to the light of Ra—provided he had been initiated.

The lower chamber of the Pyramid, accessible by way of the Descending Passage equipped with its swivel door, would continue, as always, to serve as the site of the ceremonies of the second birth, the first stage of the initiation. But for the ultimate test it was absolutely necessary to reestablish access to the central chamber, and this was certainly the purpose of the restoration work directed by Mai and Seankh-Pa, high priests of Maat and Amon, during the reign of Ramesses II.

This work involved:

1. Reblocking the old hole that had been dug in Descending Passage, under the three granite blocks.

2. Clearing the gallery of the ancestors of the debris of the royal statues, the remains of the granite plugs, and the three portcullises of the Antechamber.

3. Perforating the plaques of the two psychic ducts in the chamber of the sarcophagus, as well as piercing the part of the casing that was blocking off their ends—this in order to establish ventilation, which was indispensable.

4. Connecting the old shaft used by the descending stonecutters, which ended near the Subterranean Chamber, by digging a "well" *through the masonry*, from the location of the twenty-eighth (lowermost) statue on the west ramp of the Grand Gallery.

5. Finally, closing off the outer end of the great excavation and replacing the casing on the north face. Perhaps also a small obelisk was again placed on the platform of the Pyramid, so that when its sacerdotal college was reconstituted, it might reassume its original destination as solar temple.

THE GREAT PYRAMID FROM THE TIME OF RAMESSES II TO THE PRESENT

It can be assumed that once it was restored, the Great Pyramid again fulfilled its role as both solar temple and temple of isiac initiation. Ramesses II, in fact, reestablished a college of priests attached to the three pyramids, and the cult of Cheops, Kephren, and Mykerinos was restored to honor after over two thousand years. (This cult persisted up to the time of the Roman occupation.)

Stripped of its royal treasures, the Great Pyramid ceased to be a source of attraction to despoilers and pillagers, even during foreign occupations. Thus it remained unchanged up to the time of the Lagid Dynasty. It was visited by Herodotus, Diodorus Siculus, Strabo, and Pliny; the gnomon-obelisk had certainly disappeared, for otherwise these authors would not have neglected to mention its presence.

The Arab authors relate that pilgrims came to visit the Pyramid from all over the world, from Yemenite Arabia in particular, as the Sabeans were sun worshippers.

With the reign of Theodosius (379 A.D.), the Great Pyramid ceased to serve as an initiation temple. The early Christians wished to wipe out Egyptian paganism. Saint Cyril, the fanatical patriarch of Alexandria, ordered that all the temples and their idols be methodically destroyed. (It was at this time that Hypatia, daughter of the mathematician Theon, was stoned to death.) We should remember this fact and not lay all the blame for the acts of destruction on the Arabs; it was enough that they tore down the Great Pyramid's facing, as well as that of the pyramid of Kephren, in addition to mutilating the Sphinx's face.

The reopening of the Descending Passage's entrance, which had been filled in under Ramesses II, should probably be assigned to this period. This is also true of the excavation of the "grotto" carved in the Pyramid's "well." This cavity was occasioned by the presence of a granite block that formed the primitive curbstone of the shaft used for the stonecutters' descent while the Subterranean Chamber was being constructed. Despoilers always considered the presence of granite a sign of the possible presence of a secret chamber. It was nothing of the sort, however, and the debris from the excavation, thrown into the shaft, blocked up its connection with the Descending Passage.

Then came Arabic rule. In around 815 A.D. Al Mamun, who was visiting Egypt, took a great interest in the pyramids, particularly the pyramid of Cheops. He understood the pyramids' scientific significance and set the value of the cubit at $1/400$th the base. Upon his return to Baghdad, he had a test measurement of the meridian carried out in the desert plain of Sinjar, 150 kilometers west of the Euphrates.

But before he left Egypt, he wished to learn the Great

Pyramid's interior layout and therefore had his men reopen the great hole in the facing that Ramesses II had had repaired. The excavation that is being used as an entrance at the present time (1970) cannot be credited to Al Mamun in its entirely. According to the Arab authors, the hole he had made was only 20 cubits (9.20 meters) deep, whereas the excavation that meets the three granite blocks is 55 meters long.

There was no question as to where to pierce the casing. Since the tunnel of the Descending Passage had already been reopened, Al Mamun's men had only to pierce the extension of the old tunnel, which had simply been closed off at its northern end. Thus Al Mamun's incision was limited to perforating the facing and extracting a few blocks that had been replaced under Ramesses II.

Despite the Arab authors' accounts, it is certain that Al Mamun found no mummy, nor any valuable objects inside the Great Pyramid. The same was true of the pyramid of Kephren, which had been despoiled thousands of years earlier.

All that the Arabs discovered, after an incredible amount of work, was Mykerinos' tomb. A graffito, still clearly legible on the north wall of the chamber of the sarcophagus, mentions that "Mussa the blacksmith opened [it] in 199" (815 A.D.).

Starting with the reign of Saladin (1169 A.D.), the Great Pyramid was turned over to Arab quarriers and became a demolition site; its facing blocks were used to build the citadel and mosques of Cairo, as well as bridges and dams along the Nile. What could have been the reason for these depredations, when it would have been much easier to take the necessary blocks directly from the Turah quarries? Such a senseless act of vandalism from a scientific and historical standpoint can only be attributed to religious fanaticism.

According to the Arab authors themselves, the casings of the two great pyramids were covered with inscriptions. Abd-al-Latif, the most judicious of these authors, writes:

These stones are covered with writing of the ancient type, the significance of which is no longer known . . . These inscriptions are so numerous that, if one were to copy on paper only those visible on the surface of these two pyramids, they would fill up over ten thousand pages . . .

The same fact is related with greater precision by Qodai:

We examined the faces of these pyramids; they are crossed by longitudinal lines forming narrow parallel bands completely covered with writing that, though it is clearly visible, no one now knows how to read; its meaning is no longer understood . . .

The disappearance of the casing had an unfortunate consequence in terms of the monument's endurance. Whereas the facing blocks had been fine, solid Turah limestone, the blocks forming the masonry core are mediocre-quality limestone. Before long atmospheric agents caused serious damage and the debris from erosion, which accumulated at the foot of the Pyramid, completely covered the entrance to Al Mamun's excavation. Soon other debris, mixing with Aeolian sand washed down the Descending Passage by rainwater, clogged up the entrance to the Subterranean Chamber and filled the Descending Passage nearly up to the level of the three granite blocks closing off the Ascending Passage. Therefore the scholars accompanying the French Expedition to Egypt (1798–1801) were unaware of the existence of the Subterranean Chamber and "Al Mamun's" hole. They were forced—as were future visitors—to make the arduous climb over the granite blocks in the ancient shaft of the first despoilers.

The Subterranean Chamber and its connection with the Grand Gallery via the "well" remained undiscovered until the advent of Howard-Vyse, Caviglia, and Perring (1837).

Baraize and Barsanti undertook a methodical cleaning of the Pyramid and the surrounding area in 1916, and their work, completed in 1932, enabled me to photograph the strange Subterranean Chamber. Fortunately! For at the present time (1970), only thirty-eight years after my stay in Egypt, the Subterranean Chamber is again blocked off and inaccessible. Until that monument finally disappears, it will be necessary to subject the Descending Passage and lower chamber to a periodic cleaning.

At present, the Pyramid is entered by way of the excavation attributed to Al Mamun. One is only allowed to visit the Grand Gallery and the King's Chamber; access to the *serdab* (the Queen's Chamber) is forbidden. Unfortunately, totally inadequate electric lighting makes visiting the Pyramid rather uninteresting. Very fortunately, the delightful nocturnal "Sound and Light" show, which brings the Giza Plateau back to life, returns the avid tourist to the world of the ancient pharaohs, a world seven thousand years old.

A recent experiment made by American researchers, carried out from the lower chamber of the pyramid of Kephren, is quite interesting. Its purpose was to disclose the presence of any unknown chambers by using a computer to count the mesons detected and registered under each of the azimuths. So far, however, the attempt has afforded no definite results. For my part, I strongly doubt there are chambers within the masonry. Kephren's sepulchral crypt must be sought very deep in the bedrock beneath the pyramid; and in this case, the American researchers' method would be useless. Only the geophysical techniques the oil industry uses in its exploration would be able to provide more information.

NOTES

1. Architect for Zoser, Third Dynasty.
2. Architect for Cheops and Kephren, Fourth Dynasty.
3. "Dialogue between an Egyptian and His Spirit," in Alexandre Moret, *The Nile and Egyptian Civilization* (New York: Alfred A. Knopf, 1927), p. 223–224.

CHAPTER 7

RETURNING TO THE SOURCES

RECONSTRUCTED CHRONOLOGICAL
LIST OF THE RULERS OF EGYPT
FROM MENES TO DIOCLETIAN

NAMES	LENGTH OF REIGN (YEARS)	TOTAL PER DYNASTY	TOTAL STARTING FROM MENES	POSITION IN THE CHRONOLOGY OF ATHOTHIS	POSITION IN THE CHRISTIAN CHRONOLOGY[1]
● DYNASTY 1					B.C.
1. Menes	62			−62 to +1	5619–5557
2. Athothis	47			1–47	5557–5511
3. Kenkenes	31			47–78	5511–5480
4. Uenephes	23			78–101	5480–5457
5. Usaphaidos	20			101–121	5457–5437
6. Miebidos	26			121–147	5437–5411
7. Semempses	18			147–165	5411–5393
8. Bieneches	26	253	253	165–191	5393–5367
● DYNASTY 2					
1. Boethos	38			191–229	5367–5329
2. Kaiechos	39			229–268	5329–5290
3. Binothris	47			268–315	5290–5243
4. Tlas	17			315–332	5243–5226
5. Sethenes	41			332–373	5226–5185

NAMES	LENGTH OF REIGN (YEARS)	TOTAL PER DYNASTY	TOTAL STARTING FROM MENES	POSITION IN THE CHRONOLOGY OF ATHOTHIS	POSITION IN THE CHRISTIAN CHRONOLOGY[1]
6. Chaires	17			373–390	5185–5168
7. Nefercheres	25			390–415	5168–5143
8. Sesochris	48			415–463	5143–5095
9. Cheneres	30	302	555	463–493	5095–5065
● DYNASTY 3					
1. Necherophes	28			493–521	5065–5037
2. Tosorthros	29			521–550	5037–5008
3. Tyreis	7			550–557	5008–5001
4. Mesochris	17			557–574	5001–4984
5. Soyphis	16			574–590	4984–4968
6. Tosertasis	19			590–609	4968–4949
7. Aches	42			609–651	4949–4907
8. Sephuris	30			651–681	4907–4877
9. Kerpheres	26	214	769	681–707	4877–4851
● DYNASTY 4					
1. Soris	22			707–729	4851–4829
2. Suphis I	63			729–792	4829–4766
3. Suphis II	66			792–858	4766–4700
4. Mencheres	63			858–921	4700–4637
5. Ratoises	25			921–946	4637–4612
6. Bicheris	22			946–968	4612–4590
7. Sebercheres	7			968–975	4590–4583
8. Thamphthis	9	277	1046	975–984	4583–4574
● DYNASTY 5					
1. Usercheres	28			984–1022	4574–4546
2. Sephres	13			1022–1025	4546–4533
3. Nephercheres	20			1025–1045	4533–4513
4. Sisires	7			1045–1052	4513–4506
5. Cheres	20			1052–1072	4506–4486
6. Rathures	44			1072–1116	4486–4442
7. Mencheres	39			1116–1155	4442–4403
8. Tancheres	44			1155–1199	4403–4359
9. Onnus	33	248	1294	1199–1232	4359–4326
● DYNASTY 6					
1. Othoes	30			1232–1262	4326–4296
2. Phius	53			1262–1315	4296–4243
3. Methusuphis	7			1315–1322	4243–4236
4. Phiops	100			1322–1422	4236–4136
5. Menthesuphis	1			1422–1423	4136–4135
6. Nitocris	12	203	1497	1423–1435	4135–4123

NAMES	LENGTH OF REIGN (YEARS)	TOTAL PER DY-NASTY	TOTAL STARTING FROM MENES	POSITION IN THE CHRO-NOLOGY OF ATHOTHIS	POSITION IN THE CHRIS-TIAN CHRO-NOLOGY[1]
• DYNASTY 7	70 days		1497+2 mo.	1435	4123
• DYNASTY 8					
27 kings of Memphis	146	146	1643+2 mo.	1435–1581	4123–3977
• DYNASTY 9					
Achthoes and 18 kings of Heracleopolis	409	409	2052+2 mo.	1581–1990	3977–3568
• DYNASTY 10					
19 kings of Heracleopolis	189	189	2241+2 mo.	1990–2179	2179–3378
• DYNASTY 11					
16 kings of Diospolis	43	43	2284+2 mo.	2179–2222	3568–3378
• DYNASTY 12					
1. Ammanemes	16	16	2300+2 mo.	2222–2238	3336–3320

END OF THE FIRST BOOK OF MANETHO

2. Sesonchosis	46			2238–2284	3320–3274
3. Ammanemes	38			2284–2322	3274–3236
4. Sesostris	48			2322–2370	3236–3188
5. Lachares	8			2370–2378	3188–3180
6. Ameres	8			2378–2386	3180–3172
7. Ammenemes	8			2386–2394	3172–3164
8. Scemiophris	4	160	2460+2 mo.	2394–2398	3164–3160
• DYNASTY 13					
60 kings of Diospolis	453	453	2913+2 mo.	2398–2851	3160–2707
• DYNASTY 14					
76 kings of Xois	184	184	3097+2 mo.	2851–3035	2707–2523
• DYNASTY 15					
43 kings of Tanis and 43 kings of Thebes	151	151	3248+2 mo.	3035–3186	2523–2372
• DYNASTY 16					
32 kings of Tanis	518	518	3766+2 mo.	3186–3704	2372–1854

NAMES	LENGTH OF REIGN (YEARS)	TOTAL PER DYNASTY	TOTAL STARTING FROM MENES	POSITION IN THE CHRONOLOGY OF ATHOTHIS	POSITION IN THE CHRISTIAN CHRONOLOGY[1]
• DYNASTY 17					
1. Saites	19			3704–3723	1854–1835
2. Bnon	44			3723–3767	1835–1791
3. Pachnan	61			3767–3828	1791–1730
4. Staan	50			3828–3878	1730–1680
5. Archles	49			3878–3927	1680–1631
6. Aphophis[2]	61	284	4050+2 mo.	3927–3988	1631–1570
• DYNASTY 17, according to Josephus					
1. Salites	19			3704–3723	1854–1835
2. Bnon	44			3723–3767	1835–1791
3. Apachnan	36			3767–3803	1791–1755
4. Apophis	61			3803–3864	1755–1694
5. Sethos	50			3864–3914	1694–1644
6. Certos	29			3914–3943	1644–1615
7. Assis	20	259	4025	3943–3963	1615–1595
• DYNASTY 18					
1. Amos	25	25	4050+2 mo.	3963–3988	1595–1570
2. Chebros	13			3988–4001	1570–1557
3. Amenophthis	24			4001–4025	1557–1533
4. Amensis	22			4025–4047	1533–1511
5. Misaphris	13			4047–4060	1511–1498
6. Misaphragmuthosis	26			4060–4086	1498–1472
7. Tuthmosis	9			4086–4095	1472–1463
8. Amenophis	31			4095–4126	1463–1432
9. Orus	37			4126–4163	1432–1395
10. Acherres	32			4163–4195	1395–1363
11. Rathos	6			4195–4201	1363–1357
12. Chebres	12			4201–4213	1357–1345
13. Acherres	12			4213–4225	1345–1333
14. Armesis	5			4225–4230	1333–1328
15. Ramesses	1			4230–4231	1328–1327
16. Amenophath	19	262	4312+2 mo.	4231–4250	1327–1308
Sothic Cycle of Menophres			*4298*	*4236*	July 20, 1322 (Julian calendar)
• DYNASTY 19					
1. Sethos	21			4250–4271	1308–1287
2. Rapsaces	66			4271–4337	1287–1221
3. Ammenephthes	10			4337–4347	1221–1211
4. Ammenemnes	5			4347–4352	1211–1206
5. Thuoris	7	109	4421+2 mo.	4352–4359	1206–1199

NAMES	LENGTH OF REIGN (YEARS)	TOTAL PER DY-NASTY	TOTAL STARTING FROM MENES	POSITION IN THE CHRO-NOLOGY OF ATHOTHIS	POSITION IN THE CHRIS-TIAN CHRO-NOLOGY[1]

END OF THE SECOND BOOK OF MANETHO: 2300 + 2121

• DYNASTY 20

NAMES	LENGTH	TOTAL	TOTAL	ATHOTHIS	CHRISTIAN
1. Setnakht	2			4359–4361	1199–1197
2. Ramesses III (Uosimares)	32			4361–4393	1197–1165
3–8. Ramesses IV to Ramesses XI	101	135	4556+2 mo.	4393–4494	1165–1064

• DYNASTY 21

NAMES					
1. Smendes	26			4494–4520	1064–1038
2. Psusennes	41			4520–4561	1038–997
3. Nephercheres	4			4561–4565	997–993
4. Amenophthis	9			4565–4574	993–984
5. Osochor	6			4574–4580	984–978
6. Psinaches	9			4580–4589	978–969
7. Psusennes	35	130	4686+2 mo.	4589–4624	969–934

• DYNASTY 22

NAMES					
1. Sesonchis	21			4624–4645	934–913
2. Osorthon	15			4645–4660	913–898
3–5. *Unnamed*	29			4660–4689	898–869
6. Takelothis	13			4689–4702	869–856
7–9. *Unnamed*	42	120	4806+2 mo.	4702–4744	856–814

• DYNASTY 23

NAMES					
1. Petubates	40			4744–4784	814–774
2. Osorcho	8			4784–4792	774–766
3. Psammus	10			4792–4802	776–756
4. Zet	31	89	4895+2 mo.	4802–4833	756–725

• DYNASTY 24

NAMES					
Bochchoris	6	6	4901+2 mo.	4833–4839	725–719

• DYNASTY 25

NAMES					
1. Sabacon	8			4839–4847	719–711
2. Sebichos	14			4847–4861	711–697
3. Tarcus	18	40	4941+2 mo.	4861–4879	697–679

• DYNASTY 26

NAMES					
1. Stephinates	7			4879–4886	679–672
2. Nechepsos	6			4886–4892	672–666
3. Nechao I	8			4892–4900	666–658

NAMES	LENGTH OF REIGN (YEARS)	TOTAL PER DYNASTY	TOTAL STARTING FROM MENES	POSITION IN THE CHRONOLOGY OF ATHOTHIS	POSITION IN THE CHRISTIAN CHRONOLOGY[1]
4. Psammetichus	54			4900–4954	658–604
5. Nechao II	6			4954–4960	604–598
6. Psammuthis II	6			4960–4966	598–592
7. Uaphris	19			4966–4985	592–573
8. Amosis	44			4985–5029	573–529
9. Psammecherites	6 mo.	150+ 6 mo.	5091+8 mo.	5029–5029	529–529
• DYNASTY 27					
1. Cambyses	6			5029–5035	529–523
2. Darius	36			5035–5071	523–487
3. Xerxes the Great	21			5071–5092	487–466
4. Artabanus	7 months			5092–5093	466–465
5. Artaxerxes	41			5093–5134	465–424
6. Xerxes	2 months			5134–5134	424–424
7. Sogdianus	7 months			5134–5135	424–423
8. Darius	19	124+ 4 mo.	5216[3]	5135–5154	423–404
• DYNASTY 28					
Amyrteos	6	6	5221	5154–5160	404–398
• DYNASTY 29					
1. Nepherites I	6			5160–5166	398–392
2. Achoris	13			5166–5179	392–379
3. Psammuthis	1			5179–5180	379–378
4. Nepherites II	4 months	20+4 mo.	5241+4 mo.	5180–5180	378–378
• DYNASTY 30					
1. Nektanebes	18			5180–5198	378–360
2. Teos	2			5198–5200	360–358
3. Nektanebus	18	38	5279+4 mo.	5200–5218	358–340
• DYNASTY 31					
1. Ochus	2			5218–5220	340–338
2. Arses	2			5220–5222	338–336
3. Darius	4	8	5287+4 mo.	5222–5226	336–332
• LAGID DYNASTY					
1. Alexander the Great	8			5226–5234	332–324
2. Philip	7			5234–5241	324–317

NAMES	LENGTH OF REIGN (YEARS)	TOTAL PER DYNASTY	TOTAL STARTING FROM MENES	POSITION IN THE CHRONOLOGY OF ATHOTHIS	POSITION IN THE CHRISTIAN CHRONOLOGY[1]
3. Alexander II	12			5241–5253	317–305
4. Ptolemy I (Soter)	20			5253–5273	305–285
5. Philadelphus	38			5273–5311	285–247
6. Euergetes I	25			5311–5336	247–222
7. Philopator	17			5336–5353	222–205
8. Epiphanes	24			5353–5377	205–181
9. Philometor	35			5377–5412	181–146
10. Euergetes II	29			5412–5441	146–117
11. Soter II	36			5441–5477	117–81
12. Dionysius Neu	29			5477–5506	81–52
13. Cleopatra	22	302	5589+4 mo.	5506–5528	52–30

• ROMAN EMPERORS

NAMES	LENGTH OF REIGN (YEARS)	TOTAL PER DYNASTY	TOTAL STARTING FROM MENES	POSITION IN THE CHRONOLOGY OF ATHOTHIS	POSITION IN THE CHRISTIAN CHRONOLOGY[1]
1. Augustus	43			5528–5571	−30 to +14
Embolism, fifth year				*5531*	*August 30, 26*
A.D.				*5558*	*+1*
2. Tiberius	22			5571–5593	14–36
3. Caligula	4			5593–5597	36–40
4. Claudius	14			5597–5611	40–54
5. Nero	14			5611–5625	54–68
6. Vespasian	10			5625–5635	68–78
7. Titus	3			5635–5638	78–81
8. Domitian	15			5638–5653	81–96
9. Nerva	1			5653–5654	96–97
10. Trajan	19			5654–5673	97–116
11. Hadrian	21			5673–5694	116–137
12. Antoninus Pius	23			5694–5717	137–160

Year 2: End of the Sothic cycle of Menophres:				*5696*	*July 20, 139*
13. Marcus Aurelius	19			5717–5736	160–179
14. Commodus	13			5736–5749	179–192
15. Septimus Severus	18			5749–5767	192–210
16. Caracalla	7			5767–5774	210–217
17. Antoninus the Younger	4			5774–5778	217–221
18. Alexander Mameus	13			5778–5791	221–234
19. Maximilinus	3			5791–5794	234–237
20. Gordianus	6			5794–5800	237–243
21. Philip	7			5800–5807	243–250
22. Decius	1			5807–5808	250–251
23. Gallus	2			5808–5810	251–253
24. Galerus	15			5810–5825	253–268

NAMES	LENGTH OF REIGN (YEARS)	TOTAL PER DY-NASTY	TOTAL STARTING FROM MENES	POSITION IN THE CHRO-NOLOGY OF ATHOTHIS	POSITION IN THE CHRIS-TIAN CHRO-NOLOGY[1]
25. Claudius II	1			5825–5826	268–269
26. Aurelian	6			5826–5832	269–275
27. Probus	7			5832–5839	275–282
28. Carus and Carinus	2	313	5902	5839–5841	282–284
29. Diocletian					

End of the fourth Sothic cycle in the chronology of Athothis and beginning of the Age of the Martyrs.

1st of Mesori, year 5841 of Athothis = July 25 (in the Julian calendar), 284 A.D., year 1 of the reign of Diocletian.

1st of Thoth, year 5841 of Athothis = August 29 (in the Julian calendar), 284 A.D.

NOTE: The years of the chronology of Athothis, beginning on July 25 in the Julian calendar, overlap two successive years in the Julian calendar. As a result:

Year 1 of Athothis overlaps the years 5557 and 5556 in the Julian calendar.

The last year of Tuthmosis (Exodus) overlaps the years 1463 and 1462.

Year 1 of the Age of the Martyrs (beginning of the fifth Sothic cycle, or year 5841 of Athothis) overlaps the years 284 and 285 A.D.

This fifth Sothic cycle, beginning on the 1st of Mesori (July 25 in the Julian calendar), was confused with the reign of Diocletian, which, however, did not begin until thirty-five days later, on the 1st of Thoth (August 29 in the Julian calendar).

THE DIVINE AND PREDYNASTIC DYNASTIES
According to Manetho, Transmitted by Eusebius

Dynasty of Gods		30544 B.C.
(13,900 years)		
Dynasty of Demigods	13900	16644 B.C.
(1255 years)		
First line of kings	15155	15389 B.C.
(1817 years)		
Thirty more kings of Memphis	16972	13572 B.C.
(1790 years)		
Ten kings of This	18762	11782 B.C.
(350 years)		
Spirits of the Dead	19112	11432 B.C.
(5813 years)		
First Dynasty: Menes	24925	5619 B.C.
(253 years)		
Second Dynasty: Boethos	25178	5367 B.C.
(302 years)		
Third Dynasty: Necherophes	25480	5065 B.C.
(214 years)		
Fourth Dynasty: Soris (22)	25694	2851 B.C.
Cheops (63)	25718	4829–4766 B.C.
(4497 years)		
Thirty-second Dynasty (Lagid)	30231	332 B.C.
(302 years)		
Augustus	30515	30 B.C.
Birth of Christ	30544	Dec. 25, 1 B.C.

THE CALENDRICAL CYCLES OF EGYPT

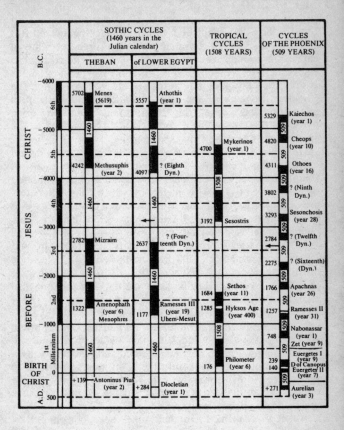

THE GREATEST ENIGMA OF ALL TIME: THE FLOOD

The reader will perhaps be astonished to see connected two subjects—the Great Pyramid and the dreadful diluvial cataclysm—which seem at first glance to bear no relation to each other. The reason for this is that the Egyptian pyramids are not the only pyramids in the world. Not to mention the Chaldean ziggurats and the Sudanese and Ethiopian pyramids, there exist in Central and South America pyramids that are oriented correctly and consecrated to the sun god, just like the Great Pyramid.

One question arises immediately: Is there any relation between the New World pyramids and the pyramids of Egypt, Ethiopia, and Chaldea? How could peoples separated by a distance of 11,500 kilometers (of which 7,000 kilometers are ocean) have had the same architectural ideas in regard to solar temples and tombs? Telepathy? Actual long-distance contact in the remote past?

Most American archaeologists date the Mexican and Peruvian pyramids at 1500 B.C. at the earliest, relegating most of them to 1400–700 B.C.; they do so without basing their claims on any specific scientific data. Is this not also true of most of our Egyptologists, who date the Great Pyramid at 2700 B.C., making an error of over 2,000 years?

Whereas Edward H. Thompson, foremost exponent of the Mexican pyramids, set himself up as a staunch defender of actual communication between the Old and New Worlds via the mysterious Atlantis before the latter was swallowed up by the ocean, his nephew, J. Eric Thompson, claims, on the contrary, that this idea is mad and is defended only by those ignorant of indigenous culture.

All new ideas have, in their time, been considered by "sensible" people to be follies. For my part, I am convinced that if the world had been inhabited only by sensible people, we would still be living in the Stone Age!

Max Planck—author of the famous quantum theory (the basis of modern physics), who was himself considered a madman and vilified by renowned scholars, the pundits of a "sensible" generation—wrote this vengeful passage:

New ideas do not usually conquer the world by means

of the adherence of their opponents, who end up becoming convinced they are true and adopting them . . . What happens is that the opponents of the new idea end up dying and the new generation is raised in the climate of this idea. Whoever possesses youth possesses the future.

To be sure, the idea that Atlantis existed is not new; indeed, it is quite old, but as it does not fit in with the biblical Genesis, it had to be ignored or combatted by Mosaic and Christian scholars.

When the earth's crust was being formed, the solidified parts, denser than water, had—because of centrifugal force—to be distributed uniformly on the liquid magma, on either side of the equator, while the water had to concentrate at the two poles.

Numerous massive cataclysms—of supraterrestrial, but in no way divine origin—then modified the distribution of the land masses and oceans, and repeatedly destroyed a major portion of the living creatures. One need only glance at a photograph of our satellite the moon in order to be convinced that the supraterrestrial cause of these cataclysms was falling asteroids, the effects of which have reverberated, through the ages to this day. The moon was incontestably the target of a cosmic bombardment. Thousands of points of impact remain clearly marked and visible because of the absence of agents of erosion; their diameters vary from a few hundred meters to 250 kilometers.

Consequently, according to Newton's law of gravity, since the ratio of the respective masses of the earth and the moon is 81:5, the earth must have been struck by nearly one hundred times as many asteroids as the moon was, and by heavier ones—thus by asteroids that were, in terms of surface, six times larger than those that struck the moon! Most of these millions of asteroids that fell to earth crashed either into the ocean or onto sedimentary terrains, where they embedded themselves deeply. Most of the mountainous land masses were simply the consequence of these cosmic shocks. "Crater Point" in the Arizona desert measures 1,200 meters in diameter and over 200 meters in depth; and it should be recalled that in Siberia, in 1908, a meteor devastated millions of square kilometers of forest. On Easter

Island the obsidian trail of the volcano Rana-Kao, pointed out by Francis Mazière, is dramatic evidence of this bombardment; its memory lives on among the islanders: "[It] fell from the Sky during the reign of King Rokoroko He Tau!"

We can easily understand that it was not without reason that our ancestors became cave dwellers at a certain stage—a stage that, unfortunately, may return any day now. Living in caves was a matter of survival since there was a good chance the sun might fall on them! This, according to Julius Caesar, was the only fear the Gauls experienced. The Olmec statue found in the park of La Venta in the state of Tabasco, who scrutinizes the sky with an anguished expression, his hands over his head, no doubt faithfully portrays the fear felt by all mankind at this time.

Let us make no mistake: Greek mythology is not pure fiction! To be sure, Hesiod and Ovid, in their cosmic tragedies, bring in Titans and imaginary gods, but the events related are real. The fight is waged with the help of enormous boulders similar to mountains! The noise of the battle causes the sky, the earth, and the oceans to tremble; Zeus hurls thunderbolts unremittingly.

Fertile tracts of land all around crackled as they burned, and immense forests roared in the fire. The whole earth and the Oceanstreams and the barren sea began to boil. An immense flame shot up into the atmosphere, so that the hot air enveloped the Titans, while their eyes, powerful as they were, were blinded by the brilliant flash of the lightning-bolt. The prodigious heat filled the Void. The sight there was to see, and the noise there was to hear, made it seem as if Earth and vast Sky above were colliding. If Earth were being smashed and if Sky were smashing down upon her, the noise would be as great as the noise that arose when the gods met in battle. The winds added to the confusion, whirling dust around together with great Zeus' volleys of thunder and lightning-bolts, and carrying the battle cries and shouts from one side to the other. . . .

Ultimately, Zeus emerges victorious, and the Titans, crushed by the boulders, are hurled down to Tartarus.

However, after an indefinite amount of time, the earth gives birth to a new Titan, Typhon, and the fight resumes. The great battle, which seemed to be over, starts up again!

The fighting is fearsome, and the entire universe is shaken. A fiery tempest is let loose between the sky and the earth. However, Zeus is again the victor; the darkened sun reappears. The cosmic drama is thus temporarily ended, but its consequences endure down to the present day.

As a sequel to Hesiod's titanomachy, it would not be unreasonable to include a more recent quote from Schliemann—the genius who discovered Troy, Mycenae, and Tiryns, and who was vilified by the official archaeologists of his day—concerning a Chaldean manuscript found in a monastery in Lhasa, Tibet.

Louis-Claude Vincent gives a French translation of the English text in the November 1912, *Magazine of the London Budget:*

When the star of Baal fell at the place where today there is only sky and sea, the seven cities with their golden gates and transparent temples trembled and shook like leaves in a storm; and behold, a torrent of flames and smoke rose from the palace. Screams of terror from the crowd filled the air. The people sought refuge in their temples and citadels, and the sage Mu—the hieretic Ra-Mu—rose and said, "Have I not predicted all this to you?" But the women and men with their jewels and brilliant garments wept and repeated, "Mu, save us!" and Mu answered, "You will all die together with your servants and your riches, and new nations will be born from your ashes! If they forget that they are superior, not because of what they possess but because of what they give, the same fate awaits them."
The flames and smoke stifled the voice of Mu; the country and its inhabitants were reduced to ashes, then engulfed by the waters.

Hesiod's two successive cosmic dramas and that of the fall of the star of Baal do not suggest any chronology.

Plato, in *Timaeus,* is much more explicit. He quotes a conversation that Solinus presumably had with a priest of

Neith belonging to the temple at Sais, in the course of a visit to Egypt during the reign of Amosis, eighth king of the Twenty-sixth Dynasty (573–529 B.C.).

According to this priest and the Egyptian annals, 9,000 years earlier (that is, c. 9600 B.C.), the Atlantean armies had attacked the countries located to the east of the Pillars of Hercules, but the Hellenic army had emerged victorious:

> But at a later time there occurred portentous earthquakes and floods, and one grievous day and night befell them, when the whole body of your warriors was swallowed up by the earth, and the island of Atlantis in like manner was swallowed up by the sea and vanished; wherefore also the ocean at that spot has now become impassable and unsearchable, being blocked up by the shoal mud which the island created as it settled down.

In the course of the conversation, the priest said to Solinus:

> The people, of your country, remember but one deluge, though many had occurred previously; and next, you are ignorant of the fact that the noblest and most perfect race amongst men were born in the land where you now dwell, and from them both you yourself are sprung and the whole of your existing city, out of some little seed that chanced to be left over; but this has escaped your notice because for many generations the survivors died with no power to express themselves in writing.

Actually, however, the Greek accounts mention two distinct floods: the flood of Ogyges and the flood of Deucalion. It is impossible to determine the date of the first. It is often confused with the biblical flood of Noah, or the Chaldean flood described by Gilgamesh, which Christian and Moslem chronologists place in 2242 A.M. (i.e., c. 3320 B.C.)—that is, toward the end of the Eleventh Dynasty, or the end of the reign of Ammanemes, first king of the Twelfth Dynasty. According to Maqrizi, the Chinese claim that there was no universal flood, for it never reached India or China. Thus, apparently, it was limited to the Mediterranean basin and the

Persian Gulf. It might have been caused by the explosion that occurred on the island of Thera.

The date of the flood of Deucalion seems to have been correctly determined by Manetho as occurring during the reign of Misphragmuthosis (Tuthmosis III), sixth king of the Eighteenth Dynasty (1498–1472 B.C.). Its effects were apparently limited to the eastern Mediterranean basin. According to Diodorus Siculus, the outlet of the Black Sea at the Cyanean Rocks was rent asunder and its waters burst forth into the Aegean Sea.

The priest in Sais was absolutely correct in informing Solinus that there had been numerous floods previous to the flood of Deucalion. Since the beginning of time such floods had unquestionably succeeded one another by the hundreds, each time destroying the animal species whose strange skeletons we are now discovering.

But I am certain that one of these floods was particularly disastrous and that it occurred when mankind had already reached an advanced stage of civilization. During which era did it occur, and what caused it? This is the enigma to be solved!

It is not unreasonable to suggest that, in view of the flood's great size, it might have been caused by the fall of an enormous asteroid—perhaps the star of Baal, as in the manuscript referred to by Schliemann—into that part of the present-day Pacific Ocean that is entirely without islands in a circle measuring over 7,000 kilometers in diameter, the center of which is located at about 10° N. and 130° W., the depth of the ocean at this point being consistently over 4,000 meters.

The unimaginable violence of the shock must have made the earth's axis tip, causing—through kinetic inertia—the oceanic waters to burst over the existing continents. This colossal marine cataclysm, a veritable universal flood sparing only the highest points of the globe, was apparently accompanied, at the point of impact and throughout its periphery, by the sinking of land masses. At the same time gigantic volcanic phenomena were unleashed, forming an infernal circle of fire that returns to haunt the mind of man.

The groups of islands that once marked the mountainpeaks of the ancient continent, now engulfed, are all that remains amid the immense ocean that became the Pacific. One might be tempted to place among the latter group Easter Island, with its mysterious, grandiose statues, handed down to us, as a final message, by a race of men that has since disappeared. (Francis Mazière provides a poignant description of these people in his book.)

I do not agree with this point of view, however, for, in my opinion, Easter Island was not part of the Polynesian continent at that time, but part of the South American continent. After the cataclysm Easter Island must have remained uninhabited for thousands of years, and it is only recently—scarcely a few centuries ago—that the Polynesians, fleeing their islands as one after another was engulfed, came to Easter Island seeking refuge.

The modern islanders' dwellings, shaped like overturned pirogues (a shape that did not escape Francis Mazière's sharp eyes), are simply the materialization of the not very distant memory of this progressive engulfment of the Polynesian islands. The islanders' only hope for salvation was the pirogue, which, was kept close at hand to take to the sea again. When King Horu-Matua and his retinue debarked on the treeless Easter Island, the only practical solution was to use the pirogues themselves as dwellings, turned upside-down and headed in the direction of the prevailing winds. The results proved satisfactory, and to this day the Easter Islanders, though reassured of the new island's stability, retain the shape of the inverted pirogue for their dwelling places.

But I find it obvious that the island's present population, composed of the descendants of Polynesian emigrants who fled overpopulated or slowly submerging islands, is totally different from the *ahu*-builders of old. For it is totally impossible that the few thousand inhabitants who could have populated what is almost a desert isle, with a surface of 118 square kilometers (of which scarcely half—6,000 acres—was capable of producing meager harvests), should have taken upon themselves the strange task of sculpting, in a compact tuff, hundreds and perhaps thousands of prefabricated colossal statues whose faces were not to be completed nor eyes opened until they were set up on the *ahu*. It is quite obvious that the Polynesian islanders must have had another, more immediate and explicit concern: that of ensuring their survival by means of fishing and an extremely aleatory agriculture.

There is no doubt in my mind that Easter Island was a high point of a part of the South American continent that was engulfed by floods: its statues are none other than those of the kings and lofty personages of the Atlantean race, for, according to Plato, Atlantis was as large as Libya and Asia put together.

It would take a whole book to prove these views, and that is not my purpose here, as this book is limited to the pyramids. I merely urge the reader to compare the colossi of Easter Island with the statues of Atlanteans found in the pyramid-temple of Tula in order to become convinced of the obvious relation between the two. The hair of these Atlantean statues is arranged like that of the Easter Island colossi, in the same knot, not to mention the long ears that are common to both.

It is impossible to go into a detailed study of the Mexican, Colombian, and Peruvian pyramids here. I will simply point out that, like the Chaldean ziggurats and the pyramid of Zoser at Saqqara, the pyramids of Tajin and Veracruz have seven recessed terraces. This must have also been true of the pyramid of Cuicuilco, which was covered by a lava stream to half its height, despite the fact that it had been placed atop a plateau.

But the strangest thing is that the pyramid of Tajin was completely painted red, like the pyramids of Cheops and Kephren; its 365 steps and red color indubitably prove that it, like Egypt's Great Pyramid, was a temple of the sun, its seven terraces, like those of the Chaldean ziggurats, being dedicated to the seven planets.

I find it incontestable that connections did indeed exist between the Old and New Worlds across the Atlantic, for it is obvious that before the universal cataclysm the division of the land masses was not as we know it today.

AN ATTEMPT TO DATE THE UNIVERSAL FLOOD

Attempting to determine the date of the titanic catastrophe that nearly destroyed the entire human race is, admittedly, a foolhardy endeavor. Nevertheless, it is not unreasonable to place it at the beginning of the dynasty of the "Spirits of the Dead," which Manetho (according to Eusebius) sets at 5,813 years before Menes, first king of the First Dynasty—that is in 11432 B.C.

This brings us a good deal closer to Plato's *approximately* 9,600 years, and it is possible that the westward drift of the American continent did not occur until somewhat later, since certain tectonic phenomena—earthquakes, appearances and disappearances of islands, volcanic eruptions—are still occurring even now along the Pacific coasts.

There is one other detail worth noting, which may be significant. The ancient Romans celebrated the feast days of the Lemuria, the "Spirits of the Dead" who had not been provided with a sepulcher, on May 9, 11, and 13 each year, that is, on the days of our "saints of ice"—St. Pancrace, St. Mamert, and St. Servais. In Gaul the celebration of these Roman feast days of the Lemuria took the form of three solemn processions, the "Rogations," occurring on May 11, 12, and 13 in the Gregorian calendar. St. Mamert, bishop of Vienna, made these feast days obligatory *c.* 450 A.D.; they are still observed today in certain villages.

An insignificant, absurd, coincidental fact? Perhaps! However, we must recall that, in the zodiacal plane, there exists around the sun a cosmic ring having its own speed of rotation; it is composed of billions of solid particles, some of which are veritable asteroids. We can see this ring by the zodiacal glow which is clearly visible in March and September.

Now, the earth traverses this cosmic ring twice a year; in the spring, from May 9 to 15, and in the autumn, from November 1 to 6. Since the sunlight is partially intercepted during this traversal, the terrestrial globe undergoes a general cooling off, concretized in the form of nocturnal frosts. At this time, only the orange and red rays of the spectrum have a wavelength sufficient to enable them to pierce the cosmic fog and reach us, while the moon, a faithful mirror, appears "reddish" to our eyes. The two annual traversals of this cosmic ring by the earth constitutes a terrible and real danger to all mankind.

Did the period May 9–13 of the year 11432 B.C. witness the great cataclysm? This is a mystery that will never be solved, barring some miraculous discovery. However, this date is not out of the question, for the biblical text Genesis 7:12 indicates that the flood began on the seventeenth day of the second month. Now, the ancient chroniclers claim that the first day of the creation of the world (the first day of the year) coincided with the spring equinox (March 21 in the Gregorian calendar), and all their calculations are based on this date. Consequently, the flood occurred on May 7, only two days before the feast day of St. Pancrace (May 9).

Obviously, one cannot give total credence to the biblical text, a defective copy of the text of the epic of Gilgamesh. It was taken from the tablets of Nineveh, which sets the duration of the diluvian hurricane as six days and six nights, whereas the story of Genesis gives forty days and forty nights. True, careful study of the biblical texts reveal clearly that in general, as well as chronologically, the number 40 is conventionally used to express an unspecified or doubtful duration. Perhaps discoveries of Babylonian or Assyrian tablets will provide us with more precise details.

It is certain that someday exploration of the oceans' depths will reveal astonishing things, while providing us with facts capable of overturning all the ideas that are currently accepted in regard to prehistory. It can be assumed that future discoveries to be made on the high plateaus of the earth's crust—Iran, Tibet, Abyssinia, Mexico, Colombia, Peru—will provide eloquent vestiges of mysterious inscriptions requiring centuries of study on the part of our paleographic scholars.

I cannot end this work without mentioning Andrew Tomas' recent book, *The Treasure of the Sphinx,* published by Robert Laffont under the title *Les Secrets de l'Atlantide* (*The Secrets of Atlantis*). This book, based on the legend of the Old and New Worlds, could be considered the product of an imagination that some people will find overactive—that is to say, morbid. However, Tomas' book is quite interesting because it leads us to reconsider all the ideas imbued in us by the official representatives of science. It exemplifies the trend toward "opening up" to revolutionary hypothetical concepts that are in no way impossible. Haven't all the shattering modern discoveries been the result of hypotheses commonly supposed to be improbable?

Tomas states his intention precisely:

This work has a precise goal and aims at a practical conclusion. It's aim is to attract the public's attention to the possibility of the extraordinary discovery of a secret legacy left by a people who are now considered mythical.

This memory of mysterious repositories in the high, secret places of the globe lives on, to this day, in the heart of certain very exclusive sects throughout the world.

Here a critical question arises: Was the Pyramid, temple of the sun and wonder of the world, not one of these high places, and is it not still the secret, *intact* receptacle of knowledge reaching far back into the mists of time?

If the chamber mentioned by Herodotus truly exists, 58 meters beneath the Pyramid's socle, there is every reason to believe that it remains inviolate, because it is protected by the waters of the Nile carried in by way of its underground canal. If this is indeed so—as I am firmly convinced—it is absolutely urgent that attempts be made to discover the chamber before the water, whose level has risen 10 meters over the last 6,750 years, destroys forever the papyruses that must have been placed there.

An appeal from UNESCO made it possible to save the temples of Nubia from destruction; the entire world is now counting upon Egypt's archaeological departments to concern themselves with saving a treasure that is perhaps unique in the world—the treasure of Cheops' sepulchral chamber.

CONCLUSION

The result of my in-depth study of the Great Pyramid is that there can be no doubt that at the time of the first recorded dynasties, the Egyptians had already attained an advanced degree of civilization; thus it amuses me to see certain renowned Egyptologists consigning these people to the Neolithic Age! The specimens of statuary, jewelry, and carpentry that have come down to us are hardly inferior to our twentieth-century masterpieces. And despite our modern methods, we would find it difficult to build pyramids as colossal as those found at Giza, Dashur, and Medum. All this implies scientific, mathematical, and astronomical knowledge that many Egyptologists are loath to concede. It is obvious that if one sets oneself the task of defending the biblical dates, it is necessary—in order to explain this undeniable fact—to have recourse to the intervention of some deity, following the example of the ineffable Father Moreux!

As far as I am concerned, there can be no doubt that the Egyptians and Chaldeans had been recording astronomical observations for over 30,000 years. Berossus refers to 432,000 years and Diodorus Siculus to 473,000 years before Alexander the Great! While these figures may seem far-fetched, they are not impossible.

As a matter of fact, Cheops seems to me to have been an exceptional king; he was both a reformer and a scholar—a magician, according to Manetho. A reformer, because he attempted a reallocation of property. At the time, the ordinary citizen was a mere slave, since most of the land in Egypt belonged to the priests and grandees of the realm, nomarchs and high-ranking officials, who handed down their powers and offices hereditarily. In a bold stroke Cheops abolished a great portion of the temples' land holdings and reserved the right to nominate high priests and dignitaries.

In addition, he attempted to found a monotheistic cult, that of the sun god Khnum, god of the cataracts, whose name, moreover, he bore: *Khnum-Khufu* ("Khnum protects me"). In so doing, he anticipated Akhnaton's hapless attempt by 3,400 years. But attempting to reduce the gods Ptah, Ra, and Amon to the rank of subordinate deities in their own territory was a dangerous endeavor: it produced a widespread rebellion which Cheops suppressed by temporarily closing the temples, according to reports by Manetho, Herodotus, and Diodorus Siculus.

The vengeance taken by the priests and feudal lords was a case of delayed action: it assumed the form of the violation, pillage, and total destruction of the interior of Cheops' tomb, in order to see to it that the memory of this heretical reformist king vanished forever. It was necessary to wait 3,550 years for the restoration of the Great Pyramid's chambers under Ramesses II before they could again be used for isiac initiations, which persisted up to the time of Roman rule.

But the memory of Cheops will always remain vivid in the mind of man. for a creation as grandiose as the Great Pyramid could never be completely destroyed. It is not, however, as a majestic tomb that his pyramid will continue to be considered the greatest wonder of the ancient world. A king's tomb, however grandiose, would not have aroused such curiosity mixed with avid fervor among the pilgrims who through the ages have flocked to it from all the countries of the Eastern Hemisphere.

Legend—true, as it happens—made it out to be the sacred temple of the sun god and stated that its dimensions were related to those of the earth. Indeed, Cheops had wished to pass down to future generations the geodesic data known or discovered during his time. By materializing—with amazing precision—the direction of the four cardinal points in the four sides of the base, he hoped to concretize both the roundness of our terrestrial globe and its dimensions.

The perimeter of the base is, in fact, the same length as the circumference having as its radius the Pyramid's height: 4c

$= 2\pi h$. Since the length of each side is 440 cubits and the height 280 cubits, we get:

$$4 \times 440 = 2 \times \frac{22}{7} \times 280 = 1{,}760 \text{ cubits.}$$

Now, the cubit in use under the Fourth Dynasty had a value of 0.5237 meter, the value determined from the dimensions of the King's Chamber. Thus, the Pyramid's height was 146.636 meters, its base 230.428 meters, and its perimeter 921.712 meters.[4]

It should be noted that value $\pi = \frac{22}{7}$ is given by the slope (α) of the facing blocks on the north face, or 51° 51′ 43″. The value of the slope does, in fact, lie between 51° 51′ and 51° 52′.

Thus, 4,500 years before Archimedes, the ancient Egyptians had determined the value of π.

But while the roundness of the earth is clearly expressed in the slope (α) of the Pyramid ($\pi = 4 \cot g\ \alpha = 4 \times \frac{11}{14} = \frac{22}{7}$), for the monument truly to be a model of the terrestrial globe, it was necessary that its perimeter correspond to an aliquot part of the meridian.

We now know the mean value of the half-minute of Egypt's meridian precisely: 923.092 meters (the perimeter of the Pyramid's base measures 921.712 meters). If—as I am convinced—the ancient Egyptians succeeded in measuring the earth in 4800 B.C. (6,800 years before the measurement made by the French scientists Delambre and Méchain in order to determine the value of the meter), their result was off by only 0.15 percent, which constitutes an amazing feat for an era in which measurements were made by royal bematists using the pace as a unit. The true value of the cubit should have been 923.092 ÷ 1,760 = 0.5245 meter, instead of 0.5237 meter; that is to say, there was an error—negligible, for all practical purposes—of 0.8 millimeter. But we must not forget that we are going by the value of the cubit derived from the dimensions of the King's Chamber, which may have undergone slight distortions under the weight of the courses above it.

Moreover, if anything should arouse our astonishment, it is the proof of the fixity of the Egyptian metric system, which was in use, without any major variation, for nearly 5,000 years. It was not, in fact, until an unknown date—certainly in the Christian era, however—that the system of measurement was modified.

How are we to explain this extraordinary stability? It cannot be ascribed solely to the pharaohs' omnipotence, for Egypt obviously went through some very troubled, even tragic times. If the cubit—as a unit of measurement and basis of the system—had been merely the average length of the human forearm, it is quite certain that its value would have undergone radical changes and would probably have been a function of either the monarchs' genetic makeup of their vanity.

There is only one possible explanation: to wit, that the Egyptian cubit represented a fraction of a unit of the geodesic arc—in fact, $1/300$th.

This unit of the arc was the stadium; that is, $1/252,000$th of the terrestrial meridian. This division into 252,000 parts was judicious and logical because it was closely related to the Egyptian methods of calculation, the number 2,520 being the smallest common multiple of the first ten integers.

However, Euergetes I (Ptolemy III), who was very interested in the sciences, instructed Eratosthenes to make a new measurement of the earth around 240 B.C. This measurement was carried out by the royal bematists along the Ptolemais–Berenice axis, on the one hand, and along the Philae–Alexandria axis on the other. The results, according to Pliny, were 4,820 and 5,000 stadia respectively. A new cubit was deduced from this: the Philaeterian cubit, having a value of 0.5277 meter.

How, then, can there by any doubt that the ancient cubit was linked to an actual measurement of the terrestrial meridian made during Cheops reign, or even earlier? I am firmly convinced that this was so; to deny it would be to display a ridiculous false pride.

But the Great Pyramid's destination is not limited to representing the terrestrial globe; it was also a solar temple dedicated to the ram-headed god Khnum, for whom were reserved two of the four solar barques discovered at its base. The Pyramid—as well as the head of Sphinx, (Harmachis, the watchful guardian of the rising sun)—was painted red, the color of the sun as it sets in the crimson west.

The Great Pyramid, unlike the other pyramids, was not topped by a black basalt pyramidion, but ended in a platform, in the center of which was raised a gnomon (spherical, I believe), whose shadow, cast on the pavement of the northern esplanade, marked true solar noon on the various days of the year. The maximal and minimal elongations of this shadow distinguished, respectively, the winter and summer solstices. Moreover—and this is an important detail that has eluded the Egyptologists who have dealt with the Great Pyramid—the faces are not at all flat, but are hollowed in such a way that for half a minute, at sunrise and sunset during the two equinoxes, only half of the north and south faces are illuminated.

Given these facts, it is not surprising that the Great Pyramid should have been considered, from the astronomical standpoint, the greatest wonder of the ancient world.

However, its renown is not only of a scientific nature, but also religious and initiatory; for the minor isiac initiatory trials and rites took place in the chaotic Subterranean Chamber, with its uterine passage and lustral well, while the Pyramid's central chamber with its granite sarcophagus, was used as the setting for the supreme initiation (reserved exclusively for the king, under the first six dynasties), during the transferral of the divine *ka* from the body of the deceased pharaoh into that of his successor.

But one question then arises: Where was Cheops inhumed?

I am inclined to believe that Herodotus' accounts are veracious: that since 4766 B.C. Cheops has lain in his crypt carved out in the bedrock at the level of the Nile's low water—that is, 58 meters beneath the Pyramid's base and 27 meters beneath the Subterranean Chamber known to us at present.

To me, this is more than a mere hypothesis, for while crawling along the blind passage, surrounded by bats, I have repeatedly had the strange impression that by striking the floor with a simple key, I made the entire Pyramid tremble! This extraordinary resonance was probably the reason why Howard-Vyse had the primitively squared lustral well deepened by 9 meters. But the depth reached was clearly not sufficient to lead to the vault of the royal hypogeum.

Current exploratory methods could readily solve the

enigma; it is certain that the day will come when the Egyptian Department of Antiquities will provide the solution. The same will be true in regard to the pyramid of Kephren, which poses the same problem. It is, indeed, inconceivable that a pharaoh of the Fourth Dynasty should have had himself inhumed in a common limestone chamber whose walls had been painted red: the chamber of the sarcophagus, known as "Belzoni's Chamber," is simply the chamber that was used in the transferral of the *ka*. It is highly probable that Kephren's granite sepulchral chamber is situated somewhere in the pyramid, very deeply imbedded, in a location that is still unknown. The great upheaval evident in all the pavement in the Pyramid's two chambers is formal proof of the despoilers' unsuccessful search.

But, getting back to the Great Pyramid, if Cheops' sepulchral crypt should indeed be discovered, there will still remain one mystery to be solved: Who was inhumed in the Great Pyramid's "central chamber"?

I've already answered that question: nobody! For once the supreme initiation of the new king had been completed, the sarcophagus, still imbued with residual emanations of the divine *ka,* had become sacred and untouchable, whence the necessity for hermetic sealing. Is this not also true of the ciborium found in Christian Tabernacles, symbol of the Holy Grail?

We are still a long way from solving the isiac mysteries of ancient Egypt, and the inscription quoted by Plutarch from a statue thought to be of Isis in a temple in Sais still holds true: "I am all that has been, and is, and shall be, and my robe no mortal has yet uncovered."

NOTES

1. See note at end of Table.
2. This king ruled in Lower Egypt, parallel to Amos, for twenty-five years.
3. The sum of $2 + 6 + 4 = 1$ year.
4. The Survey of Egypt gives 146.525 and 230.253 meters, respectively, for the height and the base, but given the Pyramid's present state, it is impossible to specify the dimensions to within 0.20 meter. Moreover, the Survey did not take into account the hollowing of the faces.